The Babe Chases 6

T0041037

The Babe Chases 60

*That Fabulous 1927 Season,
Home Run by Home Run*

JOHN G. ROBERTSON

McFarland & Company, Inc., Publishers
Jefferson, North Carolina

FRONTISPIECE: Babe Ruth, ca. 1927 (National Baseball
Hall of Fame Library, Cooperstown, New York).

The present work is a reprint of the library bound edition of
The Babe Chases 60: That Fabulous 1927 Season, Home
Run by Home Run, first published in 1999 by McFarland.

LIBRARY OF CONGRESS CATALOGUING-IN-PUBLICATION DATA

Robertson, John G., 1964–
    The Babe chases 60 : that fabulous 1927 season, home run
by home run / John G. Robertson.
        p.   cm.
    Includes bibliographical references and index.

    ISBN 978-0-7864-9367-8
    softcover : acid free paper ∞

    1. Ruth, Babe, 1895–1948. 2. Baseball players—United
States—Biography.   3. New York Yankees (Baseball team)—
I. Title. II. Title: Babe chases sixty.
GV865.R8R63 2014
796.357'092—dc21
[B]   98-33319

BRITISH LIBRARY CATALOGUING DATA ARE AVAILABLE

On the cover: Babe Ruth's 60th home run (National Baseball
Library & Archive, Cooperstown, New York)

Manufactured in the United States of America

McFarland & Company, Inc., Publishers
  Box 611, Jefferson, North Carolina 28640
  www.mcfarlandpub.com

This book is dedicated to my niece,
Laura Elizabeth Neal, who, quite
coincidentally, was born exactly 68 years
to the day after Babe Ruth hit his fifty-third
home run of the 1927 season.

TABLE OF CONTENTS

ACKNOWLEDGMENTS

The task of researching and writing a book is never a solo act. *The Babe Chases 60* would certainly never have reached fruition without the assistance of many people. I would like to express my sincere gratitude to:

• Abigail B. Clark of the photo archives department at the National Baseball Hall of Fame in Cooperstown for providing the frontispiece of Babe Ruth.

• The staff at the University of Waterloo's Dana Porter Arts Library who, during my many hours perusing microfilms of 70-year-old newspapers, provided me with ample technical assistance whenever I needed it.

• *The Society for American Baseball Research*'s Lending Library, which undoubtedly saved me hours of tedious work by allowing me to have extended access to its wonderful microfilm collection of *The Sporting News*, from which I was able to draw the boxscores for the games described in this book.

• The staff at the main branch of my hometown Cambridge (Ontario) Public Library for going far beyond the call of duty to assist me in my statistical research.

• My father, Grant Robertson, whose computer-generated research aids saved me considerable amounts of time in the library—and most certainly increased the accuracy of the boxscores that you will find in this book.

• My mother, Janice Robertson, for her unofficial but reliable proof-reading efforts.

• My good friend Fred Malatches, who inadvertently began this entire project one day by suggesting, "Why don't you write a book about Babe Ruth?"

• The late George Herman "Babe" Ruth, whose bigger-than-life personality and remarkable accomplishments continue to be an endless source of fascination.

• And lastly, the sport of baseball itself, whose timeless charm and intrigue inspired me to begin this project. As *Sporting Life* noted way back in 1884, "Verily, the National Game is great!" Indeed.

INTRODUCTION

All years are historically significant for one reason or another. However, one particular year in the twentieth century, 1927, was especially brimming with noteworthy events and achievements.

Less than two weeks after two French aviators vanished in the icy waters of the Atlantic, a courageous 25-year-old pilot, Charles Augustus Lindbergh, heroically battled exhaustion for more than 33 hours in *The Spirit of St. Louis*, his specially designed plane. His daring, nonstop solo flight from Long Island to Paris riveted public attention and ushered in the age of intercontinental air travel. (Lindbergh's amazing feat, which earned him a $25,000 prize, also resulted in the deaths of more than a dozen aviators who tried to equal or surpass it in the following months.) Lucky Lindy's triumphant return to the United States was wildly celebrated on an enormous scale, complete with grandiose ticker-tape parades witnessed by admiring millions.

Nicola Sacco and Bartolomeo Vanzetti, two anarchists found guilty of a 1920 murder and payroll robbery, exhausted their legal appeals, were denied clemency by the governor of Massachusetts, and suffered the ultimate penalty. Many people suspected the pair's convictions were based solely on their unorthodox political views rather than the actual evidence presented by the prosecution. Their highly publicized deaths by electrocution generated a tremendous uproar. Protesters as far away as Buenos Aires demonstrated against the executions and denounced the system of American justice.

The 15 millionth Model T, the relatively inexpensive automobile that transformed Americans into the most mobile population on the globe, rolled off Henry Ford's assembly line. In December it would be replaced by the more costly Model A, which could travel at twice the speed. By the end of 1927, more than nine million automobiles (approximately 39 percent of the world's total) would be registered to owners in the United States.

The twists and turns of political life created headlines in America and elsewhere. Calvin Coolidge, the colorless chief executive who had assumed

1

the presidency in August 1923 when Warren Harding suddenly died in office, surprised the nation when he unceremoniously announced he would not seek another term in 1928. Government in the Soviet Union was less precise, but equally fascinating: Leon Trotsky was abruptly expelled from the central committee of the Communist Party. Since those who fell into disfavor with the Soviet leadership often had reason to fear for their lives, it was an ominous signal for the man who had helped mastermind the sweeping changes brought on by the Russian Revolution ten years before. Turmoil also erupted in Portugal, as a short-lived civil war failed to oust the reigning government.

A new stage production, *Showboat*, was the talk of Broadway. One haunting tune from its score, "Old Man River," became an overnight sensation. The public was also singing along to "Blue Skies" and "My Blue Heaven." In other news from the world of entertainment, a petite yet buxom actress named Mae West was arrested on morals charges for staging a raunchy burlesque show provocatively titled *Sex*. (Also in 1927, a teacher in New Jersey was similarly deemed morally corrupt and was abruptly dismissed. The unfortunate young lady was caught in the act: she was seen smoking a cigarette after school hours.) In West's case, it wasn't exactly what she said but the lewd way in which she said it that got her into hot water with puritanical law officers. Predictably, the surrounding publicity boosted her career enormously. Another major stage play, *Dracula*, opened to favorable reviews. Special plaudits went to the previously unknown leading man with the odd eastern European accent, Bela Lugosi.

Hollywood was enjoying a banner year, and the studios' productions continued to flow into towns large and small. Clara Bow, an ebullient young actress, starred in a breezy flick simply titled *It*. That innocuous two-letter word became instantly synonymous with sex appeal. On a hunch, Hal Roach, the master producer of two-reel silent comedies, paired a rotund Georgian named Oliver Hardy with a scrawny Englishman named Stan Laurel for the first time. Neither had achieved noteworthy success individually, but as a team they would reach unparalleled popularity.

The first great biblical epic, Cecil B. DeMille's silent-film classic, *The King of Kings*, was released to widespread acclaim. In October 1927, though, Al Jolson's performance in *The Jazz Singer* changed movies forever. When audiences actually heard Jolson sing and ad-lib bits of dialogue, the clumsiness of reading words on the screen became instantly archaic. A few gremlins still had to be eliminated from the sound synchronization process, but the age of talking films had dawned.

The unbridled growth of another technological marvel, radio, prompted President Coolidge to establish the Federal Radio Commission in February. Its popular mandate was to regulate the nation's broadcasting signals in order to minimize interference on each station.

Literary buffs were reading Virginia Woolf's *To the Lighthouse* and

Sinclair Lewis's *Elmer Gantry*. Upton Sinclair's *Oil!* met with critical success but was officially banned by prudish civic administrators in Boston. Patrons of the arts in 1927 were discussing Henri Matisse's latest painting, *Figures with Ornamental Background*, and Edward Hopper's *Manhattan Bridge*.

New frontiers in science were being explored. Hermann J. Muller's experiments with X-rays created mutations that were both fascinating and disturbing. George Lemaitre, a Belgian, published his "big bang" theory of how the universe originated, delivering yet another assault on those who steadfastly believed in the Bible's creation story. After months of analysis, the skull of "Java Man," estimated to be 500,000 years old, was accepted by anthropologists as the oldest human fossil yet discovered. A weird electrical gadget called television was successfully tested, although skeptics openly wondered whether it could ever serve a practical purpose. Telephone customers could now call London all the way from San Francisco if they didn't mind the exorbitant rate of $25 per minute.

Sports heroes were plentiful in 1927. Bobby Jones, a modest fellow from Georgia, ruled the golf world. A quartet of talented Frenchmen, collectively known as the Four Musketeers, challenged Bill Tilden's grip on tennis supremacy. Jack Dempsey, who had lost the world heavyweight championship on points to Gene Tunney in 1926, rallied to beat Jack Sharkey in a remarkable and controversial comeback effort. Two months later, because of a few seconds of absentmindedness, Dempsey lost to Tunney again in one of boxing's most eagerly anticipated rematches.

But no sports story in 1927 could compare to the one-man show orchestrated by George Herman (Babe) Ruth of baseball's New York Yankees. Even though some of the greatest names in baseball history—Speaker, Cobb, Alexander, Johnson, Sisler, Hornsby, Frisch and Grove—were active that season, none could begin to arouse the public fascination that the Babe inspired.

Written off by baseball experts in 1925 as a has-been, Ruth electrified the American League just two summers later by launching an unheard-of total of 60 home runs. In an era when many ballparks were vast and the ball itself did not possess nearly the pop it has today, Ruth's spectacular feat seemed almost superhuman. During the 1920s, an extremely productive home run hitter was a slugger who circled the bases a mere 20 times per season. Tripling that effort was an exploit nearly beyond comprehension. That Ruth could pull off such a feat at the age of 32, after subjecting his body to a decade of high living and gastronomic abuses, was even more extraordinary. Legendary sports reporter Red Smith put everything about the Babe into perspective.

> It wasn't just that he hit more home runs than anybody else, he hit them better, higher, farther, with more theatrical timing and a more flamboyant flourish. Nobody could strike out like Babe Ruth. Nobody circled the bases with the same pigeon-toed, mincing majesty.

Oddly enough, it was not until the last month of the 1927 season that Ruth was even assured of winning the American League home run crown. Incredibly, his humble, 24-year-old teammate, Henry Louis Gehrig, was matching the Babe homer for homer through August. Richards Vidmer of the *New York Times* dubbed the fascinating slugging duel "The Great American Home Run Handicap." Many of New York's passionate baseball writers, including Vidmer, openly rooted for Ruth in the home run race, portraying Gehrig as a villain. Even though Gehrig had been a fixture in the Yankee lineup since 1925, it was considered the height of effrontery for him to challenge the immortal Babe for homer supremacy. Whomever the public was cheering for, it was a fascinating and unparalleled duel. Years later author Donald Honig discussed the situation in *Baseball America*.

> All summer long the detonations went on, and as the days flowed by, one lopsided victory after another, the rest of the league began to realize that something terrifying and diabolical was taking shape. When the cannon fire quieted and a man could take a breath and raise his head and synthesize a thought or two, it became apparent that the all-powerful king, the monstrous and unstoppable monarch of the uttermost wallop, now had right behind him in the lineup a fearsome young crown prince.

A genuine rivalry developed between the two superstars, who were worlds apart in their lifestyles. Ruth, of course, loved the spotlight. The reserved Gehrig preferred solitude. The twosome's home run battle provided far more drama than the one-sided American League pennant race of that year. (The Yankees absolutely romped to the title, finishing 19 full games ahead of the second-place Philadelphia Athletics.)

Gehrig's sudden ascension into the realm of public acclaim seemed to inspire the Babe toward the 60-homer mark. Gehrig was clearly the heir apparent to Ruth on the Yankees, but the Babe intended the 1927 campaign to be his finest. Pity the pitchers on the seven other American League clubs that season! If a hurler's deliveries happened to evade Ruth's booming bat, he immediately had to deal with the sobering reality that Gehrig was loosening up in the on-deck circle. "I don't think I ever would have established my home run record of 60 if it hadn't been for Lou," Ruth admitted near the end of his life. "He was really getting his beef behind the ball that season and finished with 47 home runs. Pitchers began pitching to me, because if they passed me, they still had Lou to contend with."

During the 1927 season, a total of 33 different pitchers allowed Ruth's 60 homers. Sixteen of them gave up more than one. Ruth belted four home runs off of two unfortunate hurlers. Seven other pitchers gave up three apiece. One member of this group, Tom Zachary, famous for giving up number 60, is unique in having the Babe homer off him while Zachary was pitching for two different teams. In later years, being remembered as one of Ruth's 1927 victims was much the same as being knocked out in the prize ring by Sugar Ray Robinson—more of an honor than a disgrace. For what it's worth, statistics indicate that a typical Babe Ruth home run during the 1927 season was hit on a Tuesday afternoon in the first inning, with no runners on base, off a right-handed pitcher, and that it sailed over the right-field fence in the opposing team's ballpark.

No team in the American League escaped Ruth's menacing swing. The Yankees faced each of their seven opponents 22 times over the course of the season. Ruth missed just four of his club's 155 games. (An official tie game had to be replayed and thus added one more contest to New York's regular 154-game schedule.) The pitching staff of the last-place Boston Red Sox was predictably the most generous to the Babe, allowing 11 homers. The Chicago White Sox were the stingiest team, permitting just six.

Ruth's humbled pitching foes were a true cross-section of the American League. He smashed homers off fellows named Joe, Slim, Sloppy, Rube, Hod, Sarge, Rip and Lefty. Two of the pitchers were in the midst of glorious careers and would eventually be enshrined in the National Baseball Hall of Fame in Cooperstown. Others had major-league stints so brief that they are remembered by only the most devoted readers of the *Baseball Encyclopedia*. (Although the era of Ruth seems light-years ago, a couple of the 33 abused hurlers were still very much alive when the 1993 edition of that indispensable reference book was published.) Two pitchers supplemented their incomes in the off-season as professional football players. One of them, oddly enough, is a charter member of the Pro Football Hall of Fame.

This book will allow the reader to revisit each game in which Babe Ruth hit a home run during the 1927 American League season. The majestic round-trippers will be described in much the same gaudy manner as New York's somewhat biased baseball writers reported on them seven decades ago. Other notable baseball happenings that occurred on the same day will be summarily recapped, reacquainting the reader with the exploits of all-time greats such as Ty Cobb, Grover Cleveland Alexander, Rogers Hornsby and the Waner brothers, and flashes in the pan such as Hod Lisenbee.

Ruth's quest for 60 homers was a dramatic adventure into uncharted territory. After the season ended, few followers of the grand old game thought Ruth's mark would ever be approached, much less eclipsed. Perhaps this game-by-game summary, which I first began to research not long after the hundredth anniversary of the Babe's birth, will provide some insight as to why Ruth's record-setting campaign was, and still is, held with such reverence by generations of baseball fans.

JOHN G. ROBERTSON
Fall 1998

BABE RUTH
BEFORE 1927

I saw it all happen, from beginning to end. But sometimes I still can't believe what I saw: this 19-year-old kid, crude, poorly educated, only lightly brushed by the social veneer we call civilization, gradually transformed into the idol of American youth and the symbol of baseball the world over—a man loved by more people and with an intensity of feeling that perhaps has never been equaled before or since. I saw a man transformed from a human being into something pretty close to a god. If somebody had predicted that back on the Boston Red Sox in 1914, he would have been thrown into a lunatic asylum. —*Harry Hooper*

As he moved, center stage moved with him. —*Roger Kahn*

He was a parade all by himself, a burst of dazzle and jingle, Santa Claus, drinking his whiskey straight and groaning with a bellyache. Babe Ruth made the music that his joyous years danced to in a continuous party. What Babe Ruth is comes down one generation, handing it to the next, as a national heirloom. —*Jimmy Cannon*

There is no shortage of well-researched biographies about George Herman Ruth. However, the best examinations of Ruth's colorful and fascinating life have all been written since 1970. During the Babe's remarkable career, his immense popularity made him virtually untouchable when it came to pointing criticism at his personal life. But after Jim Bouton's *Ball Four* was published nearly 30 years ago, presenting an honest, irreverent look at baseball players, sports historians have been more than willing to discuss the less appealing aspects of all athletes' lives, including the Babe's.

While he was alive, and for years afterwards, Ruth's biographers whitewashed his numerous character flaws. By the time his career home run mark had been eclipsed by Henry Aaron in 1974, Ruth's indiscretions were openly discussed and criticized. Dick Schaap, in an exceptionally scathing piece on the recently deposed home run king, wrote, "Babe Ruth was living proof that through sports a man could rise from common, vulgar beginnings, and remain common and vulgar. The myth of Ruth has tended to ignore that fact. It should not surprise anyone that the greatest professional athlete in American sports was a man with distorted sexual, moral, social and financial values."

Schaap is not alone in his condemnation of Ruth's private life. In *The Baseball Hall of Shame*, an amusing look at baseball's comic side, authors Bruce Nash and Allan Zullo rank Ruth among "the most disgusting role models for American youth":

> Thank God children never knew the real Babe Ruth. Imagine if they had. Millions of youngsters would have emulated their hero and indulged, like he did daily, in booze, buffets, and bimbos.
> Babe carried on a naughty, decadent life without the public's knowledge because he had the New York press corps wrapped around his fat pinky. If the same reporters who hid the truth about Babe had been covering Ivan the Terrible, he would have gone down in history as a saint.
> With the Babe, insiders looked the other way. Otherwise, he would have been up on morals charges more times than at bat. He was, for example, a gold medalist in the sexual Olympics. He didn't consider the day complete without at least one romp with a nympho or whore. His glandular prowess reached legendary status during one road trip to St. Louis when he took on an entire brothel and sampled one hooker after another. He had more contact with V.D. than he did with curveballs.

Most fans, however, prefer to remember Babe on fonder terms. Broadcaster Bob Costas, speaking on the subject of Ruth for Ken Burns's *Baseball* documentary, insisted that Ruth's plentiful shortcomings added to his allure as a national figure. Costas delightfully described the Babe as "a scruffy kid who came from the humblest of beginnings … a big, badly-flawed, swashbuckling palooka who strides with great spirit … across the American stage."

Ruth's life story, at least in abbreviated form, is well known to serious baseball fans. Still, as a prelude to his record-shattering summer of 1927, it is obligatory to present a brief biography of the man who, 50 years after his death, quite probably still holds the honor of being the most famous athlete in American history.

George Herman Ruth was born in his parents' house at 216 Emory Street near the Baltimore waterfront on February 6, 1895. (For a long time, Ruth's year of birth was listed in several reference books as 1894, but Baltimore's municipal records have confirmed 1895 as being accurate. For most of his life,

Ruth himself believed his birthday to be February 7, 1894 until he applied for a birth certificate to travel abroad in 1934 and discovered otherwise.) Although his mother, Kate, would give birth to eight children in her short life, only George and a younger sister, Mary Margaret, survived to adulthood. Ruth is said to have illogically blamed himself for his siblings' failure to live to maturity. The few surviving photos of George Sr., a proprietor of a rough waterfront saloon, leave no doubt that the youngster inherited his looks from his old man. The patriarch of the Ruth household did not hesitate to use his considerable physical force in attempts to keep his rambunctious son in line. Usually it was to no avail.

"I was a bad kid," Ruth bluntly confessed in the first sentence of his 1948 autobiography, *The Babe Ruth Story*, a project on which he collaborated with sports journalist Bob Considine. "I say that without pride, but with a feeling that it is better to say it." When he was not hanging around in his father's bar, young George was indulging in all sorts of antisocial mischief before he had reached the age of eight. Basically, Ruth was mimicking the actions displayed by the unrefined saloon customers he grew up watching. Petty theft, vandalism, and chronic truancy were character traits that his father tried literally to beat out of him. When it became apparent that the Ruths' parenting skills were incapable of controlling their son, George was legally declared "incorrigible" in 1902 and taken to St. Mary's Industrial School for Boys.

"Looking back on my early boyhood," Ruth admitted, "I honestly don't remember being aware of the difference between right and wrong. If my parents had something that I wanted very badly, I took it. I must have had some dim realization that this was stealing because it never occurred to me to take the property of anyone besides my immediate family." The fruit vendors and local merchants who lost goods to the young thief would undoubtedly disagree with Ruth's fanciful claim.

The school was not officially an orphanage (as many of the Babe's early biographers incorrectly wrote it was), but with his parents rarely bothering to visit the institution, Ruth was essentially fatherless and motherless. Except for very sporadic stays with his parents in the outside world, the school would be Ruth's restrictive home for the next 12 years.

St. Mary's was ostensibly a place where wayward youths were supposed to transfer their energies into useful trade skills. Although the institution was run by Xaverian Brothers, it housed boys of all religious denominations. Ruth would be the most notable alumnus to emerge from St. Mary's but not the only one to achieve fame. (Entertainer Al Jolson was housed there briefly in 1898.)

Like many other boys, Ruth was put to work as an apprentice shirtmaker, a task he loathed. (However, the skill never left him. Ruth's second wife, Claire, was always amused by the careful manner in which Babe handled his shirts.) By the time he was 15, Ruth had lost virtually all contact with his parents. Ruth's mother, perennially in poor health, died in 1911. His father died in his barroom in 1918 after being fatally injured in a scuffle with an unruly customer.

Ruth, of course, hated the industrial school. (Such was his disdain for the institution that Ruth, at the pinnacle of his fame, refused to acknowledge former inmates who had lived alongside him for years.) He was a frequent target of St. Mary's bullies, who taunted him about his ungainly appearance. But in an otherwise dreary life, the school offered one recreational outlet: baseball.

Brother Matthias, a Nova Scotian, was the school's towering prefect of discipline. Ruth later called him "the greatest man I've ever known." Under his authority, St. Mary's had its own internal baseball leagues comprising teams of boys usually grouped together by age. Ruth proved to be the exception. His skill at pitching and hitting were so superior to his peers' that at age eight he was competing against 12-year-olds. By the time Ruth reached 12, he had won himself a position on St. Mary's "varsity" squad, a team that had the privilege of playing opponents from outside the school in one of Baltimore's numerous amateur circuits.

By the time Ruth was 17, tales of his baseball prowess were well known in local sports circles. Not only could he belt balls better than 400 feet, he was also one of the finest left-handed pitchers in the baseball-rich city. (Ruth's first position at St. Mary's was catcher. According to one story, Ruth was belittling a pitcher who was having a poor outing. Brother Matthias then challenged Ruth, "Let's see if you can do any better." In keeping with the mythological aspects of his life, Ruth instantly discovered he was a natural on the mound.) Shortly after Ruth turned 19 in February 1914, Jack Dunn, the owner and manager of the International League's Baltimore Orioles, dropped by St. Mary's to inquire about Ruth's playing status. Dunn, who had toiled for a decade as a mediocre player in the National League, recognized that Ruth possessed star quality.

Dunn was known to the Xaverian Brothers as an upright and responsible citizen. Therefore they agreed to make Dunn, in effect, Ruth's legal guardian. Dunn's first act was to sign his charge to a minor-league contract, paying him $600 per season. The final entry about Ruth's long stay at St. Mary's was a brief notation that the school's athletic star had joined the Baltimore baseball club.

Ruth was dumbfounded by the monetary aspect of the agreement. Never before had he realized that someone could actually earn a living playing baseball. "You mean you'd pay me?" Ruth asked the Orioles' owner. When Dunn's answer was affirmative, Ruth had a feeling of giddiness descend over him. "I had some great moments in the years that followed," Ruth noted in his autobiography, "but none of my later thrills ever topped the one I got that cold afternoon at St. Mary's when $600 seemed to me to be all the wealth in the world." (The Babe quickly learned that $600 was merely a drop in the bucket. When he was at his valuable zenith with the Yankees, contract squabbles were frequent. Ruth was also known to callously flaunt his hefty paycheck in front of the noses of teammates who did not earn a tenth of what he did.)

Dunn, in honoring his obligation to look after Ruth, was so overly protective of his unsophisticated teenage charge that Ruth's Baltimore teammates began referring to him as "Dunn's Baby." It wasn't long before the nickname was shortened to Babe. The name was probably intended to be demeaning, but Ruth's Oriole teammates were immediately impressed by the obvious talent he possessed. "Babe knew how to pitch the first day I saw him," catcher Ben Egan said 48 years later. "He knew how to hold runners on base, and he knew how to work on the hitters, so I'd say he was a pretty good pitcher—on his own."

Ruth began to receive favorable press attention during his first spring training outing with the Orioles. In the March 19, 1914, edition of *The Sporting News*, correspondent E. L. Schanberger praised the newcomer, although he did butcher Ruth's name:

> Reports from this camp indicate that [Jack Dunn] has some good prospects among his rookies. For one there is a youngster named Frank Ruth [*sic*], a Baltimore boy, who has been the pitching mainstay of an industrial school team for years. He has shown Dunn so much that the manager makes the bold statement that he will stick with the team this season, both on account of his hitting and portside flinging.

Minor league baseball operated somewhat differently in 1914 than it does today. The farm system had yet to be invented, so most of the teams were independently run businesses. Club owners led a tenuous existence and generally remained financially solvent by selling their top prospects to major league teams. By the end of 1914, Ruth was sought by the Boston Red Sox, primarily as a pitcher. He had smacked a grand total of one home run as a minor leaguer. A Canadian ballpark—Hanlan's Point Park in Toronto—claims the honor of being the site of Ruth's first professional circuit clout in a regulation game. (For years, the ball which Ruth purportedly hit for his home run was in a display case at the Canadian Baseball Hall of Fame until a thief, who possessed little respect for historical artifacts, stole the ball and flung it into Lake Ontario!) Ruth's minor league batting record also contains an unusual and inexplicable statistic: two doubles and 10 triples!

During the 1914 season, Dunn was especially strapped for cash. The new, upstart Federal League had placed a club in Baltimore, and the presence of major league competition had caused a serious decline in attendance at Dunn's ballpark even though the Orioles were the class of the IL. (In fact, the IL eventually approved the transfer of the Baltimore club to Richmond, Virginia, for the 1915 season.) So, for the price of $25,000, Dunn unloaded

Ruth, Ernie Shore and Ben Egan to Boston. Dunn had first offered Ruth to Connie Mack's Philadelphia Athletics, but the A's were in the process of cruising to their fourth pennant in five seasons. With no immediate need for Ruth in his star-studded lineup, Mack politely declined the chance to acquire the man who would become baseball's greatest celebrity. Mack recalled the horrible blunder in a 1943 interview with journalist Red Smith in *The Sporting News.*

> I remember when Jack Dunn offered me two pitchers, Ruth and Ernie Shore, and told me to take 'em for nothing. I said no. I didn't turn [Ruth] down because I didn't think he was good. He was already a star in Baltimore, although I believe Shore's record was even better than Babe's down there. But Jack didn't have any money in those days and we didn't either. I remember I told him, "No, you keep those fellows, Jack, and sell 'em where you can get some money. You can use it as well as I."

The hefty price paid by the Red Sox proved to be a bargain. The Babe made his major league debut on July 11, 1914, at Fenway Park versus the Cleveland Naps (soon to be called the Indians.) The first batter he faced, Jack Graney, hit a single. But Ruth pitched well; he allowed three Cleveland runs and eight hits over seven innings before being lifted for pinch hitter Duffy Lewis. Lewis got a hit and scored a run, earning the Babe the victory. Tim Murnane of the *Boston Globe* described Ruth as "a natural ballplayer [who] will undoubtedly become a fine pitcher..." Indeed, by the end of the decade, Ruth had become the dominant left-handed pitcher in the majors.

Still, as an untested newcomer, the Babe rode the Boston bench for most of the remainder of the 1914 season. When the Philadelphia Athletics clinched the American League flag, the Red Sox sent Ruth down to their Providence farm team, which was embroiled in a pennant race. Ruth finished the season there. Ruth claimed he received just one fan letter in 1914. It was a brief note from Brother Matthias written on St. Mary's stationery. It read, "You're doing fine, George. I'm proud of you."

Harry Hooper, the great Boston outfielder, was an early teammate of Ruth's. Hooper, reminiscing years later for Lawrence S. Ritter's *The Glory of Their Times*, recalled that young Ruth made an impression on him and the other Red Sox almost immediately:

> Babe Ruth joined us in the middle of 1914, a 19-year-old kid. He was a left-handed pitcher then, and a good one. He had never been anywhere, didn't know anything about manners or how to behave among people— just a big overgrown green pea. You probably remember him with that big belly he got later on. But that wasn't there in 1914. George was six-foot-two and weighed 198 pounds, all of it muscle. He had a slim waist, huge biceps, no self-discipline, and not much education—not so very

different from a lot of other 19-year-old would-be ballplayers. Except for two things: he could eat more than anyone else, and he could hit a baseball further.

Ruth began to blossom in 1915. Re-elevated to Boston, he posted an impressive 18–8 record as a pitcher as the Bosox won the American League pennant and the World Series. (For some reason, Red Sox manager Bill Carrigan did not allow Ruth to pitch in the World Series against the Philadelphia Phillies, but he did appear once in a pinch-hitting role against Grover Cleveland Alexander. For the record, Ruth grounded out to the first baseman.) The following season, Ruth upped his pitching mark to 23–12 and led the league in both earned-run average and shutouts.

Ruth owed absolutely none of his success to a Spartan regimen. After being deprived of a social life for more than a decade at St. Mary's, Ruth intended to make up for lost time. He gorged himself at restaurants, where his table manners left a lot to be desired. He often stayed out all night drinking and carousing. Women were especially fascinating to the Babe, who had rarely seen any during his stay in the institution. In 1914 he married Helen Woodford, a 16-year-old cafe waitress he met on his first day in Boston. (The Babe was always terrible with names. In his autobiography, Ruth scarcely made mention of his first wife. When he did, he referred to her as "Helen Woodring." Teammates' names also baffled the Babe, so he called everybody "kid." Every train porter, regardless of his true name, was addressed as "George.") Nevertheless, Ruth loved Helen dearly, but he could not control his insatiable lust for the opposite sex. Veteran baseball writer John Drebinger recalled late in his life, "Ruth was the most uninhibited person I ever met. He just did things." Near the end of his own life, Ruth confessed to Arthur Daley, "I guess I could have written two books on my life—one for the adults and one for the kids."

The 1917 season was another great one on the mound for the Babe. He won 24 games, lost 13, compiled a 2.01 ERA and finished 35 of the 38 games he started. But it was the Babe's bat that was beginning to generate excitement. He batted .325, a very respectable total for a regular player—a fantastic figure for a pitcher. That season, Ruth became a footnote in one of the most fascinating games in American League history.

On June 23 Ruth was the starting pitcher against the Washington Senators. The first—and only—batter Ruth faced was Ray Morgan who walked on four consecutive pitches. In his autobiography, Ruth claimed, "Though I've cooled off a lot in the 30 years since then, I still insist that three of the four should have been strikes." Ruth took his objections with umpire Brick Owens's verdicts to an extreme by punching the arbiter on the jaw. "It wasn't a love tap. I really socked him," Ruth remembered. He was ejected, of course, and was lucky to escape with just a $100 fine from AL president Ban Johnson.

The historical significance of the game was not Ruth's punch, which years later he called a "stupid act." It had to do with Ernie Shore, who relieved Ruth on the mound. Morgan, whose leadoff walk started all the fuss, was erased from the basepaths when he was caught stealing. Shore then proceeded to retire all 26 Washington batters he faced to complete a "perfect" game. (Under today's revised and stringent scoring rules, Shore is no longer credited with this rarest of pitching achievements for two extremely good reasons: He did not throw a complete game, and a Senator did reach base.)

By 1918 Red Sox manager Ed Barrow decided to play Ruth in the outfield or at first base on the days he did not pitch. This way, Barrow figured, Ruth could help Boston offensively each afternoon instead of every fourth one. The experiment succeeded grandly. Ruth's pitching statistics dipped somewhat (he was 13–7 in 1918), but he drilled an impressive 11 homers, tying Tilly Walker of the A's for the American League lead.

Although Ruth's home run total seems paltry by today's standards, before 1921 the major leagues used a "dead ball," which historian Joseph L. Reichler quaintly described as "having the resiliency of an overripe potato." Moreover, it was quite common for an entire game to be played with five or six balls. No matter how discolored, scuffed, soiled, or warped the balls became, the umpires kept them in play. In 1918 the Washington Senators and St. Louis Browns each hit a grand total of five home runs during the entire season. Cleveland and the White Sox managed just nine apiece. Boston sports journalist Burt Whitman wrote that season, "The more I see of Babe, the more he seems a figure out of mythology."

Ruth's double duty as star pitcher and star slugger was unheard of in 1918 and absolutely unimaginable today. Daniel Okrent of *The Sporting News* put Ruth's career in perspective by noting,

> He was nearly as great a pitcher as he was a hitter. He was unquestionably the best left-handed pitcher in the American League in the 1910s. When people get into discussions about who was the greatest ballplayer in history, to me it seems utterly wasted. Let us say that Ruth was not as good an offensive player as Willie Mays. But he was also one of the greatest pitchers ever. It is as if imagining that Beethoven and Cezanne were one person producing the same work. It just can't be compared to anything else.

The legend of Babe Ruth the slugger was created in spring training of 1919. During a Red Sox–Giants exhibition game in Tampa, Ruth, facing right-hander Columbia George Smith, hit a ball farther than anyone had ever seen. In 1974, a few months before his death, Boston outfielder Harry Hooper clearly described the startling home run he had witnessed 55 years before:

I came to attention with everybody else. You watch the outfielder. He tells you how far it's going. Well, I looked up once at that ball and then I watched the right fielder. It was Ross Youngs. He was running and running into right-center, getting smaller and smaller. There was no wall or grandstand out there, just a low rail fence, way, way out. Youngs finally stopped at the fence and put his hands on his hips and stood there and watched that ball come down. Then he turned around and looked back toward the infield.

Estimates of the homer's length ranged from 579 to 620 feet. Nobody actually thought to measure it precisely. Donald Honig, in his 1985 book *Baseball America*, described the reaction to the monumental blast. "Everyone remained frozen for a few moments, as though it would have been irreverent to sit down too quickly after what they had just witnessed. Then the Red Sox players sat down en masse, wordlessly watching their young teammate trot around the bases, while Columbia George Smith stood motionless on the mound, a blank expression on his face, not quite sure whether he had been honored or humiliated."

By 1919 Ruth was the undisputed home run king of baseball, belting the phenomenal total of 29 to set a new single-season record. (The old mark of 27 homers had been set back in 1884 by long-forgotten Ned Williamson of the National League's Chicago White Stockings. If any home run record deserved to be accompanied by an asterisk, Williamson's did. He hit 25 of them over a ridiculously short left-field wall at Lake Front Park, his home playing grounds.) Whatever the Babe did on the mound was now a mere sideline. Ruth notched a 9–5 record in his last full season when he was expected to pitch. His career pitching record is an impressive 94–46 (plus a perfect 3–0 in World Series play). Ruth's lifetime ERA was 2.28. Perhaps the best indication of Ruth's pitching prowess was his 6–4 record when his mound opponent was Walter Johnson, the great Washington hurler who must rate among the top five pitchers of all time.

After winning the World Series in 1915, 1916 and 1918, the Red Sox fell on hard times in 1919, finishing a disappointing sixth in the American League. Attendance was down at Fenway Park and high-living owner Harry Frazee was in desperate need of some fast cash. Along with owning the Red Sox, Frazee was also a backer of Broadway plays. After the 1919 baseball season ended, Frazee had the opportunity to finance *No, No Nanette!*, a musical comedy that would eventually be a Broadway smash. But there was only one way Frazee could raise the capital for his theatrical production.

On January 6, 1920, the sports world was stunned upon hearing the news that Frazee had sold Ruth to the New York Yankees. In exchange for parting with the game's biggest star, Frazee received $125,000 from Yankee owner Colonel Jacob Ruppert plus a personal loan of $350,000. Baseball would never be the same again. Neither would the Red Sox. After winning four

World Series in the space of seven seasons, Boston's American League team has only played in four Fall Classics since 1919, losing all of them. "The Curse of the Bambino" is how cynical Red Sox fans conveniently explain their team's long dry spell.

In contrast, everything turned completely around for New York's formerly woebegone American League franchise. Before Ruth's arrival the Yankees had never won a pennant. By 1932 they had won seven. Commenting on the acquisition of Ruth, the *New York Times* did some bold speculating. Given that the Yankees played their home games in the Polo Grounds, a ballpark with an enticingly short right-field wall, the newspaper commented, "It would not be surprising if Ruth surpassed his home run record of 29 circuit clouts next summer."

Yankee manager Miller Huggins had little use for Ruth's pitching prowess. (Ruth went 1–0 on the mound in 1920.) Huggins opted instead to use Ruth permanently in right field. The *Times's* prediction was achieved—and then some—as a new, terrifying force was unleashed on the American League. The Babe socked the unheard of total of 54 homers and drove in 137 runs. Nobody else came close to matching Ruth's capacity to hit home runs. In fact, *no other team managed to equal Ruth's feat!* The Yankees led the American League with 115 homers, the St. Louis Browns were second with 50. Bland statisticians would call this phenomenon a disparity in talent. Baseball fans called it fascinating. Opposing teams called it frightening. After 1920, a season in which Ruth's slugging percentage was an obscene .847, he was rarely called on to pitch again.

Not long before his death, the late Red Barber, the beloved radio voice of the Brooklyn Dodgers, was interviewed for Ken Burns's nine-part PBS *Baseball* documentary. Among other things, Barber discussed Ruth's role in the sport's evolution. Said Red,

> Babe Ruth revolutionized baseball. He changed it. Ruth began hitting home runs and gave baseball its excitement. They changed everything from the ball itself, the construction of the bats, the philosophy of hitting, the philosophy of pitching. Babe Ruth changed it. We don't realize it today, but the game of baseball has never been the same since Babe Ruth started hitting home runs.

Ruth's plentiful home runs were indeed revolutionizing the sport, but some notables greatly resented what was happening. Ty Cobb, whose beloved tactical game was being transformed into a slugging match, snorted, "Given the proper physical equipment, which consists solely in the strength to knock a ball 40 feet farther than the average man can do it, anybody can play big-league baseball today. In other words, science is out the window." Rogers Hornsby noted, "The home run became glorified with Babe Ruth. Starting with him, batters have been thinking in terms of how far they could hit the ball, not how often."

Yankee manager Miller Huggins sympathized with the sentiments of Cobb and Hornsby but was forced to admit, "Real students of the game might prefer Ty Cobb's classic brand of baseball, but Babe Ruth appeals to everybody. They all flock to him because nowadays the American fan likes the fellow who carries the wallop." *Baseball Magazine* agreed. "[Ruth] has not only slugged his way to fame," said the publication, "but he has got everyone else doing it. The home-run fever is in the air. It is infectious."

Tris Speaker, Ruth's former Boston teammate, did not quite grasp the significance of what was happening. In 1921 he uttered a statement that provoked laughter even then. "Ruth made a grave mistake when he gave up pitching," said Speaker. "Working once a week, he might have lasted a long time and become a great star."

In previous years, baseball's moguls did not care much for statistical trends that shook the game's traditions. After the 1884 season, when no-hitters and shutouts were plentiful, the rules-makers, who were just adjusting to overhand pitching, decided to outlaw pitchers who threw from a running start. The desired effect was achieved as batting averages rose dramatically in 1885. When hurlers started to dominate again, the pitching rubber was moved back to 60' 6" in 1893 to give the hitters more time to react to deliveries. Given this track record, one might have expected the moguls to come up with some way of stifling the Babe's home run totals. However, with fascinated fans flocking through the turnstiles to see Ruth belt homers, nothing was done to curtail the merriment, much to the displeasure of American league pitching staffs.

The Babe was also creating a new breed of baseball fan—the home run watcher. In 1920 Cincinnati papers carried the interesting story of a local judge who was embarking on a summer vacation of indefinite length to please his son, a fanatical Ruth fan. Edward T. Dixon and his boy would travel to Cleveland on a Sunday to attend a Yankees-Indians series. As soon as Babe connected for a homer, the Dixons would return home to Cincinnati. "If the Babe makes a home run the first day out, then we will be home that day," said the judge. "We will remain with the Yankees, go where they go, and stay where they stay until Babe makes a home run. The missus knows we will be home the next morning after Babe Ruth makes his next home run."

Although Ruth hit a homer once in every 8.48 times at bat in 1920, the Dixons were gone longer than expected. The Babe drew three walks in Monday's game at Cleveland. Tuesday's contest was rained out. On Wednesday Ruth twisted his knee and had to be carried off the field. He was back in action on Thursday but went hitless. The Yankees boarded a train for Philadelphia. So did the Dixons. On Friday Ruth smacked a homer at Shibe Park. True to their pledge, the two Dixons immediately went home.

Ruth now had America's largest metropolis for his stage and quickly became a national celebrity. He tucked away Helen and his young daughter in a rural home near Sudbury, Massachusetts, while he checked into a luxurious suite in a New York City hotel. His nighttime exploits were witnessed by many but reported by few. A tacit understanding existed among sports journalists. "Ruth was a special case," acknowledged Shirley Povich, who covered baseball for the *Washington Post* for half a century. "What would have been exposed in this later day of journalism was simply ignored." The reason for the veil of silence was clear: With baseball trying to recover from the scandalous 1919 World Series, nobody wanted the sport's image further tarnished by stories about its greatest star's excesses. Ruth refused to acknowledge that Prohibition laws existed. He consumed prodigious quantities of bourbon, his favorite libation, often enhancing a gargantuan breakfast with a pint or two.

Paul Derringer, a National League pitcher, recalled encountering Ruth in a train's dining car one morning.

> In came the Babe, alone. Seeing the empty chair, he sat at my table. Ruth called over a waiter and ordered a pitcher of ice, a pint of ginger ale, a porterhouse steak garnished with four fried eggs, fried potatoes, and a pot of coffee. He told the waiter to bring him the ice and ginger ale right away.
>
> A few minutes later the waiter returned. The Babe pulled a pint of bourbon out of his hip pocket, poured it over the ice, poured in the ginger ale, and shook up the mixture. That was Ruth's breakfast juice. Sometime later, Ruth's roommate told me that was nothing more than the Babe's daily habit.

Back in his Red Sox days, Ruth also amazed people with his knife and fork. In January 1918 the Babe and Stuffy McInnis arrived at Fenway Park to sign their contracts for the upcoming season. When neither man fussed about the figure offered to him, manager Ed Barrow gave team secretary Larry Graver a five-dollar bill and told him to treat himself and the players to a hearty lunch. Under normal circumstances $5 should have been more than ample to feed three diners in 1918. However, a few hours later, Graver returned to Barrow and said, "You owe me $2.85. Have you ever seen that big guy eat? He had a whole custard pie for dessert!"

Despite his excesses, Ruth was beloved by the public, especially children. Ruth, as far back as his Baltimore days, regularly distributed handfuls of game passes to idolizing youngsters. He was also more than obliging for photographers, be it for a simple photo or as part of a promotion. No costume was too ridiculous for Ruth to put on in order to please a cameraman. Once, during their glory days, the Babe and Lou Gehrig donned cowboy duds to hype an upcoming rodeo. Gehrig looks badly out of place; Ruth, oddly enough, appears completely at home.

Ruth now ranked among the highest-paid baseball players in the majors, but his speed in parting with his cash alarmed Ruppert. Eventually the club owner began to set aside a portion of Ruth's earnings in guaranteed investments, ostensibly as security for Ruth's old age. In reality the Yankee owner wanted to prevent his slugger from bankrupting himself with his frivolous spending.

Even with Ruth's booming bat, the Yankees failed to win the American League pennant in 1920. But the New York dynasty was dawning. In 1921 Ruth continued to shock the baseball establishment by bettering his statistics from the previous year. His home run total rose to 59, certainly a record that would stand forever. A writer for the *New York Daily News* marveled, "It is impossible to watch him at bat without experiencing an emotion. I've seen hundreds of ballplayers at the plate and none of them managed to convey the message of impending doom to the pitcher that Babe Ruth did with the cock of his head, the position of his legs, and the little, gentle waving of his bat feathered in his two big paws."

Upon hitting his thirty-fourth homer in the 1921 campaign, the 26-year-old Ruth took sole possession of the all-time major league home run mark with 137 career round-trippers. (The old mark of 136 had been held by Roger Connor, who played for five different teams from 1880 to 1897.) Technically, every regular-season home run Ruth hit afterward established a new record—a feat the Bambino accomplished 577 times!

Led by Ruth's offensive outburst, the Yankees won the American pennant for the first time in 1921 but lost the final best-of-nine World Series to the Giants in eight games, much to the delight of John McGraw who resented that the secondary tenants of his Polo Grounds had become the darlings of New York City. Ruth batted .313 in his first World Series in a Yankee uniform. He hit his first of 15 post-season homers, but struck out eight of the 16 official times he came to bat.

At the end of the 1921 season, Ruth ran into trouble with commissioner Kenesaw Mountain Landis. Landis had outlawed post-season barnstorming (the practice of major leaguers traveling throughout the country to play in exhibition games). The commissioner illogically reasoned that such tours somehow demeaned the importance of the World Series. Ruth openly defied the ban and padded his wallet by appearing before awestruck crowds in the tank towns. Landis, whose word was law, promptly suspended the Babe for the beginning of the 1922 campaign. "He's just another ballplayer as far as my office is concerned," Landis insisted.

Ruth's domestic life was also experiencing some rocky times. At the beginning of 1922, Babe and Helen announced that a daughter named Dorothy had been born to them in June 1921. Not one writer could recall Mrs. Ruth showing any signs of pregnancy the previous spring. Author Ken Sabol, in his 1974 book, *Babe Ruth and the American Dream*, theorized that Dorothy was a by-product of one of Ruth's many illicit trysts, and the Babe took responsibility for the child to avoid the messy publicity of a paternity suit.

After rejoining the Yankee lineup in June, Ruth got himself into trouble again. He engaged in a series of violent rhubarbs with umpires and in his worst moment, leaped into the stands to confront a heckler at the Polo Grounds. This time Ruth was suspended by American League president Ban Johnson, who described Ruth's behavior as "warped." The Babe's numbers dropped significantly from 1921, but the Yankees made it to the 1922 World Series anyway. The Giants beat them again, this time in a four-game sweep. Versus the Giants Ruth had a disastrous time at the plate, batting just .118. At a sportsmen's banquet near the end of the year, Jimmy Walker, then a state senator, harshly criticized Ruth, telling him he was letting down the youth of America. Ruth was shamed by the accusation and promised to clean up his act.

The tenuous goodwill that had once existed between the Giants and Yankees had evaporated after 1922. Giants' manager John McGraw had allowed the Yankees to use the Polo Grounds when the American League club was clearly the less attractive of the two teams. However, with the Yankees setting new attendance records, McGraw refused to allow his financial rivals the luxury of using his ballpark any longer. Forced to find a new home, Colonel Ruppert bought a piece of property in the Bronx and authorized construction of Yankee Stadium, the gaudiest sports arena of its age.

With record speed, the vast new ballpark, which could hold 75,000 tightly packed spectators, was completed for opening day of 1923. Fittingly, Ruth homered in the inaugural game in front of a full house. Writers began calling the stadium, with some accuracy, "The House That Ruth Built." Ruth knocked out 41 homers during 1923. The Yankees won the pennant again and met the Giants for the third straight year in the World Series. This time the Yankees won in six games. It was the first in a long line of world championships for baseball's most storied franchise.

Ruth's popularity was now beyond enormous. Whenever he walked down a street, a crowd of reverent onlookers would magically assemble and follow him. A *New York Times* editorial referred to him as "the First Citizen of the United States." Newspapers vied to get new angles for stories about the man said to be the most photographed person in the world. Although Ruth was generally cordial to reporters, he rarely said anything brilliant. "He was no Rhodes scholar," Joe Dugan declared. (American League president Ban Johnson would have concurred. Once, when reprimanding Ruth, Johnson accused the Babe of having the mentality of a 15-year-old.) Ruth's conversation with Carl Sandburg, then on the staff of the *Chicago Daily News*, verified the fact.

"If some boys asked you what books to read," inquired Sandburg, "what would you tell them?"

Ruth gave a puzzled look and replied, "I never get that. They don't ask me that question. They ask me how to play ball."

Sandburg tried another approach. "What's your favorite flower?"

Ruth just laughed and blurted, "I don't care about flowers."

Still thinking he was conversing with a bookworm, Sandburg asked Ruth, "Is there any one character in history you are especially interested in, such as Lincoln, Washington, or Napoleon?"

"I've never seen any of them," was Ruth's terse reply.

In 1924 the Babe raised his home run output to 46 and led the American League with a .378 average to win his only batting championship. Even so, the Yankees lost their grip on the American League pennant, finishing second to Washington. Ruth's promise to reform did not last. Over the winter he indulged in all types of legal and illegal pleasures, becoming a favorite customer in brothels. A bookie filed suit in court in an attempt to get Ruth to pay off more than $7,700 in horse racing debts he had accrued. Helen, staggered by her husband's excesses, suffered a nervous breakdown as the couple's shaky marriage began to fall apart.

Ruth arrived for spring training in 1925 in terrible shape. His lack of fitness caught up with him. During a swing of exhibition games in the South in which the Yankees played the Brooklyn Robins, Ruth was suffering badly but still managed to put on a great show. In Atlanta the sickly Babe was placed under the care of a doctor who advised him to rest. Ruth would have none of it. He slept on a train to Chattanooga. He was too ill to practice. According to the *New York Times* the Babe "was suffering with chills and fever." Nevertheless, Ruth smashed two homers before an enthusiastic crowd of 8,000 Tennesseans who sat through a persistent rain to see their hero. One homer was said to be the longest ever hit at Andrews Field, the home park of the minor league Chattanooga Lookouts. The next afternoon, Ruth launched another home run in Knoxville, this one off Brooklyn ace Dazzy Vance.

On April 7 Ruth finally collapsed in a railroad station in Asheville, North Carolina, with a temperature of 105 degrees. British newspapers, which cared little about baseball but were always fascinated by the slugger's sizable salary, incorrectly reported that he had died. Friendly journalists claimed Ruth was suffering the aftereffects of gorging too many hot dogs.

Others believed the unlikely tale was concocted to cover up an unsavory reality: the Babe had contracted venereal disease. In an interview with author Robert Creamer nearly 50 years later, Joe Dugan, a teammate of Ruth's, dismissed the "bellyache" story as sheer nonsense. "His problem was lower than that," Dugan laughed. "He was going day and night, broads and booze." The front page of the April 8 *New York Times* claimed Ruth had "a bad case of the grip [*sic*]." Still there was optimism that Ruth would be in the Yankees' Opening Day lineup. One journalist noted "[Ruth's] indifference to colds and to injured fingers and legs and all aches and pains is well known among the players on the Yankees. Missing a ball game is something that causes Ruth severe discomfort."

In his autobiography, Ruth gave his own account of his physical collapse in North Carolina. Although Ruth avoids stating the nature of his malady, he does not give credence to the ludicrous hot dog myth, either:

> In the Asheville station I was walking with [Yankee catcher] Steve O'Neill on our way to a taxicab when I suddenly pitched forward. I would have fallen to the floor if Steve hadn't reached out and grabbed me. With some other players he helped me into a cab and I was taken to our hotel and then, when it was realized I was very sick, to a hospital. It was what the reporters called the stomach ache that was heard around the world. But I was sicker than that.

On April 8, the day after his breakdown, Ruth felt well enough to invite reporters and photographers into his bedroom. Although the official statement from the Yankee hierarchy claimed Ruth was feeling much better, the Bambino candidly informed the journalists, "Every bone in my body aches." He boarded a train for New York City, where he sought the care of team physicians. Eventually Ruth underwent an operation for "an internal abscess."

Ruth missed a good portion of the 1925 season as he recuperated in St. Vincent's Hospital. In one of baseball's quirkiest historical coincidences, Ruth made his first appearance for the Yankees on June 1, the very afternoon Lou Gehrig began his remarkable streak of consecutive games. Even with the arrival of Gehrig as the Yankees' regular first baseman, New York floundered in the standings, finishing well back in seventh place. Four decades would pass before another Yankee team would endure such an awful season.

The Babe was not much help to the club during 1925 when he did return. He learned little from what had happened in Asheville. His nonstop partying quickly resumed. With Ruth's batting average below .250, manager Miller Huggins's patience ran out. Ruth was suspended for staying out all night for two consecutive evenings during a road trip to St. Louis. Moreover, Huggins slapped Ruth with a $5,000 fine—a year's salary for some big leaguers at the lowest end of the pay scale.

Amazed by the severity of the penalty, Ruth balked at paying the huge fine and marched into Colonel Ruppert's office to complain. The club's owner, who was equally tired of Ruth's nocturnal shenanigans, strongly backed Huggins. After a time, Ruth was permitted to rejoin the team only upon making a locker-room apology to the other Yankees. (There is some doubt as to whether the fine was ever paid. Ruth, in his autobiography, claimed it was rescinded not long after Huggins's death in 1929.) By the end of the 1925 season Ruth had played in 98 games, hit 35 homers and raised his batting average to .290. They were respectable figures, all things considered.

Still, some journalists wrote mournful pieces proclaiming the Babe's best days were behind him. Veteran New York baseball scribe Fred Lieb commented, "It is doubtful that Ruth again will be the superstar he was from

1919 through 1924. Next year Ruth will be 32 [*sic*], and at 32 the Babe will be older than Eddie Collins, Walter Johnson and Ty Cobb at that age. Babe has lived a much more strenuous life."

In 1926 Ruth had fully regained his health, and the Yankees reclaimed the pennant. The Babe was once again a regular fixture in the New York lineup, hitting 47 home runs while batting .372. A new Yankee powerhouse was developing, but the St. Louis Cardinals won their first National League pennant that season and capped off a remarkable campaign by stunning Ruth and company with a seven-game triumph in the World Series. In defeat, the Babe did manage to sock four homers (including three in one game on October 6) becoming the first man to accomplish the feat in a World Series contest. Ruth's third homer of the day left broadcaster Graham McNamee in a babbling stupor.

> The Babe hits it clear into the centerfield bleachers for a home run. For a home run! Did you hear what I said? Where is that fellow who told me not to talk about Ruth anymore? Send him up here. Oh, what a shot—directly over second. The boys are all over him over there. One of the boys is riding on Ruth's back. Oh! What a shot! Directly over second base, and almost on a line, and then that dumbbell, where is he, who told me not to talk about Ruth! Oh, boy! Not that I love Ruth but, oh, how I love to see a shot like that! Wow! That's a World Series record, three home runs in one World Series game, and what a home run! That was probably the longest hit ever made in Sportsman's Park. They tell me this is the first ball ever hit in the centerfield stands. That is a mile and a half from here. You know what I mean.

Still, the heavily favored New Yorkers failed to defeat the scrappy bunch from St. Louis. If it was any consolation to the Yankees, they had a strong young team that promised to repeat as American League champions in 1927. (I won't leave you in suspense; the Yankees did indeed capture the pennant with a 110–44 mark for a winning percentage of .714. Trivia buffs love baseball numbers, and the .714 mark too closely mirrors Ruth's total of 714 career home runs to be casually overlooked!) It would be the year of "Murderers' Row," the glorious summer when Ruth, at age 32, would make an unexpected challenge at his cherished major-league record of 59 home runs, which he had set six seasons before.

2

SPRING TRAINING
1927

The most glorious season Babe Ruth would experience in his 22-year major league career started off in ominous fashion. On March 10, at the Cincinnati Reds' training site in Orlando, Florida, during the Yankees' first official exhibition game of the year, Ruth went down with a charley horse—the very same type that had afflicted him in the left leg the previous season—and hobbled off the field.

Newspapers quickly spread the disconcerting tidings to the thousands of American League baseball fans in New York City, reporting that the great Bambino, in an attempt to shift into high gear from a stationary start, had hurt himself so badly that he was forced to exit the game and the ballpark in the fourth inning. This adverse development did much to dampen the spirits of some 4,000 Floridians and tourists who had gathered at the diamond to watch the Babe. Those who opted to stay after the fourth inning saw the Yanks defeat the Cincinnati Reds 8–5.

Ruth would not be sidelined for the season; he would be riding the pines for not more than a few days. Knowledgeable folks claimed Ruth's injury was of the minor variety, but it proved that Ruth could be injury-prone below the kneecaps. Would 1927 be a bad year for injuries for America's most acclaimed and favorite home run hitter? Only time would tell.

Opposite: The 1927 New York Yankees. *Front row:* Julie Wera, Mike Gazella, Pat Collins, Eddie Bennett (mascot), Benny Bengough, Ray Morehart, Myles Thomas, Cedric Durst. *Middle row:* Urban Shocker, Joe Dugan, Earle Combs, Charlie O'Leary (coach), Miller Huggins (manager), Art Fletcher (coach), Mark Koenig, Dutch Ruether, Johnny Grabowski, George Pipgras. *Back row:* Lou Gehrig, Herb Pennock, Tony Lazzeri, Wiley Moore, Babe Ruth, Don Miller, Bob Meusel, Bob Shawkey, Waite Hoyt, Joe Giard, Pen Paschal, unknown, Doc Wood (trainer).

The Babe's problems began in the top of the fourth inning. Ruth was on second base when Mike Gazella lined a solid single into right field. Ruth tried to score on the play—and he did—but his leg muscles, still taut from doing nothing strenuous since October, were not up to the task. Ruth was clearly lame as he rounded third. Nevertheless, his momentum was great enough to carry him over the plate. Ruth was immediately attended to in the Yankee dressing room, but reports circulated that baseball's premier slugger had an ostrich-egg size knotted muscle in his leg.

The next day Ruth and his teammates were back at the Yankee spring training headquarters in St. Petersburg, where Ruth's bum leg was a major news story. The papers reported Miller Huggins's announcement that Babe Ruth would be out for several days. To those used to deciphering Huggins's coded comments, this likely meant six or seven days. Therefore Ruth was not expected to make an appearance on the field in the March 12 game with the Boston Braves, nor in the encounter with the minor league outfit from Baltimore at Auburndale the following Monday. Those who caught a glimpse of Ruth around the team could not help noticing that he was limping badly and using a cane. According to Yankees trainer Al Woods, the Babe had torn a muscle in his left leg. Woods plied the tools of his trade and massaged the knotted muscle before wrapping the entire leg in tape.

The New York Times hinted that Ruth was still engaging in his old habits. Its story concluded, "If Ruth rests, he will be all right, but try to make him rest."

Even with Ruth sidelined, Yankee owner Colonel Jacob Ruppert had a lot to smile about. Before he departed to his club's spring training headquarters in St. Petersburg, the 60-year-old baseball magnate was interviewed by the *New York Times* and used the opportunity to discuss the state of the game. Colonel Ruppert estimated the value of the American League at $25 million and the National League at a similar figure. The *Times* story recounted that when Colonel Ruppert and Colonel T. L. Huston bought the Yankees in 1915 the twosome paid only $200,000 for the entire club. Ruppert used his number-one gate attraction as an example of the economic boom times for the sport. He said that Babe Ruth's contracts over his years with the Yankees have totaled $600,000. Nevertheless, Ruppert considered it money well spent based on the gate receipts Ruth was almost solely responsible for generating since 1920.

Things were not universally rosy in the baseball world, however. The very day that Ruppert was proclaiming overwhelming public confidence in the sport, 36-year-old Buck Weaver, the slick-fielding third baseman of the disgraced 1919 Chicago White Sox, made one last attempt to have his lifetime ban lifted. Commissioner Landis flatly rejected the idea. In a letter to Weaver, Landis declared, "I regret that it is not possible for me to arrive at any other conclusion than that set forth in the decision of December 11, 1922, that your own admissions and actions in the circumstances forbid your reinstatement." Although there was no evidence that Weaver deliberately played to lose the World Series against Cincinnati, he was being punished for knowing about the fix scheme and not immediately reporting it.

Ruth was still limping on March 14 and, to no one's great surprise, did not make the trip to Auburndale, Florida, with the rest of the Yankees. Auburndale was the training site of the minor league powerhouse Baltimore Orioles. Even without the Babe New York handily trounced the International League club 11–2. Still, Ruth's nonappearance affected the attendance considerably that afternoon. According to official figures, there were only 497 customers who bought tickets. As a reward for their loyalty, this small crowd was treated to the sight of the Yanks—or, perhaps more accurately, of rookies masquerading as the Yanks—slapping baseballs all over the lot.

Ruth's health improved marginally enough for him to make a token pinch-hitting appearance the following afternoon in New York's 6–5 victory over the Boston Braves.

But this first appearance of the season in the Yankees' springtime home of St. Petersburg was somewhat of a bust. Ruth spent most of the afternoon unsuccessfully flailing at baseballs and did little more than provide a cool breeze for the overheated ballpark patrons. He failed to accomplish much when he batted for pitcher Dutch Ruether in the bottom of the sixth. George's lone at-bat consisted of three mighty swings—all of which failed to connect wood with horsehide.

But Babe still was not quite right. In a Yankee intrasquad game between the rookies and the veterans, manager Huggins placed Ruth on the newcomers' team, where he played first base in the six-inning affair. In his two times at bat Ruth grounded meekly into a pair of double plays. On March 19 Ruth fared just as miserably in a genuine exhibition game against the Boston Braves. The Yankees' four-game exhibition winning streak came to an abrupt halt—and the New Yorkers had George Herman Ruth to blame! Such is the lot of heroes.

The Bambino was an utter disappointment to his legions of friends, hangers-on and miscellaneous admirers. At the bat he produced a big, fat zero. Defensively, Ruth embarrassingly dropped a fly ball that a 40-year-old Class D player should have caught with the greatest of ease. Sure enough, a pair of runs came in on that error, and, not so coincidentally, the Yanks lost by that margin, 6–4.

Ruth's three at-bats consisted of this awful outing: He hit a grounder to the second baseman. Another grounder dribbled to the Braves' pitcher. The third trip to the plate resulted in a shabby strikeout, which sent the 2,500 paying customers into convulsions of laughter. The joke was appreciated by everyone in the park except for Mr. Ruth and his pinstripe teammates, who wanted to win the game rather than chuckle at the Bambino's off day.

Richards Vidmer penned a lengthy piece for the *New York Times* which appeared on March 21. In it he featured a fictitious conversation with the Yankee faithful regarding the team's chances to win the American League pennant in 1927. "Everyone was quite open and candid in the matter," Vidmer wrote.

> "It's the same team to a man as in 1926," they admitted.
> "What man?" I asked, waxing facetious.
> "Babe Ruth," was the immediate response.
> "Are there any good prospects?"
> "Yes. Ruth."
> "How good does the team look this year?"
> "Just as good as Ruth looks."
> "Are the Yanks working hard?"
> "Ruth is."

That same day, Ruth, still favoring his bad leg, hit a single in three trips to the plate in New York's 2–1 win over Cincinnati in St. Petersburg.

The next afternoon, the Yankees and Reds played to a five-inning 0–0 draw in Tampa that was terminated by rain. (The Babe went 0 for 1 in the abbreviated affair.) With plenty of time to spare and a column to fill, Vidmer opined that the Yankees were an atypical bunch of ballplayers, consisting mostly of loners, from manager Miller Huggins down through the entire lineup. Ruth, he noted, was almost never seen at the team's hotel and was a frequent user of room service. Nevertheless, Vidmer figured the pure power of the Yankees made up for any shortcomings in *esprit de corps*.

The rain subsided in St. Petersburg on March 23, and Ruth returned to his fine form as New York soundly thrashed the Boston Braves. He smacked out three extra-base hits, namely two homers and a double. Yankee fans hoped that Ruth had at last begun his long-distance hitting spree for the year. The Braves were totally rattled by the Ruthian outburst and succumbed to a 16–7 walloping.

Ruth began his merry-making feeling in the fifth inning with a double. Even with a bum leg, he had no trouble cruising into second base. In the very next frame, he started off by reaching first on an error. Because the Yanks strung together a lengthy rally, the Babe was up at bat again in the same inning. He took the opportunity to belt his first home run of the year, even though the springtime Florida hits would of course not count in the statistics sheet when the official numbers were tabulated in October.

Two Yankee runners were on base at the time. As soon as Ruth's bat contacted the flying spheroid, there was little doubt that three more Yankees were destined to cross the plate in an uncontested fashion. The ball landed far over the right-field fence and bounced up to the second story of a nearby apartment complex.

Just to prove that the first one was slightly more than a fluke, the Babe lashed another homer in his last at-bat of the day. The ball flew towards deep right field, smacked off the canvas that acts as a fence, and deftly ripped it away from its moorings! With plenty of momentum left over, the ball slipped under the detached canvas and rolled across the street, where it was recovered by D. L. Moody, a local St. Petersburg merchant. A giddy Mr. Moody bounded into the ballpark, acquired Ruth's signature as well as Huggins's on the ball, and soon put the object on display in an honored spot in his place of business.

On March 24 Ruth went 1 for 5 at the plate but was hardly even noticed. Umpire Frank Wilson, formerly of the American League but recently hired by the National League, ejected nine Yankees and one Brave in Boston's 10–9 win. To say the least, Wilson was having an interesting spring training. The short-tempered umpire's personal total of dismissed players was approaching 30! Earlier in the preseason, Wilson had handed the Philadelphia A's a forfeit loss the day after he had ejected mild-mannered Lou Gehrig from a Yankees game.

The Yankees were idle on March 25, but the newspapers kept Ruth's name in type by printing a few of Ruth's comments—not about baseball, but about film acting. Ruth had spent part of the winter in Hollywood starring in an utterly forgettable baseball movie. The Babe noted, "I always wondered what became of prizefighters when they got knocked out of the ring. I found out. They go into movies. They had whole regiments of them in that movie I was in, and they were all supposed to be ballplayers. And, what's worse, I was supposed to get in a clubhouse fight with them in the picture."

"Was it a good fight?" asked journalist John Kieran.

"I've had plenty of real fights with ballplayers," Ruth continued, "but that phony fight with those pugs was a darb. One of them busted my nose and another nearly knocked my eye through the back of my head. Gosh! I thought somebody had hit me with a steamer trunk. I broke one guy's arm, which was the best I could do. But I won the fight. The director saw to that. I was the hero, and the hero can't lose—in the movies."

On March 26, in a rematch of the 1926 World Series contestants, the Yankees were badly trounced, 13–2, by the St. Louis Cardinals in Avon Park, Florida. The capacity crowd was not discouraged by the lopsided score. Most stayed to the end in the hopes of witnessing a Ruth homer. They did not get their wish. Ruth did triple though. Richards Vidmer of the *Times* reported, "Babe Ruth was in the park, and it isn't every day or every year that a resident of Avon Park can see the Mighty Mauler of Manhattan. They were determined that the Ruth was mighty and would prevail—whether he did or not." Two days later St. Louis's National League club beat the Yankees again, this time in St. Petersburg, but by a more respectable 5–4 score. Ruth managed two singles in the loss. The Cards and Yanks would continue to play each other in assorted southern cities as they headed north.

On March 30 the Yankees began their northward trek. Colonel Ruppert told the press that he was pleased with the fan support his team had received in St. Petersburg. He intended to make the city the Yankees' spring headquarters through at least 1928. New York trimmed its roster to 29 players. Four more hopefuls would have to be cut by June 15. Richards Vidmer of the *New York Times* commented wryly, "It has been learned on good authority that George Herman Ruth, a left-handed outfielder, will not be among those released."

The following day's edition of the *New York Times* contained Vidmer's cautiously optimistic prediction about the Yankees' pennant chances for 1927.

> One may wonder whether if [the Yankees] are going to get off in front and lead for the last half as they did last year, or one may wonder if they are going to flop and fail as they did the year before, when they floundered and finished no higher than seventh place.
>
> In order to relieve the suspense, your correspondent will declare right here and now that he doesn't think either will happen. The Yanks aren't any stronger than they were a year ago and they will have stronger opposition. Yet they are too strong to be counted out of the running for the pennant. They may not finish first, but they certainly won't finish seventh.

That same day Ruth went 0 for 4 at bat in a 4–3 loss to Cincinnati in West Palm Beach. Oddly enough, all the runs were scored in the ninth inning. It was a thrilling finish to a generally dull ballgame, but it only partially appeased the stadium full of tourists who had turned out solely to see Babe Ruth clout a home run. He did not come even close to accomplishing the feat. All in all, he struck out once and failed to get the ball out of the infield on his other two trips to the plate.

The Yankees and Cardinals renewed their rivalry on April 1 in Jacksonville. About 10,000 persons played hooky from their normal afternoon activities and happily paid their money to see Babe Ruth. They were well rewarded for their time. Babe Ruth was the star of the game, and the overflow crowd could tell their grandchildren about it in some later decade. Not only did Ruth connect for a key double in New York's 3–2 win; he also made a sensational sprawling catch to save the game in the ninth inning.

Ruth's enormous appeal was never more in evidence than the following afternoon in Savannah, Georgia. The Yanks lost 20–10 to the Cards in a terribly played game. Still, Ruth hit a triple and a single to please the 15,000 in attendance. After the last hit, a triple—which reporters later claimed would have been an inside-the-park homer if Ruth had chosen to exert himself— there was an extraordinary display of affection from a motley collection of youngsters who were once contentedly sitting in the bleachers, the stands, and the box seats.

They gleefully dashed across the playing field with worship on their minds. Ruth had to wade through them with high-flung knees in order to reach the bench. Twice he was completely halted by the youngsters. The Yanks may have looked like a lot of bushers in this 20–10 shellacking. They were a thoroughly beaten lot, but the Babe still was a national hero as far as America's boyhood was concerned.

Montgomery, Alabama, was the next stop in the Yankees-Cardinals tour, and Ruth got two more extra-base hits, both doubles, in New York's 4–2 win. But these hits, like a few others earlier in the spring, were artificially muted. His lame leg had already held him to two bases where he could have made four on inside-the-park homers on at least three other blasts. Twice in Montgomery Ruth might have circled the bases on two lovely long drives, but the Bambino evidently figured that a double in the spring easily beat another unscheduled trip to the Yankees' infirmary.

In Atlanta on April 4 Ruth demonstrated his defensive prowess by gunning out two runners at the plate in New York's 15–8 triumph over the Cards. Newspapermen marveled that Ruth's throws "split the plate." For good measure, the Babe also stroked two more doubles.

Another Yanks-Cards clash scheduled for April 5 in Knoxville, Tennessee, was rained out. However, the equally foul weather in another part of the state did not deter the entire hamlet of Etowah, Tennessee, from gathering at its train station to greet the Bambino during a brief stop. "The township of Etowah came to worship at the shrine of the king," said the *New York Times*, "and left with a feeling of friendship. When the Babe grins, awe vanishes and he makes a pal."

The homecoming tour continued. Ruth got just one hit in five at-bats in Chattanooga on April 6 in a 5–4 Yankee victory in 10 innings. On April 7 in a game played at Nashville, the Babe went 1 for 3 in a 10–8 loss to St. Louis. Such was the importance of Ruth's arrival that Tennessee's House of Representatives adjourned early so the elected members could attend the game en masse.

By April 9 the Yankees were back in metropolitan New York. In the first of a two-game exhibition series against Brooklyn at Ebbets Field, Ruth homered and singled in New York's 6–5 victory in front of 15,000 wind-chilled fans. The next afternoon, before 25,000 spectators (a Brooklyn preseason attendance record), Ruth rapped out three more singles as the Yankees won 4–3.

The preliminaries were now complete. The Yankees' home opener was scheduled for April 12. The Philadelphia Athletics would be the first visitors at Yankee Stadium in 1927. Ruth was healthy and fit, and his batting stroke was honed. He would now begin his run at one of the most cherished individual marks in the annals of team sports.

THE 1927 SEASON

⚾1 April 15
Athletics at Yankees

Athletics	ab	r	h	po	a
E. Collins, 2b	4	0	0	0	3
Lamar, lf	4	0	0	3	0
Cobb, rf	4	0	1	1	0
Simmons, cf	4	1	2	1	0
Hale, 3b	2	0	0	3	1
Poole, 1b	2	0	1	6	2
Perkins, c	3	0	1	2	1
French, pr	0	1	0	0	0
Foxx, c	1	0	0	5	0
Boley, ss	2	1	1	2	0
Ehmke, p	2	0	0	1	1
Dykes, ph	1	0	1	0	0
Pate, p	0	0	0	0	1
Walberg, p	0	0	0	0	1
Totals	29	3	7	24	10

Yankees	ab	r	h	po	a
Combs, cf	4	1	2	4	0
Koenig, ss	5	0	2	0	4
Ruth, rf	4	2	2	3	2
Gehrig, 1b	1	1	0	13	0
Meusel, lf	4	0	2	1	0
Lazzeri, 2b	4	0	1	2	4
Gazella, 3b	3	2	2	2	5
P. Collins, c	3	0	1	2	0
Pennock, p	4	0	0	0	3
Totals	32	6	12	27	18

Philadelphia	0 0 0 0 0 0 3 0 0 - 3
New York	1 1 1 1 0 0 2 0 x - 6

The New York Yankees were three games into the 1927 campaign before Babe Ruth managed to hit his first home run of the season. The opponents that Good Friday afternoon at Yankee Stadium were Connie Mack's Philadelphia Athletics, who had already dropped the first two contests of the three-game series to New York. This did not bode well for the A's, who were considered the best bet of the other seven American League clubs to upset the defending champions in the long chase for the pennant.

Before spring training began, Ruth had returned his contract unsigned to Yankee owner Colonel Jacob Ruppert. It was something of a ritual for Ruth, who always felt his services were worth far more money than the

33

Yankees' original offer indicated. Eventually, Ruth agreed to play the 1927 season in exchange for $70,000 of Ruppert's gate receipts. The sum was $18,000 more than the Babe was paid in 1926, and amounted to nearly a 35 percent pay hike. As far as anybody knew, Ruth was receiving the highest salary ever paid to any ballplayer in history. (Lou Gehrig, not yet the household name he would soon be, would receive the mere pittance of $7,000 in 1927. This would prove to be a tremendous bargain for Ruppert as Gehrig proceeded to match Ruth home run for home run for the first five months of the season.)

Babe Ruth and Herbert Pennock were the heroes for the Yankees in their 6–3 victory on the fifteenth of April. While Pennock's fine pitching was drawn out over the course of the whole afternoon, Ruth's noteworthy blow occurred early in the contest—in the bottom of the first inning, to be exact. Veteran Athletics hurler Howard Ehmke paid dearly for trying to sneak a slow curveball across the outside corner of the plate. The Bambino, always able to adjust to any variance in speed that an opposing moundsman might attempt, was not fooled by the offspeed pitch.

Ruth feasted on Ehmke's generous offering and majestically belted it deep into Yankee Stadium's right field bleacher seats to give the home team a quick edge. Upon the ball's descent into the admiring spectators, the crowd of about 20,000 heartily roared its approval.

Apart from the solo home run, Ruth made a defensive gem in the top of the second inning to snuff out a Philadelphia scoring threat. Al Simmons of the A's was stationed at second base with two out when teammate Jim (Easy) Poole hit a solid single that landed in front of Ruth in right field. Ruth grabbed the bounding ball and fired a rocket toward catcher Pat Collins. The accurate throw arrived in the catcher's mitt on one hop. Collins applied a perfect tag to Simmons's foot, and the A's were retired.

Although the Yankees opened up a seemingly comfortable 4–0 lead, the Athletics put together a serious rally in the top of the seventh. Connie Mack's club scored three times to get within a run of the home team. The Yankees immediately retaliated, scoring twice more in the bottom of the seventh to establish a 6–3 lead, which they held until the end of the game. Herb Pennock was credited with the victory, his first of the young season.

New York's win gave them a perfect 3–0 record to begin the season. However, they were not alone at the top of the standings. The Washington Senators, American League pennant winners in both 1924 and 1925, had also swept their first three tilts against the Boston Red Sox to occupy a share of the league lead. Throughout the entire 1927 season, the Yankees would always hold at least a partial share of first place. Fifty-seven seasons would pass before another club, the 1984 Detroit Tigers, would similarly go "wire to wire" in a major league baseball season.

Howard Ehmke, the Babe's first homer victim of 1927, is known to baseball scholars as an improbable hero of the 1929 World Series. After appearing in just 11 games for the A's that season, Ehmke was slotted by Connie Mack as his surprise starter to open the World Series against the Chicago Cubs. Using his repertoire of off-speed pitches, Ehmke completely baffled the Cubs, recording 13 strikeouts in Philadelphia's 3–1 victory to establish a Series record that stood for 24 years.

Before the season started, those in charge of major league baseball had serious concerns that scandalous revelations uncovered during the 1926 season involving Ty Cobb and Tris Speaker, two of the American League's finest players, might hamper attendance in 1927. (Speaker and Cobb had both been implicated in a game-fixing scandal dating back to 1919.) For the first three dates at Yankee Stadium, nearly 125,000 fans passed through the turnstiles in less than ideal weather, including the 72,000 souls who turned out on Opening Day. The owners' fears of lingering bitterness in the hearts of the paying customers were quickly put to rest.

Yankee owner Jacob Ruppert really was a colonel; the rank was bestowed on him when he served in the Seventh Regiment of the National Guard. He became sole proprietor of the Yankees in 1923 by buying out co-owner Tillinghast Huston's half of the club for $1.2 million. Ruppert was a lifelong bachelor and a member of the New York social register. Late in his life he noted, "I found out a long time ago there is no charity in baseball. Every club owner must make his own fight for existence. I went into baseball purely for the fun of it. I had no idea I would spend so much money. The only return I ever sought was to make ends meet."

Other Baseball News

- George Sisler, the man whose astonishing total of 257 hits in a single season has remained in the record books for 78 years, went 2 for 2 in the Browns' abbreviated game versus the Detroit Tigers in St. Louis. With the game tied 2–2 after five innings, persistent rain forced the termination of the contest. Because five full innings had been played, everyone's statistics counted.

- Tris Speaker, who was nearing the end of his marvelous career, barely showed any signs of advancing age. He scored three runs in Washington's 7–1 home victory over Boston, which kept the Senators briefly on pace with New York.

- The first noteworthy disturbance of the 1927 season occurred at a National League game in Philadelphia between the visiting New York Giants and the Phillies. Umpire Pete McLaughlin ruled that Edd Roush's hot grounder past third base was a fair ball, much to the displeasure of the Phillies and their fans. After Philadelphia manager Stuffy McInnis was ejected for his prolonged protests, the 17,000 angry Philadelphia fans reacted by flinging leather seat cushions, scorecards, paper wads, hot dogs, and other debris onto the diamond. Once order was restored, the Giants won the game 6–3.

• The Pittsburgh Pirates' first three games of the season were played in Cincinnati, but the unfriendly surroundings did not stop the Pirates from launching themselves into first place in the National League standings. Pittsburgh concluded their three-game sweep of the Reds with a convincing 10–6 victory in which all nine Pirate starters got at least one hit apiece.

2 April 23
Yankees at Athletics

Yankees	ab	r	h	po	a		Athletics	ab	r	h	po	a
Combs, cf	5	0	1	2	0		E. Collins, 2b	2	1	0	4	3
Koenig, ss	5	0	2	5	4		Dykes, 2b	1	0	0	0	2
Ruth, rf	5	1	1	0	1		Cochrane, ph	1	0	0	0	0
Gehrig, 1b	4	1	1	10	2		Lamar, lf	4	0	2	2	0
Meusel, lf	4	0	2	2	0		Cobb, rf	4	2	2	2	0
Lazzeri, 2b	3	1	0	3	3		Simmons, cf	2	0	2	2	0
Gazella, 3b	4	0	2	2	2		Hale, 3b	4	0	2	0	2
Grabowski, c	3	0	1	1	0		Branom, 1b	4	0	1	12	0
Ruether, p	3	0	0	1	1		Perkins, c	3	0	1	4	0
Paschal, ph	1	0	0	0	0		Wheat, ph	1	0	0	0	0
Moore, p	0	0	0	0	1		Boley, ss	4	1	2	1	4
							Walberg, p	4	0	1	0	4
Totals	37	3	10	26	14		Totals	34	4	13	27	15

New York   2 0 0 1 0 0 0 0 0 - 3
Philadelphia 1 0 2 0 0 0 0 0 1 - 4

One of baseball's numerous charms is that it is a game with sudden and subtle shifts of momentum—and no clock to prevent them from happening. Take the April 23 game between the Yankees and the Philadelphia Athletics at Shibe Park as a prime example.

On the strength of two consecutive solo homers by Babe Ruth and Lou Gehrig, New York vaulted to a quick 2–0 in the top of the first inning. As demoralizing as this probably was for the A's, there was still plenty of baseball to be played, and ample time for Philadelphia to reverse the trend and erase the Yankees' lead. Sure enough, the plucky Athletics fought their way back into the game and managed to win it in the bottom of the ninth inning, albeit on a throwing miscue. With a rare infield error, the visitors from the Bronx finally did themselves in, falling 4–3 to the hometown team. As far as

Yankee manager Miller Huggins was concerned, his club was also badly short-changed in a couple of key umpiring decisions earlier in the afternoon, and he was not above complaining about it.

But first things first: Let's examine Ruth's home run, his second of the young campaign. Like his first homer of the season, the clout was recorded in the score books in the very first inning of play. It was a solo shot, courtesy of Rube Walberg's pitching arm, that carried over Shibe Park's right field wall to put the visitors briefly ahead by a 1–0 count. Next into the batter's box strode Lou Gehrig, who quickly proceeded to duplicate the Babe's feat—and then some. Gehrig's magnificent homer flew clear out of Connie Mack's home ballyard, crash-landed on the roof of a Twentieth Street home and bounced several times before vanishing from sight. The grandeur of Gehrig's belt even brought some throaty cheers from the fickle fans of Philly.

Despite the quick offensive output, the New Yorkers failed to hold on to their early lead. By the time Philadelphia and the Yankees had entered the home half of the ninth inning, things had changed considerably and the game was tied 3–3. The home side, sensing the kill, immediately mounted a threat by putting runners at second and first bases with just one out. Manager Mack inserted Mickey Cochrane as a pinch hitter for Jimmy Dykes. However, at first glance, the substitution appeared to have been a wasted one. Cochrane hit what should have been an inning-ending, routine double-play grounder toward Yankee second baseman Tony Lazzeri.

Lazzeri fielded the ball with his customary ease and fired it accurately to shortstop Mark Koenig, who was covering second base on the play. The second out of the inning was recorded—one more to go. Koenig's attempt to turn the twin killing and send the game into extra innings went awry, however. His off-line throw to Lou Gehrig sailed past the first baseman's head and allowed Joe Boley to score Philadelphia's fourth run absolutely uncontested all the way from second base. Although there was considerable disagreement among the gentlemen of the press regarding to whom the error should have been assigned (many witnesses feeling that Gehrig should have been able to snare the throw even if he had to vacate the bag to do it), it went down in the official records as Koenig's blunder.

New York's frustration at losing this closely fought contest in such a sloppy fashion was compounded by two arguments they had with umpires earlier in the game. Earle Combs was declared out in the top of the fifth inning while running between first and second base. The play began when Mark Koenig slapped a ground ball towards A's second baseman Eddie Collins. Combs jumped to avoid being hit by the batted ball, but virtually landed in Collins's lap. Before Collins could utter a word of protest, Combs was quite properly ruled out for interfering with Collins's attempt to field Koenig's grounder. Diminutive Yankee manager Miller Huggins unsuccessfully tried to argue that Combs's collision with Collins resulted from his runner's genuine efforts to avoid being hit by the ground ball, which, as any serious student of baseball's rules knows, is totally irrelevant on such a play.

In the bottom of the fifth, Huggins thought his team was victimized again by a questionable umpiring decision when Al Simmons was awarded first base after being hit by a very slow Dutch Ruether offering. Huggins claimed that Simmons hardly made any effort to avoid being struck by the harmless pitch and should have been awarded nothing more than a ball in the count. "In both debates," commented James Harrison of the *New York Times,* "Huggins ran second in a field of two."

When contemporary fans think of Miller Huggins, invariably they remember him as the manager of the first dynastic Yankee team. However, Huggins did have a noteworthy playing career. From 1904 to 1916 Huggins was a very competent second baseman with the Cincinnati Reds and St. Louis Cardinals. Standing just 5'6", Huggins was not physically gifted; he had to work hard to excel in the majors, a character trait many great managers over the years have possessed. He was always among the league leaders at his position in putouts, assists, and double plays. Huggins's unimpressive lifetime batting average of .265 belies his true value as a leadoff hitter. His 1,002 career walks and 324 stolen bases generated a lot of runs. Sports writers called him "the Mighty Mite," an apt title to be sure.

On this day the Athletics were full value for their slim one-run victory. Philadelphia connected for 13 hits, including two from the bat of 40-year-old Ty Cobb, who was playing in his twenty-third American League campaign. Cobb had certainly lost some of his youthful speed, but his raging intensity on and off the field was still the same as it was when he was a raw Detroit Tiger rookie in 1905. During the course of the 1927 season, Cobb would display more than the occasional flash of his batting talents, and also a glimpse of his unrivaled competitive fury.

The loss to the Athletics dropped the Yankees' record to 7–3 after 10 games. The St. Louis Browns now occupied second place, but their stay near the top of the standings would be a short one.

Other Baseball News

- Flint Rhem, whose 20 victories had sparked the St. Louis Cardinals to an unexpected World Series championship the previous season, looked to be in peak form when he shut out the visiting Chicago Cubs 7–0.

- A costly blunder by a veteran relief pitcher was the key moment in Cincinnati's surprising 6–4 win at Pittsburgh's Forbes Field. Johnny Morrison of the Pirates, who answers to the colorful nickname Jughandle Johnny, committed a balk that forced in the tie-breaking Red tally late in the game.

• The Boston Red Sox converted three doubles and two singles in the third inning into four important runs as they edged the Washington Senators by a 5–4 score at home. It was the first win at Fenway Park in 1927 for the last-place Red Sox.

♪3 April 24
Yankees at Senators

Yankees	ab	r	h	po	a		Senators	ab	r	h	po	a
Combs, cf	5	0	0	0	0		Rice, rf	4	1	1	0	0
Koenig, ss	5	0	1	3	4		Harris, 2b	2	0	1	2	5
Ruth, rf	4	1	3	3	0		Speaker, cf	4	0	0	3	0
Gehrig, 1b	3	0	1	13	0		Goslin, lf	4	0	2	4	0
Meusel, lf	4	2	2	1	0		Judge, 1b	4	0	2	15	1
Lazzeri, 2b	3	1	0	0	8		Myer, ss	4	0	0	1	4
Gazella, 3b	3	1	2	2	1		Bluege, 3b	4	0	1	1	3
Collins, c	2	0	0	4	0		Ruel, c	4	0	0	1	3
Grabowski, c	0	0	0	1	0		Thurston, p	2	1	1	0	1
Shocker, p	3	0	1	0	2		Marberry, p	0	0	0	0	1
Durst, ph	1	1	1	0	0		Burke, p	0	0	0	0	2
							Cullop, ph	1	0	0	0	0
							West, ph	1	0	0	0	0
Totals	33	6	11	27	15		Totals	34	2	8	27	20

New York   0 1 0 0 0 5 0 0 0 - 6
Washington   0 0 0 0 1 0 1 0 0 - 2

It did not happen often during the 1927 season, but sometimes Babe Ruth could hit a home run in a Yankee win and not be lauded by the fawning New York press as the star of the game. Such was the case on April 24 in Washington's spacious Griffith Stadium when Miller Huggins sent unheralded Cedric Durst up to the plate as a pinch hitter in the sixth inning. The substitute hit a triple that rolled all the way to the edge of the greensward in right center field. This timely triple, one of three that Durst would hit over the course of the season, propelled the Yankees to a 6–2 win over the Senators, before the eyes of some 20,000 disappointed residents of the nation's capital. What's more, it made Miller Huggins look like a brilliant strategist for inserting Durst into the batting order at that particular moment.

Durst was a tall, lean Texan who stood 5'11" but weighed only about 160 pounds. He had been around the American League since 1922 as a member of the St. Louis Browns. Before the 1927 season got underway, Durst, who would turn 31 in August, was acquired by the Yankees and served as one of the club's capable utility players that remarkable summer. He would appear in 65 games for New York that season, making 21 pinch-hit appearances and playing an occasional stint in the outfield or first base. (With Lou Gehrig near the start of his iron man streak of 2,130 consecutive games, Durst's play at first base would come only after Gehrig's name had been safely recorded in the daily box score.) In 1930, Durst would be shipped to the Boston Red Sox in exchange for Charles (Red) Ruffing, a right-handed pitcher who would be a mainstay of the great Yankee staffs for the rest of the decade.

Babe Ruth hit his third home run of the 1927 season in his favorite direction—over the right field fence. It was a shot worthy of Ruth, who absolutely crushed an offering by Senators' pitcher Hollis (Sloppy) Thurston that was estimated to have traveled in excess of 400 feet. The 45-foot-high right field wall at Griffith Stadium is located some 328 feet from home plate. But this hardly proved to be a daunting obstacle for Ruth, who was in fine form. Ruth's blast left the ballpark in a great hurry, soaring over the top of a neighboring tree before disappearing from the view of the impressed audience gasping within the confines of the stadium.

Another Yankee, Bob Meusel, also homered that afternoon. His blast came in the top of the second inning. The victory raised New York's record to 8-3, two and a half games ahead of the second-place St. Louis Browns.

The winning pitcher for New York that day was Urban Shocker, who went the distance, allowing eight hits to the Senators. Born Urbain Jacques Shockcor in 1890, Shocker is one of the most underappreciated pitchers in the history of baseball. He began his major league career with the Yankees in 1916 before being traded to the St. Louis Browns after the 1917 season. For seven utterly frustrating summers, he led the Browns' pitching staff. Unfortunately for Shocker, the Browns' greatest years came at a time when the first dominant Yankee team was emerging. A consummate professional, Shocker never had a losing season on the mound. He won 27 games in 1921 and 24 more a year later. Shocker returned to the Yankees in 1925 and compiled a 49-29 record over the next three years. Poor health forced his retirement at the end of the 1927 season. Less than a year later, he was dead at age 38 from what was described as "an overstrained athlete's heart."

Other Baseball News

• The St. Louis Browns won 9-4 in Cleveland in a strange contest. Tom Zachary, who would later serve up three of the Babe's 1927 homers, allowed 12 Cleveland hits, but was continually rescued by the stellar defensive work of his teammates. The Indians left 13 runners on base.

• The Philadelphia Athletics participated in an exhibition game in New Haven, Connecticut, against a team of minor league all-stars from the Eastern League. Manager Connie Mack used his regulars only sparingly and allotted plenty of playing time for his substitutes. A late rally by the all-stars earned them a popular 3–2 win. Before the game, New Haven's mayor presented Ty Cobb with a hunting rifle and Connie Mack with a clock. Both gifts were manufactured locally. The 65-year-old Mack had not yet begun to worry about the passage of time. He would still be the owner-manager of the A's for another 23 years.

• Forty-year-old Grover Cleveland Alexander, still basking in the glory of his famous relief pitching effort in the previous year's World Series, gave up seven hits to the Chicago Cubs, but his team, the St. Louis Cardinals, still won 2–1.

4 April 29
Yankees at Red Sox

Yankees	ab	r	h	po	a	Red Sox	ab	r	h	po	a
Combs, cf	4	2	0	5	0	Wanninger, ss	3	0	0	3	3
Koenig, ss	5	1	2	4	5	Rothrock, ss	2	0	1	1	1
Ruth, rf	4	3	3	3	0	Haney, 3b	3	0	0	1	1
Gehrig, 1b	4	1	1	11	1	Tobin, rf	3	0	0	1	0
Meusel, lf	5	0	2	0	0	Flagstead, cf	3	0	1	2	0
Lazzeri, 2b	4	1	2	3	4	Jacobson, lf	4	0	1	1	0
Dugan, 3b	5	1	1	0	0	Todt, 1b	3	0	1	12	1
Collins, c	5	0	1	1	0	Regan, 2b	4	0	1	1	3
Ruether, p	3	0	0	0	3	Hofmann, c	2	0	0	5	0
						Rollings, pr	0	0	0	0	0
						Sommers, p	0	0	0	0	1
						Shaner, ph	1	0	0	0	0
						Harriss, p	1	0	0	0	3
						Rigney, ph	1	0	0	0	0
						Lundgren, p	0	0	0	0	0
						Hartley, c	2	0	1	0	0
Totals	39	9	12	27	13	Totals	32	0	6	27	13

New York   1 0 4 0 3 1 0 0 0 - 9
Boston   0 0 0 0 0 0 0 0 0 - 0

The first American League stadium that Babe Ruth called home was Boston's Fenway Park. Any reasonable scholar of baseball history knows that Ruth was a star pitcher for the Red Sox before being sold to the New York Yankees in 1920 in one of the sport's most shortsighted deals. Ruth's first career home run, oddly enough, came against a New York hurler, Jack Warhop, in 1915. (Warhop's name would likely be forgotten by today's baseball fans if it were not for that tiny piece of trivia.) However, Ruth victimized Boston while he was a Yankee far more often than he had stung New York as a member of the Red Sox.

This phenomenon was not merely a coincidence. The fortunes of the Red

Sox severely plummeted after they sold Ruth to New York. From 1903 through 1918, Boston's American League club was among the most talented in baseball. The Red Sox won six pennants and five World Series titles. (Boston could very well have won six world championships, but the 1904 World Series was never played. The National League champions that season, John McGraw's New York Giants, despised the American League so much that they simply refused to participate in a postseason series against its pennant winner.)

When Ruth was sold, Red Sox owner Harry Frazee unloaded most of the team's remaining stars as well. Many of them ended up in Yankee pinstripes.

Harry Hooper played on Boston's championship clubs of 1912, 1915, 1916 and 1918. Years later, when he was reminiscing for Lawrence Ritter's book *The Glory of Their Times*, Hooper was still offended by the sudden decline of the Red Sox fortunes:

"Harry Frazee became the owner of the Red Sox in 1917, and before long he sold off all our best players and ruined the team. [He] sold them all to the Yankees—Ernie Shore, Duffy Lewis, Dutch Leonard, Carl Mays, Babe Ruth, then Wally Schang, Herb Pennock, Joe Dugan and Sam Jones. I was disgusted. The Yankee dynasty of the Twenties was three-quarters the Red Sox of a few years before. All Frazee wanted was the money. What a way to end a wonderful ball club!"

The decline of the Red Sox actually began in 1919, Ruth's last year with the team. From that year until 1933, Boston never finished higher than fifth in the American League standings. During those lean times, the Red Sox were often mired in the cellar. Such was the case in the 1927 season, when Boston would finish the year at 51–103 and was the only American League club that suffered the indignity of enduring 100 or more losses.

One of those losses was the April 29 game at Fenway. The Yankees' Dutch Ruether pitched a complete-game shutout, and Babe Ruth generously provided a great portion of New York's offensive clout in the Yanks' thorough 9–0 whitewashing of the Sox before a crowd that saw little from the home side to make them cheer.

Despite the wind-whipped conditions that made things a little chilly for the spectators, umpires, and players alike, George Ruth's bat was sizzling hot. With tremendous gusto, the Babe made the pitching staff of Boston manager Bill Carrigan suffer. Among Ruth's contributions to the easy triumph were three hits: a home run that was snagged by a lucky spectator in the distant right field bleachers, a double that smacked soundly off the fence deep in left center field, and, to make the day complete, an RBI single.

The geography of Fenway Park quite probably reduced Ruth's home run output from two to one. His double was hit as hard as his circuit clout and bounced backward so swiftly to Red Sox center fielder Ira Flagstead that Ruth had to be content with a mere two-bagger instead of a more gratifying circuit clout. The fact that New York held a commanding 8–0 lead at the time of the tragedy probably soothed Ruth's feelings somewhat.

Entering the game, Ruth's total of runs batted in was exactly identical to his home run count. By game's end he was finally able to drive across the plate someone other than himself. With the afternoon's efforts safely recorded in the statistical journals, Ruth's home run to RBI ratio now stood at 4:5. For good measure, Ruth also scored three of New York's runs himself.

All in all, it amounted to a joyous homecoming for Ruth, who still retained his status as a fan favorite among the local patrons of Fenway Park despite the fact it had been eight long seasons since he last wore a Red Sox uniform.

Ruether allowed just six Boston hits in recording the shutout. The Yankees upped their record to 9–4, only half a game better than the charging Philadelphia Athletics, who had recovered from the three-game pasting administered by New York to open the season. The A's, after enduring a mid-season slump, would rally to provide the greatest threat to the Yankees' march to the pennant for the rest of the 1927 schedule.

Ruth always remained a beloved figure in Boston, even decades after Harry Frazee had sold his contract to the Yankees. In 1968, a boulevard in South Boston was renamed Babe Ruth Park Drive; in 1983 he was elected by Red Sox fans as the club's best left-handed pitcher on the "All-Time Dream Team"; and in 1995 Ruth was one of the first inductees into the newly created Boston Red Sox Hall of Fame.

Other Baseball News

- The Philadelphia Athletics solidified their hold on second place in the American League standings with a come-from-behind 8–7 win over the Washington Senators at Shibe Park. The A's scored seven runs in the sixth inning to edge the visitors. The amazing and ageless Ty Cobb had a productive afternoon belting a triple, a double, and a single.

- The Yankees were not the only New York–based ball club to upend a team from Boston. John McGraw's New York Giants crushed the Boston Braves 10–3 in a National League game at the Polo Grounds. Home runs from Freddie Lindstrom, Bill Terry and Albert (Ty) Tyson were the telling blows.

- Jumbo Jim Elliott pitched a four-hitter to lead the Brooklyn Robins to a 7–0 win at Ebbets Field over the visiting Philadelphia Phillies. The Brooklyn victory was a rarity. It was just their third in 15 outings thus far in the season.

♟ 5 & 6 May 1
Athletics at Yankees

Athletics	ab	r	h	po	a
E. Collins, 2b	5	0	2	1	2
Lamar, lf	4	0	1	2	0
Cobb, rf	4	0	2	0	0
Simmons, cf	3	0	0	2	0
Hale, 3b	4	1	1	1	3
Branom, 1b	3	1	1	12	0
Foxx, ph	1	0	0	0	0
Poole, 1b	0	0	0	1	0
Perkins, c	4	1	2	5	0
Boley, ss	4	0	1	0	5
Quinn, p	2	0	1	0	4
Willis, p	0	0	0	0	1
Dykes, ph	1	0	0	0	0
Walberg, p	0	0	0	0	0
Galloway, ph	1	0	1	0	0
Totals	36	3	12	24	15

Yankees	ab	r	h	po	a
Combs, cf	4	0	0	3	0
Koenig, ss	2	2	0	1	4
Ruth, rf	4	2	2	4	1
Gehrig, 1b	3	2	2	11	1
Meusel, lf	3	1	1	5	0
Lazzeri, 2b	3	0	0	1	3
Dugan, 3b	4	0	0	1	1
P. Collins, c	3	0	0	1	0
Pennock, p	3	0	0	0	4
Totals	29	7	5	27	14

Philadelphia 0 1 0 2 0 0 0 0 0 - 3
New York   2 0 0 0 0 2 0 3 x - 7

The mark of any great team in any sport is its ability to consistently win games that, at least on paper, should have been rightfully entered into the loss column. Such was the situation on May 1 for the Yankees when the visiting Philadelphia A's, buoyed by a five-game winning streak, got 12 hits off Herb Pennock yet were still defeated 7–3 in a game at Yankee Stadium, even though the home team managed to hit safely just five times throughout the course of the entire contest. If the Athletics had indeed managed to upend the Yankees, Connie Mack's club would have gained sole possession of first place in the American League.

As some 65,000 paying customers gazed upon the action, New York regained the coveted sole leadership spot in the junior loop thanks to three home runs—two of them courtesy of the potent bat of George Herman Ruth. Actually, only two of the Yankees' homers were genuinely needed to the Athletics. Babe Ruth's first round-tripper of the afternoon, a mighty clout that came to rest amongst the friendly faces in the right field bleachers, occurred with a teammate aboard. Not to be outdone in the productivity department, Lou Gehrig later accomplished the same feat. To make the day wholly satisfactory for his loyal legions of worshippers, Ruth notched a second homer into the very same section to record his first multiple home run game of 1927.

Veteran Athletics hurler Jack Quinn, whose career in the American League dated back to when Ruth was starring as an amateur pitcher for his Baltimore trade school, was a bit of a hard-luck loser, surrendering just two hits before being yanked in the bottom of the sixth inning. Charles Willis and Rube Walberg relieved Quinn and did not do much to stop the New York onslaught.

Ruth's initial homer occurred in the bottom of the first inning with teammate Mark Koenig occupying first base courtesy of a walk issued by the aforementioned Mr. Quinn. Unlike many of the Babe's trademark blasts, this one had no grandiose arc for fans to lovingly watch and admire; it was hit nearly on a line to the exit gap in the bleacher section. From the moment the crack of Ruth's bat was audible, there was little doubt the Bambino had connected for a homer. Old Ty Cobb was patrolling that particular patch of the outfield for the A's, and Tyrus hardly wasted any effort chasing the obvious home run. He merely raised his head skyward and watched it sail into the seats along with everyone else at Yankee Stadium.

Ruth's second home run of the afternoon was equally impressive. This time the delivery man was Mr. Walberg. No teammates accompanied the Babe around the bases on this occasion. However, by that time in the game, the small issue of which team was going to post the win had been almost certainly decided.

Richards Vidmer, who was covering the game for the *New York Times*, must have been a prescient baseball journalist. Even though less than one-tenth of the season had been played at this point, Vidmer was already pondering the Babe's home run pace and calculating whether he could possibly match his terrific campaign of six years before. He reported that "Ruth's two homers brought his total to six for the season, which put him ahead of the schedule he created in 1921 when he set a season's record with 59. That year he hit his sixth homer on May 2. However, it was in his thirteenth game. Yesterday's contest was his fifteenth of 1927."

Lou Gehrig, too, played a key offensive role in the New York victory. The Yankee clean-up hitter blasted a home run in the sixth inning, and his single, following Ruth's second homer of the afternoon, began a rally that added two more runs to the Yankee total. The win boosted New York's record to 10–5 in the American League, one full game ahead of the defeated A's.

Other Baseball News

• The Brooklyn Robins eked out a thrilling victory, a rare sight in 1927 for their die-hard supporters at Ebbets Field. Two runs in the bottom of the ninth gave the home team a 4–3 win over their archrivals, the New York Giants. Pinch runner Max Carey won the game when he scored on a sacrifice fly that was caught just a few feet beyond the infield dirt by second baseman Edd Roush. Carey scored well ahead of Roush's throw, as the runner's reckless (and highly successful) charge to the plate surprised everyone in the park.

- Horace (Hod) Lisenbee, a rookie pitcher for the Washington Senators, made a spectacular major league debut by shutting out the Boston Red Sox 6–0 before an appreciative hometown gathering at Griffith Stadium.

- Frankie Frisch of the St. Louis Cardinals had a tremendous day at Sportsman's Park. Frisch rocked Cincinnati pitchers for a home run, two doubles and a single in St. Louis's 12–4 rout of the visiting Reds.

7 May 10
Yankees at Browns

Yankees	ab	r	h	po	a		Browns	ab	r	h	po	a
Combs, cf	4	2	2	4	0		O'Rourke, 3b	4	0	2	1	0
Koenig, ss	4	1	0	2	4		Adams, 2b	4	0	0	1	7
Ruth, rf	4	1	1	2	0		Sisler, 1b	2	1	0	10	0
Gehrig, 1b	4	1	2	8	2		Williams, lf	2	0	0	2	0
Meusel, lf	2	1	1	1	0		E. Miller, lf	3	0	1	1	0
Lazzeri, 2b	4	0	0	3	3		Rice, rf	3	2	2	2	0
Bengough, c	0	0	0	0	0		Schulte, cf	4	1	1	3	0
Dugan, 3b	3	0	0	1	1		Gerber, ss	3	1	0	2	2
Pennock, p	0	0	0	0	1		Schang, c	3	2	1	5	1
Collins, c	2	0	0	4	0		Gaston, p	2	0	1	0	0
Grabowski, c	1	0	1	1	0							
Gazella, 3b	0	1	0	0	0							
Pipgras, p	2	0	0	1	0							
Giard, p	0	0	0	0	0							
Moore, p	1	0	0	0	3							
Paschal, ph	1	0	0	0	0							
Morehart, ph	1	0	0	0	0							
Durst, pr	0	1	0	0	0							
Totals	33	8	7	27	14		Totals	30	7	8	27	10

New York	3 0 0 0 0 2 0 0 3 - 8	
St. Louis	0 0 1 2 3 0 0 1 0 - 7	

    In a contest much like that of May 1, when the Yankees lost the statistical battle with the Philadelphia Athletics yet somehow won the game, New York defeated the St. Louis Browns 8–7 at Sportsman's Park on May 10. It must have been thoroughly discouraging for the also-rans of the American League in 1927.

    Twice in this contest, the Browns could have put the Yankees away, but victory eluded them nevertheless.

    Such frustration was frequent. Often the best efforts by New York's rivals, even when combined with a poor Yankee performance, still ended up as another Yankee win. In Donald Honig's *Baseball America*, a quote by George

Pipgras, one of New York's stellar pitchers that legendary year, underscored the team's attitude of invincibility, which mushroomed with each success: "When we got to the ballpark, we knew we were going to win," he said. "That's all there was to it. We weren't cocky. I wouldn't call it confidence either. We just knew. It's like when you go to sleep you know the sun is going to come up in the morning."

The home club's first opportunity to hand the vaunted Yankees a loss came in the top of the ninth inning. St. Louis was clinging to a tenuous 7–6 lead. Two Yankees had already been retired, but two others stood anxiously in scoring position. All that Browns pitcher Milt Gaston had to do to pick up the win was retire Lou Gehrig. Instead, Gehrig prolonged matters by zipping a base hit past the startled Gaston and driving home both the tying and go-ahead runs.

Feeling charitable themselves, New York allowed St. Louis ample opportunity to get back in the ballgame in the home half of the ninth. The Browns loaded the bases with one out via a base on balls, a George Sisler single, a sacrifice bunt, and an intentional walk. Wally (Spooks) Gerber stepped into the batter's box with a chance to win the game for St. Louis. Instead, the Browns' shortstop hit into a textbook 6–4–3 double play that went from Koenig to Tony Lazzeri to Gehrig.

Ruth's homer, his seventh of the young campaign, occurred in the very first inning with two of his teammates aboard. Earle Combs's single just eluded the reach of Browns third baseman Frank O'Rourke, and Mark Koenig reached on an error by second baseman Spencer Adams. The opportunistic Ruth capitalized on the Browns' generosity by depositing one of Gaston's offerings into the right field pavilion. The ball landed on top of the concrete front wall and bounded far back.

It turned out to be Ruth's only hit of the day, although he did draw a critical walk in the dramatic ninth inning, and another time he sent center fielder Fred Schulte scurrying to the base of the wall to haul in a long fly ball.

New York used four different pitchers in the game. Such lineup shuffling was a highly unusual maneuver for any major league club in 1927, never mind the powerful Yankees. Relief pitching had not evolved into the specialized art form of today. Often, a pitcher would go the full nine innings even if he allowed five or six runs and his club trailed badly. Pipgras started the game on the mound for New York. He was replaced in turn by Joe Giard, rookie Wilcy Moore (who was credited with the win) and Herb Pennock.

Ruth's seventh home run of the season tied him with Gehrig for the American League lead in that department. In losing, the Browns outhit the Yankees 8–7. New York's victory raised their record to 15–8, two full games ahead of the Chicago White Sox, who had surged past Philadelphia into second place.

The pitcher who surrendered Ruth's homer on this day was Milt Gaston. Gaston had broken into the majors with the Yankees in 1924 but was with the team for only one season. Along with pitching for the Browns, the well-traveled Gaston also played with the Senators, Red Sox and White Sox. He possessed a lively forkball that puzzled as many catchers as batters. Twice he led the American League in losses.

Gaston was well into his nineties when he was interviewed for Ken Burns's lengthy *Baseball* documentary. His topic, of course, was Babe Ruth. "He was one of a kind," the elderly Gaston noted. "There was never anyone else like him. They broke the mold when they made him. He had a world of talent. He didn't live long, but he lived fast."

Other Baseball News

• Detroit baseball fans flocked to Navin Field to witness the return of Ty Cobb to the city that made him famous. Cobb had spent every season from 1905 to 1926 in Tiger colors, winning 12 batting championships and setting records for hits and stolen bases that many fans believed would stand forever. He had even acted as Detroit's player-manager from 1921 to 1926. Cobb's first appearance in Detroit as a member of the Philadelphia A's was cause for a grand celebration. Ty Cobb Day attracted 30,000 fans to the park. Cobb was honored with a pregame parade and a postgame testimonial dinner. During the afternoon, Cobb laced a double in Philadelphia's 6–3 win.

• In a battle of two teams at the bottom of the American League standings, Boston tallied five runs in the top of the fifth inning to edge the Cleveland Indians at Dunn Field. The Red Sox victory did not change the teams' positions. Boston remained in last place in the eight-team circuit. Cleveland stood seventh.

• Three members of the Chicago Cubs (Hack Wilson, Gabby Hartnett and Riggs Stephenson) all connected for home runs as the Cubs recorded a road win in Philadelphia. The other three National League games scheduled that afternoon were rained out.

• Alphonse (Tommy) Thomas of the White Sox hurled a complete game in Chicago's 4–3 home win over Washington. Thomas helped his own cause considerably by driving in three runs himself. Chicago's other run came courtesy of a homer by Alex Metzler. It was the first home run hit by a member of the White Sox since Comiskey Park had been remodeled.

8 May 11
Yankees at Browns

Yankees	ab	r	h	po	a
Combs, cf	3	0	0	3	0
Koenig, ss	4	1	0	2	4
Ruth, rf	4	2	2	0	0
Gehrig, 1b	4	0	2	13	1
Meusel, lf	3	0	0	2	0
Lazzeri, 2b	4	1	1	2	3
Dugan, 3b	3	0	0	1	1
Grabowski, c	3	0	1	3	2
Shocker, p	2	0	1	1	2
Totals	**30**	**4**	**7**	**27**	**13**

Browns	ab	r	h	po	a
O'Rourke, 3b	4	0	3	1	4
Adams, 2b	3	0	0	3	3
Melillo, 2b	1	0	0	1	0
Sisler, 1b	4	0	0	14	2
Williams, lf	3	0	1	1	0
Rice, rf	4	1	1	2	0
Schulte, cf	4	1	2	1	0
Gerber, ss	3	0	1	2	5
O. Miller, ss	0	0	0	0	1
Schang, c	4	0	0	2	1
Nevers, p	3	0	0	0	4
O'Neill, ph	1	0	0	0	0
Bennett, ph	1	0	0	0	0
B. Miller, ph	1	0	0	0	0
Totals	**36**	**2**	**8**	**27**	**20**

New York	2 1 1 0 0 0 0 0 0 - 4	
St. Louis	0 2 0 0 0 0 0 0 0 - 2	

The 1926 World Series is remembered fondly by baseball fans for the underdog St. Louis Cardinals' unexpected and dramatic victory over the powerful New York Yankees. The Cards' surprise win was punctuated by the pitching heroics of Grover Cleveland Alexander.

The one-time 30-game winner had been cast off by the Chicago Cubs as a drunkard and was picked up by St. Louis only with the greatest of reluctance. Alexander won game six at Yankee Stadium to even the series at three games apiece. He was then summoned by player-manager Rogers Hornsby as a reliever to quell a New York rally late in game seven. Despite the handicap of a lingering hangover, Alexander struck out Tony Lazzeri with the bases loaded and silenced the Yankee bats for the rest of the game. His performance made Alexander the stuff of legends. In 1950, just after Alexander's death, Ronald Reagan portrayed him in a biographical film titled *The Winning Team*.

Even though the Yankees surprisingly lost the World Series in 1926 (Babe Ruth made the final out when he was foolishly caught trying to steal second base), Ruth did capture his share of glory. In game four at Sportsman's Park, Ruth connected for three home runs. One of these was a tremendous shot that landed deep in the distant center-field bleachers. Veteran St. Louis sports journalists claimed it was the first time that a batter had ever deposited a baseball there.

Sportsman's Park did double duty as the home grounds for both the National League Cardinals and American League Browns. On May 11, 1927, Ruth returned to the site of his towering blast and came very close to reproducing it.

The blow went a long way to ensure that New York's mastery of St. Louis's American League representatives continued.

According to those with good memories, Ruth's eighth homer of the 1927 campaign was hit higher than the one he had launched the previous autumn versus the Cards, but it did not travel quite as far. In fact, this one, hit in the opening inning of hostilities, barely eked its way into the second row of bleachers—if one can demean such a long hit—before bouncing up further into the largely vacant seats. Mark Koenig cruised home ahead of the Babe after the home run was duly signaled by the umpires.

The score ended up 4–2 in favor of the visitors from the Bronx. New York recorded seven hits during the chilly afternoon. Urban Shocker allowed eight to the Browns' batters in a lifeless contest played before a sparse crowd. Ruth's impressive clout provided the lone spark of excitement and all the scoring was completed after the top of the third inning. The win lifted the Yankees' seasonal mark to 16–8, two games ahead of the Chicago White Sox.

Ernie Nevers, the St. Louis pitcher who served up Ruth's homer in this game, was a fascinating athlete in his own right. He was the Bo Jackson of his time. After starring as a collegiate football player, Nevers played three professional sports simultaneously. During the summer months he pitched for the Browns. In the autumn, Nevers could be found playing halfback in the NFL. (He eventually assumed the job of player-coach for the Chicago Cardinals.) Once football season ended, he spent his winters as a professional basketball player in the Chicago area. On November 28, 1929, Nevers scored all of his team's points in the Cardinals' 40–7 Thanksgiving Day victory over the Chicago Bears at Comiskey Park. He scored six touchdowns and kicked four extra points in the rout. Nearly seven decades later, Nevers' name still graces the pages of the record book; no other NFL player has ever had a more prolific day on a professional gridiron. When the Pro Football Hall of Fame opened in Canton, Ohio, in 1963, Nevers was one of the charter inductees.

Other Baseball News

• American League president Ban Johnson handed down $200 fines to both Al Simmons and Ty Cobb of the Philadelphia Athletics because of their unsportsmanlike behavior in an A's–Red Sox game the previous week. In a lengthy and flowery letter written to A's owner-manager Connie Mack, Johnson declared, "The conduct of a player, by word or action, that would tend to excite the partisan element of a baseball crowd to wrath against the decision of an umpire is one of the most reprehensible occurrences that can happen in a game and stamps the offender as entirely devoid of the highest principles of manhood."

• Horace (Hod) Lisenbee, the rookie Washington pitcher who had started the season with a sparkling 3–0 record, finally tasted defeat at the hands of the Chicago White Sox. Chicago's 4–1 win at Comiskey Park was made possible by Aaron Ward's bases-loaded double in the sixth inning.

• A spirited National League contest at Braves Field in Boston ended in an unsatisfactory 4–4 tie. Pittsburgh led the home team 4–2 entering the bottom of the eighth. The Braves scored two runs and were still batting in the unfinished inning when heavy rains made further play impossible.

♫9 May 17
Yankees at Tigers

Yankees	ab	r	h	po	a		Tigers	ab	r	h	po	a
Combs, cf	3	2	2	4	0		Blue, 1b	4	0	0	6	2
Koenig, ss	6	2	3	5	4		Warner, 3b	4	0	1	0	0
Ruth, lf	4	1	1	2	0		Heilmann, rf	5	0	1	1	0
Gehrig, 1b	4	3	3	9	0		Fothergill, lf	4	1	2	3	0
Durst, rf	4	1	2	1	0		Manush, cf	5	1	4	6	0
Lazzeri, 2b	5	0	2	3	6		McManus, 2b	3	0	0	4	3
Dugan, 3b	2	0	0	1	3		Tavener, ss	2	0	0	6	1
Grabowski, c	4	0	1	2	1		Woodall, c	4	0	1	1	1
Pennock, p	4	0	1	0	1		Collins, p	3	0	2	0	5
							Carroll, p	0	0	0	0	0
							Neun, ph	1	0	1	0	0
Totals	36	9	15	27	15		Totals	35	2	12	27	12

New York   0 0 3 0 1 2 0 3 0 – 9
St. Louis   0 2 0 0 0 0 0 0 0 – 2

It was not uncommon for renowned athletes during the 1920s to accept acting roles in silent films as an easy way to pad their bank accounts. Because the primitive technology did not require the participants to learn any dialogue, many sports figures were willing to don the pancake makeup and give the celluloid pantomime world their best efforts. Heavyweight champion Jack Dempsey, believe it or not, played romantic roles opposite Estelle Taylor, his Hollywood starlet wife. Dempsey was no threat to Rudolph Valentino, John Barrymore or Wallace Reid, and his career in films was mercifully brief.

Babe Ruth, being the most famous athlete in the United States (if not the world), was constantly being offered lucrative movie roles as early as 1921. Almost all of them were in baseball flicks in which the Babe would emerge as the hero of the day by blasting the inevitable game-winning home run. Most of the scripts handed to Ruth were ridiculously juvenile, yet the producers banked on the notion that the Babe's enormous fame would draw patrons to the movie houses regardless of how silly the plots happened to be. Such was the appeal of Ruth that many people in small-town America who could never hope to see their hero in an actual major league game gladly forked over their nickels for a chance to see his flickering image on the screen.

Here is the plot summary of *Babe Comes Home*, Ruth's cinematic offering for 1927: Ruth plays a Los Angeles ballplayer, Babe Dugan, who disgusts the team's laundry girl with the tobacco stains he gets on his uniform. The girl throws a fit but has a change of heart when she actually meets the Babe. Naturally, she immediately falls in love. However, the girl is a reformer who insists that Dugan give up his sloppy chewing habit. The Babe, equally smitten, agrees but quickly falls into a dreadful batting slump. With the pennant on the line in the crucial game, the girl hands Dugan a plug of tobacco, which, of course, inspires him to produce the winning hit.

Such forgettable fare was routine in Ruth's film career—with one conspicuous exception. In 1942 Ruth would play himself quite convincingly in an MGM talking film, *The Pride of the Yankees*, Lou Gehrig's biography. Many people consider it the best baseball movie ever made.

As a noted screen star and baseball player of some repute, Ruth pleased both his athletic admirers and cinema buffs in Detroit on May 17, 1927. On that day, in that city—if one were so inclined—one could see the Babe play baseball at Navin Field in the afternoon; then, when the game had concluded, the same fan could catch Ruth's latest celluloid masterpiece at a local motion picture theater for just a few pennies more.

Those in the majority, however, were quite satisfied to see Ruth perform solely on the diamond, and they were witnesses to his ninth home run of the 1927 season. It was a thrilling spectacle, as usual. Ruth's shot sailed over the scoreboard in left-center field this time, a most unlikely direction for the pull-hitting lefthander—and landed with a thud in the front lawn of a local resident. It was the crowning achievement in New York's resounding 9–2 triumph over the local Detroit nine.

Ruth's blow was utterly unnecessary in the grand scheme of things. Runs came the Yankees' way in bunches. Two Tiger hurlers, Rip Collins and Owen Carroll, were victimized by the New Yorkers' lively bats and combined to surrender 15 hits of assorted severity.

The Yankees' run total could have been far higher, as could the Tigers'. There was no shortage of offensive opportunities for both teams. Each club stranded 13 runners on base. Herb Pennock went the distance for New York, but his performance on the mound was hardly a thing of beauty. Detroit collected 12 hits off him as well as five walks. The victory enabled the Yankees to become the first team in the majors to reach the 20-win plateau in 1927. Their 20–8 record put them four full games ahead of their nearest rivals, the Chicago White Sox.

Other Baseball News

- In a marathon encounter, the visiting Chicago Cubs edged the Boston Braves 4–3 in 22 grueling innings. Bob Smith, beginning his third season in the majors, was the hard-luck loser for Boston, going the distance before being replaced by an unsuccessful pinch hitter in the home half of the twenty-second. Incredibly the score had remained 3–3 since the bottom of the seventh when the Braves had evened matters. Charlie Grimm was the Cubs' hero, driving in Hack Wilson from second base with a single in the top of the decisive inning. The Braves had participated in the longest game in major league history seven years earlier on May 1, 1920, a 1–1 tie with the Brooklyn Robins that had been terminated by darkness after 26 innings.

- The Philadelphia Phillies surprised their followers by temporarily moving into third place in the National League standings with a 4–3 home win over the St. Louis Cardinals. Jack Scott pitched a complete game for the victors, and Grover Cleveland Alexander went the distance for the vanquished. It was the high-water mark for the Phillies, who would finish the 1927 season in last place.

- In a wild International League game in Buffalo, the home team managed to squeak out a 1–0 win in 14 innings over the visiting Toronto Maple Leafs. Frequent brawls marred the pitchers' duel and resulted in the ejection of eight players. Police were summoned to the field on three separate occasions to prevent overly exuberant fans from joining in the battles.

10 May 22
Yankees at Indians

Yankees	ab	r	h	po	a
Combs, cf	5	2	2	5	0
Koenig, ss	5	2	2	3	1
Ruth, rf	2	2	1	1	0
Gehrig, 1b	4	0	2	11	1
Paschal, lf	4	0	2	1	0
Lazzeri, 2b	4	0	1	1	4
Dugan, 3b	4	1	1	2	1
Grabowski, c	4	0	0	2	2
Shocker, p	2	0	0	1	1

Indians	ab	r	h	po	a
Summa, rf	5	0	0	1	0
Jamieson, lf	3	1	1	4	0
Fonseca, 2b	4	0	0	3	7
Burns, 1b	4	1	2	10	0
J. Sewell, ss	4	0	1	1	2
L. Sewell, c	2	0	1	3	1
Myatt, c	2	0	1	1	0
McNulty, cf	4	0	2	3	0
Lutzke, 3b	4	0	2	1	1
Shaute, p	0	0	0	0	0
Karr, p	2	0	1	0	0
Miller, p	0	0	0	0	1

Yankees	ab	r	h	po	a
Totals	34	7	11	27	10

Indians	ab	r	h	po	a
Spurgeon, pr	0	0	0	0	0
Uhle, ph	1	0	0	0	0
Totals	35	2	11	27	12

New York   0 0 3 0 0 4 0 0 0 - 7
St. Louis   0 0 0 0 0 0 0 2 0 - 2

Major league ballparks have never been uniform in their dimensions. The absence of symmetry in classic stadiums such as Wrigley Field and Fenway Park actually adds a degree of charm to those ancient places. In Babe Ruth's era, there was a huge disparity among the sizes of American League parks. Yankee Stadium and Comiskey Park were cavernous enclosures that could accommodate enormous crowds. At the other end of the scale was minuscule Dunn Field in Cleveland. The home of the Indians in 1927 was an antiquated and cramped ballpark that could barely host 20,000 souls.

Usually, the vast stadiums had thousands of seats to spare for an ordinary game. Any crowd larger than 20,000 was noteworthy. Because most major league games began in the late afternoon, it was impractical for many working people to attend in large numbers. However, important weekend games often drew gatherings that tested the spatial limitations of places like Dunn Field. Instead of turning away those who were too late to buy seats in the grandstand or bleachers, it was customary for owners to sell standing-room tickets and herd the people onto the playing field in foul territory. Occasionally, if this measure proved insufficient, even portions of fair territory were allocated to the patrons. Sometimes the overflow crowd was corralled by a rope. Other times, when there was no barrier at all, the umpires could only pray that the unhindered spectators would not create too much interference.

The appearance of Babe Ruth and his fabulous teammates for a late May weekend series in Cleveland generated tremendous excitement. The crowds, estimated at about 23,000—moderate by today's standards—were so far beyond Dunn Field's limited capacity that foul ground was completely overrun by excited spectators.

Those folks saw their hometown heroes drop a 7–2 verdict to the mighty visitors and also saw Babe Ruth collect his tenth home run of 1927. Despite the unfavorable results for the locals, they seemed thoroughly delighted that Ruth had honored them with one of his circuit clouts.

A mighty blast it was not. In most other parks where big league baseball is contested, what passed that day for a pathetic Ruth homer would have been long forgotten as a harmless little pop fly. But things being what they were in the bantam Cleveland ballyard, Ruth got credit for a four-bagger in spite of it all. Ruth's hit went nearly as high as it did long and may have scraped the outer side of the right field wall on its descent. The concrete barricade stood a mere 300 feet or so from the point of home plate. Ruth actually looked embarrassed when his fly ball was counted as a genuine home run and he was forced to make the obligatory trip around the bases.

Nevertheless, it was definitely the Babe whom the locals had gleefully paid their coins to see. During one lull in the action after the fifth inning had concluded, a band of Indians (the kind one sees in Western movies, not the baseball-playing Cleveland variety), who were part of a touring rodeo, excitedly beckoned Ruth to join them in foul ground. Once persuaded to accept their invitation, the Great Bambino was formally presented with a headdress of colorful feathers. The umpires pretended not to notice as Ruth played the full inning in the irregular headgear.

New York put the game out of reach with a four-run barrage in the sixth inning. Included in the total was Ruth's anemic home run. The win concluded the Yankees' road trip, in which they won 10 of 13 games. Their overall mark was a solid 22–10. Urban Shocker pitched the full nine innings for the victors, allowing 11 Cleveland hits.

Other Baseball News

- More than 40,000 shocked fans at the Polo Grounds saw the Pittsburgh Pirates thump the New York Giants 9–4 to sweep a four-game series. Pittsburgh's success vaulted them into first place in the National League standings. The Pirates rocked the Giant pitching staff for 17 hits, including two by winning pitcher Vic Aldridge.

- The Brooklyn Robins had no trouble solving the Philadelphia Phillies' pitching at Ebbets Field in a 20–4 rout in front of their loyal but cynical fans. Brooklyn recorded 22 hits. Twenty of them were singles.

- The Philadelphia Athletics got 10 hits in their 6–1 victory over the White Sox in Chicago. However, Ty Cobb failed to get one, thus bringing an end to his 21-game hitting streak.

♫11 May 23
Yankees at Senators

Yankees	ab	r	h	po	a		Senators	ab	r	h	po	a
Combs, cf	4	0	0	1	0		Rice, rf	4	0	0	1	0
Koenig, ss	3	0	0	3	2		Harris, 2b	4	0	1	2	3
Ruth, rf	4	1	2	5	0		Speaker, cf	3	0	1	2	0
Gehrig, 1b	3	1	1	6	0		Goslin, lf	4	1	1	2	1
Durst, lf	3	0	0	4	1		Judge, 1b	3	0	0	12	0
Meusel, lf	0	0	0	0	0		Ruel, c	3	0	1	3	0

Yankees	ab	r	h	po	a	Senators	ab	r	h	po	a
Lazzeri, 2b	4	0	0	0	5	Tate, c	0	0	0	2	0
Dugan, 3b	4	0	1	1	0	Rigney, ss	3	1	2	3	5
Collins, c	3	0	2	3	0	Bluege, 3b	1	0	0	0	2
Thomas, p	3	0	1	1	0	Thurston, p	2	0	1	0	3
Shawkey, p	0	0	0	0	0	Braxton, p	0	0	0	0	0
Morehart, ph	1	0	0	0	0	Marberry, p	0	0	0	0	0
Gazella, pr	0	0	0	0	0	Stewart, pr	0	1	0	0	0
Wera, pr	0	0	0	0	0	Tucker, ph	0	0	0	0	0
Grabowski, ph	1	0	0	0	0	McNeely, ph	0	0	0	0	0
Totals	33	2	7	24	8	Totals	27	3	7	27	14

New York   2 0 0 0 0 0 0 0 0 - 2
Washington   0 0 1 0 0 0 2 0 x - 3

Babe Ruth and Lou Gehrig both continued their home run swatting in this match at Griffith Stadium against the Washington Senators, but despite a homer from each man, the Yankees still went down to defeat by an agonizing 3–2 count.

Both homers came early in the game. In the top of the first inning, George Herman propelled a hit into the center field bleachers. Before the crowd had settled down, Gehrig kept up his share of the pace by hitting a homer of his own over the right field fence. Ruth now leads Gehrig 11–10 in home runs in 1927 as the two continue their battle for American League and team superiority in that noteworthy department.

What looked to be a day of offensive fireworks for Miller Huggins's crew quickly fizzled from that point onward. No more New Yorkers crossed the plate the rest of the afternoon. Undaunted by the Yankees' early 2–0 advantage, the Senators gamely chipped away at the deficit. They took the contest by scoring one run in the third inning and two others in the decisive seventh when they sent New York starter Myles Thomas to an early shower.

The Senators may have been aided by a disputed call on the basepaths in the top of the seventh inning when the Yankees were threatening to score again. After Yankee catcher Pat Collins had singled, Thomas tried to move him to second with a sacrifice bunt. Pitcher Sloppy Thurston fielded the bunt and fired the ball to second base, where umpire Bill Dineen declared Collins out. Moments later, manager Huggins was storming onto the field in an ill-fated attempt to correct the injustice, but he could not convince the arbiter of his misjudgment. The unpopular verdict—unpopular from a New York point of view, that is—took the starch out of the Yankees' comeback aspirations. They never really mounted a serious challenge again, and Washington resourcefully took the lead in the home of that same inning.

Both home runs were hit off of right-handed pitcher Hollis John (Sloppy) Thurston, a 28-year-old veteran from Fremont, Nebraska, who was playing for his third American League team in five years. He inherited his unique nickname from his father, a restaurateur whose poor skills at serving soup frequently resulted in liquid messes on his dining counter. But the moniker did not fit his son. Hollis was anything but sloppy in his personal habits. During the 1920s he was renowned as one of the sharpest and most meticulous dressers in the American League. After several years with the White Sox, Thurston was shipped to Washington in 1927 largely because Chicago player-manager Eddie Collins believed Thurston's arm was dead. Thurston, who died in 1973, still holds a share of a major league record, although he was not exactly proud of the accomplishment: Near the end of his career, while pitching for the Brooklyn Dodgers in 1932, he allowed six home runs in one game.

But on this day, Thurston pitched well enough to chalk up a victory. After the back-to-back home runs Thurston gave up to Ruth and Gehrig in the top of the first inning, he completely shut down the Yankees through the seventh.

Umpire Dineen, unkindly known as Wild Bill during his pitching days, won three games for the Boston Pilgrims during the first modern World Series in 1903. When Dineen's pitching career came to an end in 1909, he was hired immediately by the American League as an umpire. Given his lack of preparatory training for such an assignment, his second baseball-related career was remarkably successful. He was considered one of the best in his profession until his retirement in 1937. Back in the era when World Series umpires were selected solely on merit, Dineen was a regular fixture in the Fall Classic, working a total of 45 games. Not surprisingly, as a plate umpire, Dineen tended to favor pitchers by broadening the strike zone. Batters who looked for walks had little luck. Statistics indicated his games behind the plate were usually the shortest by any umpire in the American League.

On this Monday afternoon at Griffith Stadium, the momentum of the game turned on Dineen's debatable call at second base. After the New York rally was quelled, Washington scored twice in the bottom of the seventh (after Thurston had been lifted for a pinch hitter) to rally from a 2–1 deficit. Myles Thomas, the losing pitcher, is a largely forgotten member of the 1927 Yankees' staff. Even though he received little attention, the 29-year-old hurler from Pennsylvania posted an adequate 7–4 record for the season. It would be his best output. By the end of 1930 Thomas would be out of the major leagues.

Both the Yankees and the Senators got seven hits in the game. The bitter loss dropped New York's seasonal record to 22–11, two and a half games ahead of the surprising Chicago White Sox.

Other Baseball News

- The Cleveland Indians and Detroit Tigers split a lively doubleheader at Dunn Field. The Indians won the first game by a 9–4 count, but the Tigers rallied to win the second game 7–5.

- Pittsburgh pitcher Johnny Morrison gave up 12 hits to the Reds in Cincin- nati, yet still went the distance and recorded the win in an 8–5 Pirates vic- tory. The win solidified Pittsburgh's grip on first place in the National League.

- One day after being shellacked by Brooklyn in Ebbets Field, the Philadel- phia Phillies returned home and handed the Robins a 7–1 defeat at the Baker Bowl. Clarence Mitchell, who was a member of Brooklyn's pitch- ing staff during their championship season in 1920, hurled a complete game for the win, scattering seven Brooklyn hits. He was aided by Fresco Thomp- son, who had a pair of doubles.

12 May 28
Senators at Yankees

Senators	ab	r	h	po	a		Yankees	ab	r	h	po	a
McNeely, cf	2	0	0	1	0		Combs, cf	4	1	0	3	0
Harris, 2b	3	0	0	3	3		Koenig, ss	4	2	2	2	1
Speaker, cf	3	0	0	3	0		Ruth, rf	4	1	3	5	0
Wert, rf	4	0	1	4	1		Gehrig, 1b	3	1	0	7	0
Goslin, lf	4	0	1	0	0		Meusel, lf	3	2	2	2	0
Judge, 1b	4	0	1	12	3		Lazzeri, 2b	4	0	1	5	4
Ruel, c	4	0	0	0	1		Dugan, 3b	3	0	1	0	2
Rigney, ss	4	0	2	1	1		Grabowski, c	3	1	1	3	0
Bluege, 3b	4	0	0	2	2		Shocker, p	3	0	0	0	0
Thurston, p	3	2	3	1	5							
Totals	35	2	8	27	16		Totals	31	8	10	27	7

Washington	0 0 1 0 1 0 0 0 0 - 2
New York	0 0 0 0 0 3 5 0 x - 8

Famous goats are found throughout baseball lore. Usually they are pitch- ers who had the misfortune to give up memorable or crucial home runs. Ralph Branca, Mitch Williams and Ralph Terry quickly come to mind. Though not a pitcher, Tony Lazzeri was considered by some to be the goat of the 1926 World Series between the Yankees and the St. Louis Cardinals. His crime was striking out with the bases loaded late in game seven against old Grover Cleveland Alexander. Lazzeri lined Alexander's first pitch just to the wrong side of the left-field foul pole for a long strike. It was his best shot at being a hero. Alexander whiffed him shortly thereafter.

Lazzeri's career statistics got him posthumously elected into the Hall of Fame in 1991; nevertheless, he is best remembered for failing in that one famous time at bat. Still, serious baseball scholars recall that Lazzeri was one of the most reliable hitters in Yankee history. He still holds the American League record for RBIs in a game: 11, in a 1936 contest versus the Philadelphia A's when he was at the tail end of his terrific career. However, on May 28, 1927, Lazzeri, the Yankees' second baseman, was legitimately a goat. His absentmindedness during the top of the eighth inning in the second game of a doubleheader gave Washington a crucial insurance run in a closely fought contest before an enthusiastic crowd estimated at 45,000.

In the first game, George Herman Ruth connected for his twelfth home run of the season, which spurred the home side to a comfortable 8–2 win. Still wanting to compete in the pennant race, the Washingtonians fought their way back to a 3–2 win in the second encounter.

The second game was almost salvaged by Miller Huggins's crew, but Fred (Firpo) Marberry, the Senators' ace reliever, preserved the Washington victory when he was summoned to the mound with the tying run on second base and two men out.

As for Ruth, he had a stellar day at the plate. Over the course of the two games, the Bambino tallied a homer, a triple, and a single in just four official times at bat. The triple and single were wasted efforts as far as scoring goes, but the home run was both terrific and productive. It sailed in amongst the happy patrons of the right-center field bleachers. Two of the Babe's teammates were on base in the bottom of the seventh inning when Ruth's bat made all the noise.

The home run came in the middle of a big inning that put the game away for New York. The Yankees scored five times in the seventh. The Babe's three-run blast was followed by a Bob Meusel homer two batters later. Washington had led 2–0 at one juncture in the contest. Ruth also made a sparkling defensive play in right field, lunging to make a catch that robbed Bucky Harris of an extra-base hit.

The second game, won by Washington, was described by James R. Harrison of the *New York Times* as being "as pretty a duel as ever graced any ball field." The mound combatants were Wilcy Moore of New York and the Senators' Firpo Marberry. Two key plays in the top of the eighth propelled the visitors to victory. With the score tied 1–1, Harris stepped on Lou Gehrig's ankle on a play at first base as he tried to beat out a ground ball. While Gehrig was crumpled over in pain, Marberry alertly scored on the play. There was concern that Gehrig's tender foot might keep him out of New York's lineup. Lou somehow managed to play the following day—and in every Yankee game for the next 12 years.

Later that inning, Tony Lazzeri committed a major mental miscue when he failed to cover second base during a rundown play. Earl McNeely should have been picked off. Instead, he ended up scoring the run that eventually decided the game. The Yankees scored once in the ninth but came up a run short when their rally died.

Fred Marberry's nickname—Firpo—was given to him by teammates who thought he resembled Luis Firpo, the enormous Argentine heavyweight who knocked Jack Dempsey through the ropes during their famous 1923 title fight at the Polo Grounds.

The split of the doubleheader gave the Yankees a 24–13 record, putting them a game and a half in front of Chicago.

Tony Lazzeri died tragically in 1946 when he suffered an epileptic seizure and tumbled down a flight of stairs.

Other Baseball News

• The International League's Reading Keys were making headlines with their inept play. Reading lost both ends of a doubleheader to Newark, extending their losing streak to 29 straight games. The last-place Keys' record stood at an embarrassing three wins and 39 losses.

• The Cincinnati Reds broke a five-game losing streak in convincing fashion, winning 8–0 against the Cubs in Chicago. Wally Pipp, the former Yankee first baseman whom Lou Gehrig had replaced in 1925, went 3 for 5 at the plate for Cincinnati. One of his hits was a double. Reds pitcher Peter Donohue gave up just six hits in a complete-game victory.

• The Philadelphia Athletics swept a doubleheader against the last-place Red Sox in Boston by scores of 8–6 and 4–3. Lefty Grove finished both games in relief for the A's. Philadelphia scored six runs in the first inning of the first game but had to hang on for the victory as Boston scored six times in the bottom of the fifth. Red Sox catcher Grover Hartley had two doubles in the big inning.

♣13 May 29
Red Sox at Yankees

Red Sox	ab	r	h	po	a		Yankees	ab	r	h	po	a
Tobin, rf	5	1	1	0	0		Combs, cf	4	2	1	6	0
Haney, 3b	2	1	1	0	2		Koenig, ss	5	1	3	0	1
Rollings, ph	0	0	0	0	0		Ruth, rf	5	2	2	2	0
Todt, 1b	5	2	2	9	0		Gehrig, 1b	5	1	1	8	0
Flagstead, cf	2	2	1	3	0		Meusel, lf	5	1	3	2	0
Jacobson, lf	3	0	1	3	0		Paschal, lf	0	0	0	0	0
Myer, ss	3	0	0	4	4		Lazzeri, 2b	4	1	1	1	1
Rothrock, 2b	4	0	1	1	4		Dugan, 3b	3	2	0	0	1
Hartley, c	4	1	1	4	1		Wera, 3b	0	0	0	0	0
Wiltse, p	2	0	0	0	2		Grabowski, c	4	3	4	8	0
Wingfield, p	0	0	0	0	0		Reuther, p	1	0	1	0	2
MacFayden, p	1	0	0	0	0		Thomas, p	3	2	1	0	4

Red Sox	ab	r	h	po	a		Yankees	ab	r	h	po	a
Rogell, ph	0	0	0	0	0							
Russel, p	0	0	0	0	0							
Carlyle, p	1	0	0	0	0							
Totals	32	7	8	24	13		Totals	39	15	17	27	9

Red Sox	2 1 3 0 0 0 1 0 0 - 7
New York	0 1 2 4 1 0 0 7 x - 15

For many years those who drew up major league baseball schedules had to contend with a special logistics problem: Many cities had active bylaws on their books that forbade Sunday baseball. Out of respect for the Lord's day, Sabbath or "blue" laws, as they were commonly known at the time, prevented professional sports of any kind from taking place on Sundays in numerous locales small and large. Some of these statutes stayed on the books well into the 1950s. To counter this problem, the schedule-makers had to be creative at times. Late May of 1927 was one example.

The Yankees had just finished a series at home against the visiting Washington Senators. The final game was played on May 28, a Saturday afternoon. Another series, this time with the Philadelphia Athletics, was scheduled to begin at Shibe Park on Monday, May 30. (Philadelphia had perhaps the strictest and most enduring municipal blue laws, which prevented their big set of games with the Yankees from beginning on that Sunday.) In a scheduling twist that would be considered strange by today's standards, Bill Carrigan's hapless Boston Red Sox came into New York—where pro baseball was perfectly legal seven days of each week—to play a single game against the powerful Yankees on Sunday May 29. After the afternoon's business was completed, both teams quickly loaded up their gear and headed out of town.

Such travel arrangements were quite common during Ruth's era, especially late in the season when important rained-out games had to be made up. Boston was already firmly entrenched in the American League basement by late May and showed no signs of imminent improvement. Their one-day trip into New York City probably was not fondly anticipated by the battered Red Sox pitching staff, who were keenly aware of Gehrig's and Ruth's recent hot streaks. Boston's total collapse in this game versus the Yankees, after they had broken out to a surprising and sizable lead, was indicative of their dismal 1927 season.

When the worst team in the American League pays a brief call on the class of the field, one might expect a lot of runs to be scored. Such indeed was the case on this day, but not too many of the locals who made up the crowd of 35,000 baseball fans expected seven of those runs to appear on Boston's side of the ledger. On the other hand 15 of the game's 22 runs were credited to the Yankees. Four hapless Boston hurlers had to share the blame for this one.

Although seven tallies was an impressive output for the shabby Red Sox club this year, New York actually managed that amount in one inning alone. To be precise, that inning would be the home half of the eighth, when Yankee batters were so effective that Ruth actually got to bat twice. He started the avalanche of scoring with a home run that fell into the seats in left field—quite a rarity for the Babe. Approximately ten minutes later, he was digging into the batter's box again. Wasting little time, Ruth hit a single with the bases full of Yankee teammates and recorded two more RBIs.

The homer raised Ruth's personal total for 1927 to 13. Gehrig was now two back of the Babe at 11. Ruth was on pace to equal his home run–happy year of 1921, when he set the sports world abuzz with 59 circuit clouts. Other types of hits, though, were not quite as plentiful for the Bambino in 1927 as in past seasons.

Even though the score indicates a one-sided New York romp, the Red Sox actually led by a 6–1 count going into the bottom of the third inning. Starting Yankee pitcher Dutch Ruether was totally ineffective and was replaced by Myles Thomas after the second inning. Thomas put in a fine outing in relief, holding Boston to just one more run over the remaining seven innings. His efforts earned him the victory.

New York's victory kept them one and a half games ahead of their nearest challengers, the pesky Chicago White Sox, at the top of the American League standings.

Other Baseball News

- The St. Louis Cardinals thumped the Reds 11–3 at Cincinnati. Grover Cleveland Alexander defied the calendar once again, allowing just six hits to the home team. Frankie Frisch had a great day for the Cards, going 3 for 5 at the plate and making two impressive defensive plays at second base.

- Al Simmons pounded out two doubles and a triple to lead the Philadelphia Athletics to a 6–1 victory over the Senators in Washington. Rube Walberg picked up the win for Philadelphia, scattering just four Washington hits. A throwing error by Mickey Cochrane brought in the only Senator run, ruining Walberg's bid for a shutout.

- The Reading Keys continued their losing ways in International League play. The Keys dropped their thirtieth straight decision. This time they were drubbed 17–6 at home by the Baltimore Orioles. Reading allowed 21 hits and trailed 11–0 after the top of the third inning.

⚡14 May 30
Yankees at Athletics

Yankees	ab	r	h	po	a	Athletics	ab	r	h	po	a
Combs, cf	5	2	3	5	0	E. Collins, 2b	6	1	2	1	2
Paschal, cf	1	0	0	0	0	Lamar, lf	5	1	3	2	0
Koenig, ss	4	0	0	1	1	Cobb, rf	4	1	1	6	0
Collins, c	2	0	0	1	0	Simmons, cf	3	0	0	1	0
Ruth, lf	4	3	2	0	0	Dykes, 3b	3	0	1	2	1
Gehrig, 1b	6	0	4	13	0	Cochrane, c	2	0	0	4	1
Meusel, rf	5	0	1	3	0	Perkins, c	3	1	2	6	0
Lazzeri, 2b, ss	5	0	0	3	8	Poole, 1b	5	0	2	9	0
Dugan, 3b	2	0	1	0	0	Boley, ss	4	0	0	2	3
Gazella, 3b	3	0	0	1	1	Gray, p	2	0	0	0	2
Grabowski, c	4	0	1	6	0	Walberg, p	1	0	0	0	0
Morehart, 2b	1	0	1	0	2	Foxx, ph	1	1	1	0	0
Pennock, p	2	1	0	0	2	Bishop, ph	1	0	0	0	0
Moore, p	2	0	0	0	0	Wheat, ph	1	0	0	0	0
Totals	46	6	13	33	14	Totals	41	5	12	33	9

New York   0 0 2 0 0 0 3 0 0 0 1 - 6
Philadelphia 0 0 0 1 0 3 1 0 0 0 0 - 5

Few people in the annals of sport are so immediately identified with one team as Connie Mack is with the Philadelphia Athletics. From the team's birth in 1901 (the inaugural season for the American League) through the summer of 1950, Connie Mack was both the club's owner and its manager. He was a revered figure. Always wearing a business suit instead of a uniform, Mack's mere presence on the bench was enough to put his players on their best behavior. Even men who had been on the A's roster for years never dared call him anything but Mr. Mack. Because he felt it was improper to step out on the field to question an umpire's decision without a uniform, Mack delegated the duty to one of his senior players. The May 30 doubleheader at Shibe Park was one instance in which Mack felt compelled to dispute a ruling. In front of some 40,000 spectators, veteran Eddie Collins was dispatched to politely inform the umpires that Mr. Mack intended to file a protest.

The morning game went smoothly enough, at least for Philadelphia, who managed to emerge on the front end of a 9–8 decision despite the fact that Lefty Grove allowed 15 hits to the visitors.

Mack's protest came in the afternoon game, provoked by umpire Van Graflan's ruling on a strange and somewhat comical play in the bottom of the fourth inning. At the time, New York held a 2–0 lead, but the A's had the seeds of a rally planted with Eddie Collins on second base and Ty Cobb on first with just one out.

The always dangerous Al Simmons was Philadelphia's next batter. He lofted a high foul ball near the home team's bench. Yankee catcher Johnny

Grabowski hustled over to make a brilliant, acrobatic catch, but his momentum propelled him head first over an iron railing and in amongst Connie Mack's boys! Then the fun began.

Grabowski hit the floor of the A's dugout and was awkwardly sprawled down a flight of stairs leading to the stands. With his feet kicking frantically in the air, Grabowski was assisted by several sportsmanlike A's who kindly tried to extricate the Yankees' catcher from his uncomfortable resting spot. However, because Grabowski had made the catch, the ball was still live. Alert to the situation, both Collins and Cobb tagged up and headed for home. Both men scored easily as Grabowski was indisposed, but it was not long before Miller Huggins was out on the field demanding the umpires reanalyze the situation.

After due consideration, the gentlemen in blue rewarded lawyer Huggins with a partial victory: They ruled that Collins could score all the way from second base on the play, but Cobb could advance no further than third, since two bases was the proper award on such an odd occurrence. This was the ruling that prompted Mack to send Collins on his mission of official protest.

But the ruling turned out well enough for the Yankees. Cobb never did score that inning. Had his run counted, there would have been no eleventh inning—and none of Ruth's home run heroics, for Ruth's fourteenth home run came in the top of the eleventh and proved to be the difference in New York's 6–5 victory.

Eventually, Ban Johnson upheld the umpires' decision on the play. The split in the doubleheader put the Yankees' record at 26–14, one and a half games ahead of the White Sox, who divided a twin bill of their own with St. Louis.

Johnny Grabowski was not the regular catcher for the Yankees in 1927. Pat Collins carried the bulk of the work behind home plate that summer. Still, Grabowski has his fans. A few years ago, a contestant on *Jeopardy!* mentioned that he was a passionate consumer of baseball trivia. When Alex Trebek asked him what was the most obscure fact he knew about his favorite sport, the man quickly replied, "Johnny Grabowski was the back-up catcher for the 1927 Yankees."

Journalist Red Smith got to know Connie Mack quite well over the last ten years of Mack's tenure at the helm of the Athletics. Like others who encountered Mack, Smith had kind words about baseball's elder statesman but was well aware of Mack's paradoxical nature. "He could be as tough as rawhide," Smith wrote, "and gentle as a mother, reasonable and obstinate beyond reason, and courtly and benevolent and fierce. He was kindhearted and hardfisted, drove a close bargain and was suckered in a hundred deals. He was generous and thoughtful and autocratic and shy and independent and altogether lovable."

Other Baseball News

- Walter Johnson, entering his twenty-first season with the Washington Senators, finally made his first pitching appearance of 1927. It was impressive. Johnson, now nearly 40, pitched a complete-game shutout against the Red Sox in the first game of a doubleheader in Washington. (He also got a hit in three trips to the plate.) In the Senators' 3–0 win, "The Big Train" struck out just one Boston batter, but it increased his major-league record for career strikeouts. Johnson had injured himself in spring training and had missed the first six weeks of the season.

- The St. Louis Cardinals swept a doubleheader from the struggling Cincinnati Reds, who resided in the National League cellar. Jesse Haines won the opener for the Cards, upping his personal winning streak to eight games.

- The Reading Keys finally ended their horrendous slump and won a ball game in the International League. The Keys lost the first game of a home doubleheader to Baltimore by a 4–2 score, but managed to squeak out a 9–8 decision in 11 innings in the second game. The loss in the opener extended Reading's losing streak to an appalling 31 straight games.

♪15 May 31
Yankees at Athletics

Yankees	ab	r	h	po	a
Combs, cf	5	1	1	3	0
Koenig, ss	5	2	2	1	6
Ruth, lf	4	2	1	2	0
Gehrig, 1b	5	3	3	11	0
Meusel, rf	4	0	3	3	0
Lazzeri, 3b	5	1	1	1	1
Morehart, 2b	4	0	0	3	3
P. Collins, c	2	1	1	3	0
Hoyt, p	3	0	1	0	3
Totals	**37**	**10**	**13**	**27**	**13**

Athletics	ab	r	h	po	a
E. Collins, 2b	3	1	1	1	2
Bishop, 2b	2	0	0	0	1
Lamar, lf	5	0	2	2	0
Cobb, rf	3	0	0	1	0
French, rf	1	0	0	1	0
Simmons, cf	3	0	1	2	0
Wheat, cf	1	0	0	1	0
Dykes, 3b	4	2	3	1	1
Cochrane, c	1	0	0	2	0
Perkins, c	1	0	0	3	0
Poole, 1b	4	0	3	12	0
Boley, ss	4	0	0	1	5
Quinn, p	1	0	0	0	0
Willis, p	0	0	0	0	0
Pate, p	2	0	1	0	1
Yerkes, p	0	0	0	0	2
Branom, ph	1	0	0	0	0
Totals	**36**	**3**	**11**	**27**	**12**

New York	3 0 1 1 3 0 2 0 0 - 10
Philadelphia	1 0 0 0 0 1 0 1 0 - 3

♪ 16 May 31

Yankees at Athletics

Yankees	ab	r	h	po	a
Combs, cf	6	4	5	5	0
Koenig, ss	6	3	3	1	3
Ruth, lf	6	2	3	3	0
Paschal, lf	0	0	0	1	0
Gehrig, 1b	5	1	2	11	0
Meusel, rf	1	0	1	0	0
Durst, rf	4	1	1	3	0
Lazzeri, 3b	6	3	4	0	0
Morehart, 2b	6	0	0	1	5
Grabowski, c	5	2	2	2	2
Shocker, p	3	2	3	0	2
Totals	48	18	24	27	12

Athletics	ab	r	h	po	a
E. Collins, 2b	5	0	0	1	5
Lamar, lf	3	0	1	1	0
Wheat, lf	2	1	1	0	0
Cobb, rf	4	2	3	0	0
Simmons, cf	3	0	1	1	0
French, cf	1	0	0	1	0
Dykes, 3b	4	1	2	2	3
Cochrane, c	3	0	1	3	1
Foxx, c	1	1	1	2	0
Poole, 1b	4	0	2	14	0
Boley, ss	4	0	0	2	3
Ehmke, p	1	0	0	0	3
Rommel, p	1	0	0	0	0
Pate, p	1	0	0	0	1
Branom, ph	1	0	0	0	0
Totals	38	5	12	27	16

New York   1 1 0 0 6 7 0 3 0 - 18
Philadelphia   1 0 0 1 0 1 1 1 0 - 5

Connie Mack's A's took it on the chin again from the front-running Yankees this day, but the two-day total of 105,000 paid admissions into Shibe Park must have pleased the Athletics' frugal owner. Mack (whose given name was Cornelius McGillicuddy) often put finances ahead of winning on his priority list. Realizing that Ruth and his mates were a tremendous draw, Mack had scheduled the May 30 Memorial Day doubleheader as separate morning and afternoon games. This way, any fans who wanted to watch both games had to buy tickets twice.

Over the years Mack's Athletics had fluctuated wildly from greatness to ineptness largely because of Mack's interest in the team's ledgers. Not once in their 54-year history did the A's draw a million fans to their home games in a season. Therefore, Mack frequently broke up his championship teams by selling his star players to rival owners. One quote from Mack summed up his business attitude toward the game: "It is more profitable for me to have a team that is in contention for most of the season but finishes about fourth. A team like that will draw well enough during the first part of the season to show a profit for the year, and I don't have to give the players raises when they don't win."

Even though the 1927 Athletics featured old veterans such as Ty Cobb and Eddie Collins (another geezer, Tris Speaker, would be added to the roster in 1928), there was a nucleus of young talent too. The A's would win three straight American League pennants from 1929 through 1931. However, Mack, as usual, sold off his stars to other clubs not long afterward. The A's would not return to the World Series again until 1972, long after the club had severed its ties with Philadelphia.

The games of May 30 had been real nail-biters, each decided by a single run. On the 31st, however, the New Yorkers had little trouble romping to easy victories in both skirmishes. The final scores were 10–3 in the first encounter and 18–5 in the second.

Ruth had a lot to do with how things progressed over the course of the afternoon. Home run number fifteen for the Bambino came in the first game, followed by his sixteenth in the second affair. The latter was especially pleasing to the eye. There were no concerns about its length, but plenty that it might drift foul. Much to the Babe's pleasure, the ball cleared the right field wall about a foot fair before flying over a two-story house across the street.

Ruth's two homers made up just a portion—albeit an impressive portion—of the overall Yankee display of raw power on this day. Lou Gehrig and Pat Collins matched the Babe's homer in the opener with four-bag smashers of their own. Tony Lazzeri and Mark Koenig equaled Ruth's feat in the nightcap. Altogether, in the space of two games, the defending American League pennant holders managed to collect 24 hits. Along with the six homers, the Yankees also contributed four doubles and two triples.

In the second game, the Yankees had consecutive innings where they batted through their order. New York scored six times in the fifth inning and seven runs in the sixth. The Yankee seasonal record stood at 28–14, two full games ahead of the Chicago White Sox.

Other Baseball News

• Joe Harris of the Pirates had a perfect day at the plate, going 5 for 5 in Pittsburgh's 10–9 win over Chicago. Harris got a triple to lead off the bottom of the ninth and scored the winning run on a single by Roy Spencer.

• Former Brooklyn pitcher Bob McGraw, recently acquired by the St. Louis Cardinals, made a successful debut with his new team. McGraw pitched a complete-game shutout as St. Louis beat the Reds 1–0 at Sportsman's Park. The fast-moving game took just 76 minutes to play.

• Johnny Neun, Detroit's first baseman, recorded the second unassisted triple play in the major leagues in two days as the Tigers beat Cleveland 1–0. Neun's defensive work saved the day for Detroit and concluded the afternoon's entertainment. The first two Cleveland batters in the top of the ninth reached base. Glenn Myatt was on second base, Charlie Jamieson was on first. The next hitter, Homer Summa, smacked a line drive directly at Neun. Both runners left their bases on the crack of the bat. Neun caught the ball, then ran over and tagged Jamieson between first and second base. Neun continued toward second base and stepped on it before Myatt could return.

- Neun had read newspaper accounts of the unassisted triple play made by Jimmy Cooney of the Chicago Cubs against the Pirates in Pittsburgh the previous afternoon. Because of the great fanfare Cooney's play generated, Neun was determined to duplicate the feat if the chance ever arose. After making the first two outs on the play, Neun could have easily completed the triple play by tossing the ball to Jackie Tavener, his shortstop, who was standing on the bag and expecting Neun's throw. Years later, Neun remembered yelling to Tavener, "Oh, no. I'm going to go down in the history books!" Neun's triple play received only a fraction of the attention that Cooney's had because it occurred so soon afterward. In retrospect, it should have gotten more recognition. There would not be another unassisted triple play in the major leagues until Ron Hansen of the Washington Senators turned the trick 41 years later in 1968.

✦ 17 June 5
Tigers at Yankees

Tigers	ab	r	h	po	a		Yankees	ab	r	h	po	a
Warner, 2b	4	0	2	1	1		Combs, cf	3	1	0	3	0
Neun, 1b	4	0	0	9	0		Koenig, ss	3	1	2	3	2
Manush, cf	5	0	2	2	0		Ruth, rf	4	1	2	3	0
Fothergill, lf	5	0	1	2	0		Gehrig, 1b	2	1	0	12	0
Heilmann, rf	3	1	1	0	0		Paschal, lf	2	1	1	0	0
DeViveiros, pr	0	0	0	0	0		Lazzeri, 3b	4	0	2	2	2
Gehringer, 2b	5	0	1	3	3		Morehart, 2b	2	0	0	2	7
Tavener, ss	4	1	2	3	4		Grabowski, c	3	0	0	2	0
Wingo, ph	1	0	0	0	0		Moore, p	1	0	0	0	3
Bassler, c	3	1	2	4	0		Thomas, p	1	0	0	0	0
Whitehill, p	4	0	1	0	5							
Totals	38	3	12	24	13		**Totals**	25	5	7	27	14

Detroit	0 0 1 1 0 0 1 0 0 - 3
New York	0 0 0 2 0 1 0 2 x - 5

The visiting Detroit Tigers gamely battled the front-running New York Yankees for the better part of eight innings on June 5 before succumbing to the weight of the home team's bats. Babe Ruth was a key factor in the Yankee win, accounting for one-third of his team's total hits. However, he waited until late into the game before he unleashed his game-saving offensive assault on Detroit pitcher Earl Whitehill.

One of his timely hits just happened to be his seventeenth home run of the 1927 campaign. The other was a piddling, wee single, but all in all it went a long way in propelling the Yankees to a tight 5–3 win.

Ruth's noteworthy blast, as far as circling the bases is concerned, was witnessed by some 35,000 Sunday spectators in the bottom of the sixth. The crowd cheered, bellowed, and went into various forms of hysterics when the ball descended into Ruth's favorite section of Yankee Stadium—the lower right field seats.

Two innings later, with the game's outcome still very much in question, George did it again. His base hit broke a tie with the determined bunch from the Motor City and gave the Yankees a lead they would never relinquish. The hard-fought victory added another half game to the lead the heady New Yorkers held over the oncoming Chicago White Sox.

The Sunday entertainment for the patrons was interrupted by a rainstorm that delayed the proceedings for about 80 minutes. Those who decided to wait through the inconvenience not only got to see Mr. Ruth circle the bases in his home-run trot, but for the same price of admission saw several first-rate catches and a few miscellaneous thrills. Nobody was seen demanding his money back. The game was a genuine cliff-hanger until the Bambino took matters into his own trusty hands and delivered his two key blows.

Detroit outhit New York 12 to 6. Three players (two of them Tigers) also reached base after being hit by pitches. The long rain delay interrupted play when Detroit was batting in the top of the third inning. The resumption of the game after such a lengthy delay was unusual for the time. Modern drainage systems were still years away from being standard equipment at major league parks. Often a heavy rain would render a field unplayable because of mud and puddles.

Ruth really did have a distinctive home-run trot, although it was not nearly as showy as those of later players such as Reggie Jackson or Mark McGwire. In a 1998 article discussing this particular baseball art form, *Sports Illustrated*'s Rick Reilly said, "Babe Ruth ran with little mincing steps, as though he were trying not to step on cracks."

The Detroit pitcher who served up Ruth's home run on this afternoon was Earl Whitehill, a native of Cedar Rapids, Iowa. During Whitehill's 17-year career in the major leagues, he was famous for being a sharp dresser and having a volatile personality. He was one of the few people who dared to argue with temperamental Ty Cobb. When Whitehill broke into the Detroit lineup, Cobb acted as the Tigers' player-manager. Whitehill stood for no criticism of his choice of pitches, even from the legendary Georgia Peach. He would often yell at Cobb if he saw him approaching from center field to offer advice. Whitehill was also a constant complainer as far as umpires were concerned. Teammates who were suspected of giving less than a total effort were special targets of Whitehill's ire.

Although Whitehill is little remembered by contemporary fans, he did win a respectable total of 218 games in his career. His best yearly victory total was 22, which he achieved with the Washington Senators in 1933. Whitehill made his only World Series appearance that same year, pitching a complete-game shutout against the New York Giants in game three in his lone assignment on the mound. It was the only game the Senators won in that series.

Whitehill's lifetime earned-run average of 4.36 is the highest of any 200-game winner in baseball history. When his pitching career ended after the 1939 season, Whitehill stayed in baseball as a coach, first with Cleveland then with the Philadelphia Phillies.

Other Baseball News

• The New York Giants blew an early lead of 6–0 and a ninth-inning 9–7 advantage and lost to Cincinnati by a 10–9 score at Crosley Field. Billy Zitzmann's timely double in the ninth inning made the difference for the Reds. It drove in the tying and winning runs.

• National League president John A. Heydler and 23,000 other fans were on hand at Wrigley Field to watch the Chicago Cubs defeat the Boston Braves 7–0. John (Sheriff) Blake recorded the shutout for the Cubs, scattering five Boston hits.

• A precedent was established by England's two most prestigious universities when Oxford and Cambridge played their first baseball game against each other. Oxford won 10–0 in a game that featured no English players. The students who participated in the historic contest were Americans, Canadians and Japanese. Oxford's American pitcher was the star of the game, striking out 19 opponents. Cambridge allowed seven runs in the second inning to fall hopelessly behind. Sixty-eight-year-old Arlie Latham, one of the handful of players to appear in three major leagues (American Association, National League, and Players' League), acted as the game's sole umpire. The unsophisticated crowd of 2,000 at Stamford Bridge Stadium was puzzled by the occasional yell of "Kill the umpire!" which jokingly came from the teams' benches. Latham had moved to England with his wife after his playing career had ended. With the Second World War approaching, Latham moved back to New York, where he worked into his nineties as a press-box attendant at the Polo Grounds, delighting writers with his firsthand accounts of pre–1900 baseball lore.

♪ 18 June 7
White Sox at Yankees

White Sox	ab	r	h	po	a
Metzler, cf	4	0	0	3	1
Hunnefield, ss	5	0	1	2	2
Barrett, rf	4	0	1	1	0
Crouse, c	4	0	0	3	0
Falk, lf	2	0	1	5	0
Kamm, 3b	4	0	0	0	1
Clancy, 1b	4	1	3	8	0
Ward, 2b	4	0	1	2	2
A. Thomas, p	3	0	0	0	0
Wilson, ph	1	0	0	0	0
Totals	35	1	7	24	6

Yankees	ab	r	h	po	a
Combs, cf	4	0	0	1	0
Koenig, ss	3	0	0	1	2
Ruth, rf	3	1	1	7	0
Gehrig, 1b	4	2	2	8	0
Durst, lf	4	0	1	4	0
Lazzeri, 3b	1	0	0	1	1
Morehart, 2b	3	0	1	0	3
Collins, c	3	1	1	4	0
Hoyt, p	3	0	0	1	3
Totals	28	4	6	27	9

Chicago	0 0 0 0 0 0 1 0 0 - 1	
New York	0 0 0 2 0 1 1 0 x - 4	

The visiting Chicago White Sox came into Yankee Stadium with a legitimate chance to extend their winning ways and overtake New York in the American League standings. Manager Ray Schalk gave the ball to his promising young pitcher, Alphonse (Tommy) Thomas, who was in the midst of an impressive personal winning streak. The extremely confident pitcher was brought down a peg or two by the combined efforts of Babe Ruth and Lou Gehrig. The "Homer Twins," the nickname given to the slugging twosome by the New York media, delivered back-to-back special blows to humble the cocky youngster. This came as a personal tragedy not only to Alphonse, but more importantly to his fellow Chicago White Sox, who had designs on catching the league-leading Yankees in the pennant race. Thomas had entered the fray with a 10–2 won–lost record. Now it was 10–3.

It was during the fourth inning, that Ruth discovered Thomas's much-talked-about fastball was not much different from any of the others he had been banging out of American League ballparks in 1927. Babe's graceful swing carried it some 50 yards southeast of the large scoreboard that adorned the outfield, despite the presence of a stiff breeze blowing towards home plate. The wind nearly made this homer into an out. The ball stayed aloft long enough for a quorum of Chicago outfielders to make a last, desperate lunge at it. Alas, for them, it was to no avail. The ball landed with a crash a few feet on the other side of the fence.

Immediately following Ruth's impressive clout, Lou Gehrig stepped up to the plate and connected for his fourteenth home run of the year. There were two other homers in the game, one by Pat Collins of the Yankees and another by White Sox rookie Bud Clancy. Technically Clancy was a fourth-year player, but statistically he was still considered a rookie. He played in 13 games in 1924, just four in 1925, and 12 in 1926. Clancy would be the regular first baseman for the White Sox for just two seasons and would fade out of the majors by 1934. He died in 1968 in Ottumwa, Iowa, a small town best known to television sitcom fans as the home of Radar O'Reilly, M*A*S*H's company clerk.

Although pitcher Tommy Thomas enjoyed a fast start, he would struggle for the rest of 1927, losing more games than he won. He finished the season with a mark of 19–16. After winning 32 games for the International League's Baltimore Orioles in 1925, Thomas was in the middle of his second season in the majors. He would pitch until 1937, but he never won more than 17 games again, gaining a reputation as a hard-luck hurler who seemed to fall short when faced with important challenges. Twice more in 1927 Thomas would surrender home runs to Ruth. Both of them were gigantic.

Other Baseball News

• There was no shortage of offense at Shibe Park in Philadelphia. The Athletics and Browns combined for a total of 32 hits in the A's 11–9 win. St. Louis's George Sisler could not be blamed for his team's loss. He managed to get a hit in each of the four official times he came to bat. Sisler also stole three bases.

• Rogers Hornsby hit a home run, but his team, the New York Giants, lost 9–6 to the Pirates in Pittsburgh. The loss dropped the Giants into fourth place after they had led the National League early in the schedule. The game was highlighted by sparkling defensive plays by Pittsburgh's Joe Harris and New York's Freddie Lindstrom.

• The Boston Braves climbed up to fifth place in the National League standings by routing the Cardinals 12–5 in St. Louis. Vice president Charles Dawes was in attendance at Sportsman's Park to witness Boston's 14 hits. Two of them were home runs by third baseman Andy High.

♫ 19 & 20 June 11, 1927
Indians at Yankees

Indians	ab	r	h	po	a		Yankees	ab	r	h	po	a
Jamieson, lf	4	0	0	1	0		Combs, cf	5	0	1	3	0
Eichrodt, cf	4	1	1	3	0		Morehart, 2b	5	1	3	2	4
Fonseca, 2b	4	0	1	4	3		Ruth, rf	3	2	2	1	1
Burns, 1b	3	1	3	9	0		Gehrig, 1b	3	1	0	8	0

Indians	ab	r	h	po	a
J. Sewell, ss	3	0	0	3	1
Hodapp, 3b	4	1	0	0	5
Summa, rf	1	0	1	0	0
Cullop, rf	0	1	0	1	0
L. Sewell, c	4	0	1	3	0
Buckeye, p	2	0	0	0	2
Karr, p	0	0	0	0	3
Neis, ph	1	0	0	0	0
Shaute, p	1	0	1	0	0
Totals	31	4	8	24	14

Yankees	ab	r	h	po	a
Meusel, lf	5	0	2	3	1
Lazzeri, 2b	4	1	2	4	3
Dugan, 3b	4	0	1	1	1
Collins, c	4	0	1	5	1
Thomas, p	3	1	2	0	0
Moore, p	0	0	0	0	0
Totals	36	6	14	27	11

Cleveland 0 0 0 0 0 1 0 0 3 - 4
New York   0 0 2 0 2 1 1 0 x - 6

During his career Babe Ruth impressed his adoring public not only with the quantity of home runs he hit but also with their amazing distance. Yankee Stadium seemed specially designed for Ruth in 1923 with its short right field and low wall. However, the length and height of many of the Babe's homers were so formidable that they were capable of clearing the fences of any ballpark. On June 11 Ruth launched two more awe-inspiring blasts against Garland Buckeye of the Cleveland Indians. The first one was so tremendous that Cleveland catcher Luke Sewell suspected something might be amiss.

For those 30,000 fans who saw the Yankees edge the Indians 6–4 at Yankee Stadium, the final score might eventually be forgotten, but the memory of that magnificent home run would linger considerably longer. Even those who got an extremely close look at it had trouble understanding its full magnitude. Indians' catcher Luke Sewell is a prime example.

After the ball had fallen into the center field bleachers directly in front of the scoreboard, Sewell seized Ruth's bat and made a quick inspection. Whatever he was looking for, he failed to find. After several comical moments of gazing at the offending piece of lumber, Sewell was forced to concede that the home run had been hit fair and square, and he simply shrugged his shoulders.

Many longtime Yankee followers claimed it was the second-longest home run hit in the five seasons since New York's American League club was evicted from the Polo Grounds. Not surprisingly, the champion home run was delivered by the same George Herman Ruth back in 1925. Although the 1927 blast benefited from a favorable tailwind, almost all of the power was generated by the Babe himself. The ball carried over the fence in right-center field and neatly bisected the section of seats in front of the scoreboard, landing six or seven rows up.

Oh, yes: Another Ruth homer followed. This one came in the fifth inning and landed in the right field bleachers, just a few rows from the top. It was a pretty fair poke, but nothing compared to the earlier blow.

After Ruth's second home run of the game, Lou Gehrig and Tony Lazzeri both reached base. With Gehrig on third and Lazzeri on first, the Yankees executed a double steal to perfection. Lazzeri broke for second, drawing Sewell's throw. After the Cleveland catcher had released the ball, Gehrig dashed for the plate. Lazzeri was safe at second and the return throw to home was bobbled by Sewell. According to the journalists on hand, the catcher's mishandling of the ball did not make any difference. Gehrig would have been safe on the play regardless.

People who picture Lou Gehrig as a lumbering slugger might be surprised to learn that Gehrig was no slouch on the basepaths. In his magnificent career, Gehrig pilfered 102 bases. This total includes the 15 times he accomplished the sport's toughest baserunning feat—stealing home. Even hardcore fans obsessed with baseball statistics find that particular snippet of data hard to believe. A 1978 journal published by the *Society for American Baseball Research* featured an article called "Lou Who Stole Home 15 Times?" Gehrig was also an intelligent baserunner. Throughout his days with the Yankees, he constantly displayed his ability to judge situations wisely. Gehrig's keen analytical sense enabled him to capitalize on his opponents' moments of indecision or their subtle miscues and turn them into extra bases.

Baseball writers liked to refer to Cleveland pitcher Garland Buckeye as a "mammoth southpaw." Big he was, especially by 1927 standards. He weighed in the neighborhood of 260 pounds. Buckeye had his best season in 1925 when he was 13–8 for the Indians. But size did not translate into victories for the big left-hander. Buckeye's career won–lost record was an unimpressive 30–38. Because of his obvious bulk, Buckeye was lured into the world of professional football during the off-season. He thus joined the company of Ernie Nevers as one of two gridiron athletes who surrendered home runs to Babe Ruth during the 1927 season.

Other Baseball News

- The Detroit Tigers capitalized on costly throwing errors by Jimmy Dykes and Jimmie Foxx in the ninth inning to edge the Athletics 6–5 in Philadelphia. Heinie Manush had a hot bat for the victors, hitting two doubles.

- Grover Cleveland Alexander won his fourth straight game as the St. Louis Cardinals beat the Philadelphia Phillies 4–2 at home. Losing pitcher Hub Pruett allowed nine walks before getting the hook in the sixth inning. Pruett is well known to baseball historians as Babe Ruth's unlikely nemesis. When Pruett was a youthful hurler with the St. Louis Browns, he fanned the Babe 10 out of the 16 times he faced him.

- Hack Wilson's home run proved to be the difference as the Chicago Cubs edged the New York Giants 2–1 at Wrigley Field. Edd Roush hit a triple and a homer in a losing cause for New York.

🏃 21 June 12
Indians at Yankees

Indians	ab	r	h	po	a
Jamieson, lf	4	2	2	2	0
Spurgeon, 2b	4	2	3	2	3
Burns, 1b	5	2	2	10	0
J. Sewell, ss	4	0	3	5	4
Hodapp, 3b	3	0	0	1	0
Lutzke, 3b	1	0	0	0	1
Summa, rf	2	0	0	0	0
Eichrodt, cf	4	1	1	2	0
L. Sewell, c	3	1	0	5	0
Hudlin, p	3	0	0	0	3
Uhle, p	2	0	0	0	1
Totals	35	8	11	27	12

Yankees	ab	r	h	po	a
Combs, cf	5	1	3	3	0
Morehart, 2b	4	2	1	2	4
Ruth, rf	5	1	2	0	0
Gehrig, 1b	5	0	1	14	0
Meusel, lf	2	0	0	1	0
Durst, lf	2	0	0	1	0
Lazzeri, ss	4	1	2	1	4
Dugan, 3b	0	0	0	0	0
Wera, 3b	4	1	1	0	3
Grabowski, c	4	0	1	5	1
Koenig, ph	1	0	0	0	0
Hoyt, p	0	0	0	0	1
Pipgras, p	4	1	2	0	1
Totals	40	7	13	27	14

Cleveland   2 5 0 0 0 0 1 0 0 - 8
New York   0 2 0 0 2 0 1 1 1 - 7

It was an unusual game for the New York Yankees. The visiting Cleveland Indians rocked Yankee starter Waite Hoyt for a 7-0 lead before two innings had been completed. It was a rare occasion in 1927 when Miller Huggins's team fell behind so drastically. But being the defending champions of the American League and the current sole occupants of first place, the New Yorkers did not want to embarrass themselves. They nearly came back, almost erasing the Indians' seemingly secure lead. In the end Cleveland held on to win by a single run.

Babe Ruth's performance was deemed a disappointment, even though he hit home run number 21. The blow occurred in the seventh inning, and the ball ended up in the possession of a bleacher patron in right field, one of the 45,000 souls who bought tickets to the Stadium.

The Yankees' starting pitcher was definitely sub-par on this day. Waite Hoyt lasted less than two innings. George Pipgras came in and did his best. He allowed only one Cleveland score in the remaining innings, but that lone run would prove costly.

George Uhle was Ruth's home run victim. Ruth's third homer in the space of two days must have angered Mr. Uhle, who stuck around long enough for revenge.

Most newspaper men covering the game deemed Ruth to be a failure that afternoon despite the long home run. Twice he struck out to end Yankee rallies. In the ninth inning, with the tying and winning runs in scoring position, Ruth waved at three of Uhle's pitches and did not hit so much as a foul ball. Ruth, who lived to be the hero of every game, was seen sulking on the bench for several minutes after his final strikeout ended all hope for a Yankee comeback.

George Pipgras, who pitched very well in relief for New York, had a surprisingly productive day at the plate, pounding out a homer and a double. It was a rare outburst for Pipgras. His home run off of Uhle was the only one he would hit during the 1927 season—and accounted for half of his lifetime total of two.

During the 1932 World Series versus the Chicago Cubs, Pipgras established a dubious batting record that remains unchallenged. He became the first player to strike out five times in a World Series game. His career batting average was .163.

Winning pitcher George Uhle was nicknamed "The Bull" because of his capacity to pitch complete games. Twice he led the American League in that category. (Two other seasons he topped the league in innings pitched.) One memorable afternoon in 1919, Uhle defied fatigue to hurl a 20-inning shutout. Such outings were costly, though. Late in his career, the Bull suffered from a sore arm that greatly reduced his effectiveness. Even though he won exactly 200 career games, Uhle's greatest contribution to baseball was inventing the term "slider" to describe his innovative pitch. In 1923 Uhle rapped out 52 hits, a record total for a pitcher.

The loss dropped the Yankees' record to 35–17, but they remained four full games ahead of the slumping Chicago White Sox.

Other Baseball News

- Lester Bell's two-run homer in the bottom of the ninth gave the St. Louis Cardinals a dramatic 5–4 win over the Philadelphia Phillies at Sportsman's Park. Phillies outfielder Johnny Mokan had the best day in his seven-year big-league career, going 5 for 5 at the plate. He would be out of baseball by the end of the season.

- The Chicago White Sox failed to capitalize on New York's loss to Cleveland. The Sox lost 6–1 in Washington. The Senators roughed up Chicago's pitching staff for 15 hits. Washington's Hod Lisenbee allowed just five.

- George Pipgras was not the only reliever to show some clout at the plate this afternoon. Brooklyn's Norman Plitt, the fourth pitcher for his team that day, drove in the winning run as the Robins edged the Pittsburgh Pirates 11–10.

♪22 June 16
Browns at Yankees

Browns	ab	r	h	po	a
O'Rourke, 3b	4	0	2	3	0
Melillo, 2b	4	0	3	3	2
Sisler, 1b	2	0	0	7	0
E. Miller, lf	4	0	0	1	0
Rice, rf	4	0	0	2	0
Schulte, cf	4	1	1	2	0
Schang, c	3	0	1	3	1
Gerber, ss	2	0	0	3	3
Zachary, p	0	0	0	0	0
Gaston, p	3	0	0	0	3
Williams, ph	1	0	0	0	0
Totals	31	1	7	24	9

Yankees	ab	r	h	po	a
Combs, cf	3	1	1	5	0
Morehart, 2b	3	1	1	3	3
Ruth, rf	4	2	2	2	0
Gehrig, 1b	4	2	2	11	1
Paschal, lf	4	1	1	0	1
Lazzeri, ss	2	1	1	0	4
Dugan, 3b	4	0	0	0	2
Grabowski, c	4	0	1	5	0
Hoyt, p	4	0	0	1	1
Totals	32	8	9	27	12

St. Louis   0 0 0 0 0 0 1 0 0 - 1
New York   3 0 5 0 0 0 0 0 x - 8

It was one of those fascinating moments in history when two legendary figures crossed paths: Charles Lindbergh met Babe Ruth. During his stay in New York, "the Lone Eagle" agreed to be the guest of honor at Yankee Stadium where the American League leaders were hosting the St. Louis Browns. Although Lindbergh's visit to the stadium was well intended, his late arrival, due to the huge crowds he encountered elsewhere, fouled things up considerably.

The famous aviator was supposed to make an appearance on the field, take a few bows, meet the players, and be comfortably seated for the first pitch at 3:30 P.M. With Lindbergh still nowhere in sight nearly 30 minutes past the appointed time, plate umpire George Hildebrand had a dilemma on his hands. Would he be breaching protocol if he were to start the game without the colonel being present? In the interest in getting nine full innings in before darkness fell, Hildebrand ordered the clubs to begin play.

Lindbergh's lateness prevented him from seeing Ruth's twenty-second homer of the 1927 campaign. "I had been saving that homer just for Lindbergh," Ruth joked with the press corps afterward, "and he doesn't show up. I guess he thinks this is a twilight league."

Even though the colonel missed Ruth's clout, 15,000 others saw it quite clearly. Ruth's homer came in the first inning when people were still waiting for the celebrity to arrive at the stadium. Earle Combs was on second base with one out. Browns hurler Tom Zachary got ahead of the Babe with a couple of quick strikes. A third pitch appeared to have him fooled. Ruth made what looked like a half-hearted, defensive swing at the ball, but the contact he made was enough to push Zachary's offering into the left-center field bleachers.

Still faking anger at Lindbergh's absence, Ruth told reporters, "I held back as long as I could, but it had to come. When you get one of those things in your system, it's bound to come out."

Lou Gehrig followed the Babe's home run with one of his own, putting his personal total at 15. By the time Lindbergh eventually entered Yankee Stadium in the eighth inning, the game was no longer in doubt. New York had opened up an 8–0 lead by the home half of the third, thanks to some sloppy St. Louis fielding.

Umpire Hildebrand's verdict to begin the game without the conquering hero in the stands turned out to be sound. Waiting for Lindbergh would have delayed proceedings for two hours, which would not have sat well with the 15,000 paying customers. There also was the chance, albeit a slim one on June 16, that the game might have been imperiled by darkness if it happened to be unusually lengthy.

Hildebrand was the central figure in baseball's most dubious darkness call. He was working the plate in Game One of the 1922 World Series. After nine innings, the Giants and Yankees were tied 3–3 in a thrilling contest. In an utterly mysterious decision, Hildebrand terminated the game due to darkness even though there was still enough daylight left for at least one inning if not two. Commissioner Kenesaw Mountain Landis was so embarrassed by Hildebrand's controversial ruling that he donated the entire gate receipts from Game One to New York City's war charities. It was largely a gesture to irate fans who accused baseball's hierarchy of conspiring to gouge the public.

The Yankees' convincing 8–1 win over the Browns upped their seasonal record to 37–17, four and a half games ahead of Chicago.

Other Baseball News

• Bill Terry and Rogers Hornsby combined for seven hits as the New York Giants beat the Cardinals 10–5 at St. Louis. The home team honored their former player-manager by declaring the afternoon to be "Rogers Hornsby Day." Before the game, Hornsby was presented with a watch and a floral horseshoe.

• Paul Waner extended his hitting streak to 19 straight games in Pittsburgh's 6–0 victory over the Boston Braves at Forbes Field. Lee Meadows pitched the shutout.

• George (Sarge) Connally of the Chicago White Sox threw a 4–0 shutout against the Athletics in Philadelphia. Bill Hunnefield led the White Sox with a home run and a double.

♪23 & 24 June 22
Yankees at Red Sox

Yankees	ab	r	h	po	a
Combs, cf	5	1	3	2	0
Morehart, 2b	3	0	0	1	2
Meusel, ph	0	0	0	0	0
Gazella, ss	1	0	0	0	0
Ruth, lf	4	2	2	4	0
Gehrig, 1b	2	1	0	15	0
Paschal, rf	3	1	1	1	0
Lazzeri, ss, 2b	4	0	1	2	4
Dugan, 3b	3	0	0	0	2
Collins, c	2	0	2	1	3
Wera, pr	0	0	0	0	0
Grabowski, c	1	0	0	1	0
Thomas, p	1	0	0	0	1
Moore, p	2	1	0	0	5
Totals	**31**	**7**	**9**	**27**	**17**

Red Sox	ab	r	h	po	a
Tobin, rf	4	1	3	3	0
Haney, 3b	3	1	1	1	0
Carlyle, lf	4	1	2	0	0
Flagstead, cf	4	0	1	2	0
Todt, 1b	4	0	0	13	0
Myer, ss	4	0	0	1	4
Regan, 2b	4	0	1	2	4
Hartley, c	3	0	0	5	0
Wiltse, p	2	1	0	0	4
Rogell, pr	1	0	1	0	0
Harriss, p	0	0	0	0	0
Rollings, ph	1	0	1	0	0
Totals	**34**	**4**	**10**	**27**	**12**

New York	0 0 0 2 1 0 4 0 0 - 7
Boston	0 0 3 0 1 0 0 0 0 - 4

The woeful Boston Red Sox, deeply entrenched in last place in the American League, played host to the New York Yankees for two Wednesday afternoon contests. By this time, the Yankees' closest challengers, the Chicago White Sox, were beginning to drop further and further behind the league leaders. Sixty games into the 1927 season, Babe Ruth was beginning to hobble with a leg injury. His physical problems hardly mattered on this day, though, as the Bambino pounded out two more gigantic home runs, both of which came in New York's 7–4 win in the opener. Ruth was now ahead of his record home run pace of 1921.

Babe clouted his first of the afternoon in the top of the fifth inning, an impressive shot that cleared the wall in Fenway Park's left-center field. Two innings later, a longer blow came from Ruth's bat and caused a minor skirmish outside the park. The ball went between the two stands, rolled across a vacant lot, and came to rest near the wall of a neighboring garage, where a merry scuffle among eight Ruth admirers ensued for the souvenir.

The Bostons actually assumed a quick lead in the opener by parlaying three hits and some shoddy fielding by Ben Paschal into three runs. However, being unaccustomed to such an advantage, Boston hurler Hal Wiltse could not nurse it.

The Yankees managed to erase the lead with Ruth's first clout. Ruth's second homer capped a four-run seventh inning. Earle Combs was on base at the time for this one.

The defensive star of the game undoubtedly was second baseman Tony

Lazzeri, who had been honored at an Italian-American function the previous evening. Lazzeri's skillful play saved the second game in the ninth inning when Boston appeared to be rallying.

With New York clinging to a 3–2 lead, Phil Todt opened the bottom of the ninth for the Red Sox with a two-base hit. Wilcy Moore replaced Urban Shocker on the mound for New York. Buddy Myer bunted Todt to third base. Then Bill Regan bounced a grounder towards the Yankee pitcher who fielded it above his head.

Suddenly Todt found himself in a rundown between third and home, but Moore nearly botched it. As Moore chased Todt back toward the bag, he flung a wild toss that sailed over third baseman Joe Dugan's head. Thinking he had home plate all to himself, Todt reversed his direction and made a beeline for the dish.

However, the swift Lazzeri had cleverly backed up third base. He scooped up the ball on one hop and made a perfect throw to catcher Johnny Grabowski, who applied a deadly tag to the surprised Todt.

Phil Todt was among the most liked players in the American League. He possessed a cheerful attitude even though he played first base on Red Sox teams that finished last for six straight seasons. He was never much of an offensive threat, batting just .258 in his career. However, Todt was talented with his mitt. His .997 fielding average in 1928 was the best among American League first basemen.

The Yankees' sweep of the doubleheader put New York's record at 43–17, nine full games ahead of the fading Chicago White Sox.

Other Baseball News

- The St. Louis Browns and Chicago White Sox split a doubleheader at Comiskey Park. St. Louis won the first game 3–2 in ten innings when George Sisler's sacrifice fly drove in Frank O'Rourke. Tommy Thomas picked up his eleventh victory of the season as Chicago won the second game 8–5.

- The St. Louis Cardinals moved into second place in the National League standings by defeating the Chicago Cubs 11–5 at home. Grover Cleveland Alexander volunteered to pitch out of turn so he could face the club that dropped him in 1926. Frankie Frisch got three hits for St. Louis, raising his batting average to .381.

- Pittsburgh rallied from an early 5–0 deficit to beat Cincinnati 11–9 at Forbes Field. The Reds' Curt Walker had three hits in the game, including a double and a triple.

♪ 25 June 30
Red Sox at Yankees

Red Sox	ab	r	h	po	a		Yankees	ab	r	h	po	a
Tobin, rf	3	1	2	0	0		Combs, cf	6	0	3	2	0
Tarbert, rf	1	0	1	0	0		Morehart, 2b	6	3	2	0	6
Rollings, 3b	1	0	0	0	1		Ruth, rf	4	2	2	1	0
Rogell, 3b	4	0	0	0	0		Gehrig, 1b	5	2	3	13	0
Carlyle, lf	5	1	2	0	0		Meusel, lf	4	2	3	1	0
Regan, 2b	3	1	0	4	2		Durst, lf	1	0	0	0	0
Todt, 1b	5	1	2	9	0		Lazzeri, ss	4	1	2	1	1
Myer, ss	4	1	1	2	4		Dugan, 3b	4	0	1	0	1
Shaner, cf	4	1	1	4	0		Wera, 3b	0	0	0	0	0
Hofmann, c	4	0	0	5	1		Collins, c	3	2	2	9	0
Moore, c	0	0	0	0	0		Thomas, p	1	1	1	0	2
Harriss, p	2	0	0	0	0		Moore, p	4	0	0	0	2
Welzer, p	2	0	0	0	3							
Totals	38	6	9	24	11		Totals	42	13	19	27	12

Boston   0 0 6 0 0 0 0 0 0 - 6
New York   3 2 1 3 1 3 0 0 x - 13

The great drama of each baseball season, especially in the days when the major leagues were not broken up into divisions, was in the pennant races. But one of the sport's strengths is that it has the capacity to attract a following even when one team, such as the 1927 Yankees, is a virtual cinch to win the flag. Subplots always seem to emerge, and one did in late June of that year.

Incredibly, young upstart Lou Gehrig, had risen to even terms with Babe Ruth in the home run standings. When the Babe hit his twenty-second homer of the season, one New York writer joked that the man who followed George in the batting order was only seven home runs behind him. The "only" was meant in a derogatory manner. At the time, the idea that the shy fellow from Columbia might actually challenge the Babe for home run laurels seemed completely ridiculous. Suddenly, though, Gehrig went on a power-hitting tear, and the writers were forced to reevaluate their perceptions. Going into the Yankees' June 30 game against Boston, Gehrig and Ruth were level at 24 homers apiece.

Most of the 3,000 or so paying customers at Yankee Stadium that day probably cared little about the ballgame; the main attraction was the ongoing home run duel. For those who were interested, New York prevailed over the lackluster Boston Red Sox by a convincing 13–6 margin.

Gehrig briefly assumed the lead in the contest with a home run in the first inning. This four-bagger, among other things, drove home Babe Ruth, who now found himself in second place.

Ruth, however, refused to capitulate the home run laurels and evened the count in the fourth inning. As was the case with Gehrig, Slim Harriss was the obliging pitcher for Ruth, as he had been for Gehrig. Gehrig's homer was hit on a 2–0 pitch. So was Ruth's. Ruth's home run crashed through the thick air and eventually settled in the right field bleachers.

Ruth's homer was perhaps more aesthetically pleasing with its higher arc, but Gehrig's was sharper and more powerfully struck.

Many of the New York writers covering the Ruth versus Gehrig home run splurge liked to fantasize that Ruth and Gehrig were saying and thinking nasty things about one another after hitting their respective home runs. Actually in 1927 their relationship was friendly, though in later years it would deteriorate. The two rarely saw eye to eye as Gehrig blossomed into a bona fide star. Gehrig disapproved of Ruth's hedonistic lifestyle. Ruth did not care for Gehrig's mother, who frequently traveled with her son. Over the years their feud became increasingly bitter. The most famous photo of the two men was taken during Lou Gehrig Appreciation Day at Yankee Stadium in 1939, when Gehrig, having been diagnosed with amyotrophic lateral sclerosis, had his uniform retired. Ruth is seen giving his old teammate a big bear hug. The next time you see the photo, look at it closely. Gehrig, who still harbored ill feelings despite the passage of time, is not hugging Ruth in return.

Although the frenzy of Gehrig and Ruth home runs was captivating the vast majority of America's baseball fans, there were some dissenters who were appalled. One was journalist Joe Vila. Suspecting the 1927 version of the official game ball had been juiced up, Vila criticized the orgy of four-baggers in a piece in the June 30 edition of *The Sporting News*. "Baseball today has become a game of home runs," declared Vila. "The season isn't half over, yet the big league sluggers have recorded more than 400 homers, indicating nearly 1,000 at the end of the pennant race. Isn't it about time to call an end to this farce? If the present ball could have been pitched to sluggers like [Cap] Anson, [Dan] Brouthers, [Sam] Thompson, [Ed] Delahanty, [Napoleon] Lajoie, [Hugh] Duffy, [Tip] O'Neill and others of long ago, the public would have cried out in protest against the countless home runs which would have marred the scientific games we old-timers once enjoyed."

On this afternoon Boston put a scare into the home team by scoring six times in the third inning, but it was not nearly enough. The Yankees put runs on the board in each of the first six innings to win comfortably.

Red Sox pitcher Slim Harriss (whose legal name was William Jennings Bryan Harriss) was an odd physical specimen. He stood 6'6" and weighed just 180 pounds. He would lead the American League in losses in 1927 with a total of 21.

The 13–6 victory lifted New York's record to 49–20. (In stark contrast, last-place Boston had a pitiful 15–51 mark.) The Washington Senators, in the midst of an impressive winning streak, took over second place from the White Sox but were still 13½ games behind the frontrunning Yankees.

Other Baseball News

• Goose Goslin's single scored Sam Rice in the bottom of the ninth to give the Senators a 6–5 win over Philadelphia at Griffith Stadium. The A's had held the lead on three separate occasions.

• Charlie Gehringer's homer started a three-run rally in the eighth as the Detroit Tigers beat Cleveland 6–5 at Dunn Field.

• Pirate shortstop Glenn Wright was having a tough week. After being beaned by a wild pitch in St. Louis, he was sent home to Pittsburgh to recuperate. During his trip on the Pennsylvania Railroad, his train derailed near Denison, Ohio. Wright and the other passengers were jostled, but were otherwise uninjured.

🏃 26 July 3
Yankees at Senators

Yankees	ab	r	h	po	a		Senators	ab	r	h	po	a
Combs, cf	5	1	1	3	0		Rice, rf	5	1	1	5	0
Morehart, 2b	3	1	0	1	5		Harris, 2b	3	1	1	0	4
Shawkey, p	0	0	0	0	2		Speaker, cf	4	1	2	3	0
Ruth, rf	3	1	1	2	0		Goslin, lf	3	2	1	2	0
Gehrig, 1b	4	0	2	13	0		Judge, 1b	4	1	2	10	1
Meusel, lf"	5	0	1	0	0		Ruel, c	4	0	2	5	0
Lazzeri, ss, 2b	5	1	1	2	3		Bluege, 3b	4	0	1	0	2
Dugan, 3b	4	0	0	1	1		Reeves, ss	4	0	2	2	3
Gazella, ss	0	0	0	0	1		Lisenbee, p	2	0	0	0	0
Grabowski, c	3	0	0	2	0		Braxton, p	0	0	0	0	0
Bengough, c	0	0	0	0	0		Marberry, p	0	0	0	0	0
Shocker, p	1	1	1	0	1							
Thomas, p	1	0	1	0	1							
Giard, p	1	0	0	0	0							
Collins, ph	0	0	0	0	0							
Durst, ph	1	0	0	0	0							
Paschal, ph	1	0	0	0	0							
Wera, 3b	0	0	0	0	1							
Totals	37	5	8	24	15		Totals	33	6	12	27	10

New York 1 0 2 0 0 0 1 1 0 – 5
Washington 2 0 1 0 3 0 0 0 x – 6

First it was the Philadelphia Athletics. Then came the Chicago White Sox. Now it was the turn of the surprising Washington Senators to challenge the New York Yankees' grip on first place in the American League. Bucky Harris, who had managed the Senators to consecutive championships in 1924 and 1925, had witnessed his club quietly putting together a winning streak that at least caused people to wonder if the powerful Yankees were capable of faltering. (Few of New York's partisan baseball writers even considered the possibility of the Yankees blowing the pennant. Most discussed the idea of Ruth and his teammates participating in October's World Series as a fore-gone conclusion.) Nevertheless, the Senators' unexpected surge into second place did wonders for fan interest in Washington. All of a sudden, the Yan-kees' visit to Griffith Stadium had pennant implications, and great hordes of hopeful spectators—a capacity crowd and then some—turned out in the early July sunshine to see baseball's two hottest teams battle one another.

The Senators had won nine straight games; the Yankees, seven. Some-thing had to give, and it turned out to be the Yankees' run of triumphs. Wash-ington won 6–5.

Despite the loss, Babe Ruth smacked his twenty-sixth home run of the season, which leveled his personal race with teammate Lou Gehrig. Ruth's homer, which landed deep into the center field bleachers, was said to be the longest ever hit at Griffith Stadium. Tony Lazzeri, no slouch himself, also notched a homer for the defending pennant winners.

The game was a thriller. Washington broke out to a 6–3 lead but very nearly saw their advantage evaporate in the late innings. New York managed to score one run in the seventh and another in the eighth, but they could not put the tying marker across the plate. Although Lou Gehrig did not connect for a home run, he did enjoy a productive day, belting a triple and a double.

The overflow crowd was indirectly responsible for two episodes of comic relief during the bottom of the fifth inning. Washington's Joe Judge was awarded a ground-rule double when he hit a fair ball that struck a refresh-ment vendor! Apparently the crowd at Griffith Stadium was so large that the resident hawkers could not negotiate the aisles with their usual ease. Many responded to the cramped quarters by conducting their business from foul territory. However, when Judge's hit struck a surprised vendor who had strayed onto fair ground, the umpires ordered all the salesmen back into the stands for the remainder of the game.

Shortly after the ground-rule double occurred, another crowd-control incident delayed the proceedings further. An inebriated fan in the distant bleachers (who clearly brought his own libations to the ballpark) opened a gate in center field, staggered onto the field, and sat down on the grass to enjoy the game. "The umpires waved sternly at him," reported *New York Times* reporter James R. Harrison, "and he courteously waved back." When Ruth approached the man to persuade him to leave, the trespasser simply brayed like a donkey at the Babe. Security staff eventually led the man out of the stadium.

New York's loss dropped their record to 51–21, 9½ games in front of the charging Senators.

Other Baseball News

- The Cincinnati Reds edged the Pittsburgh Pirates 5–4 at Crosley Field. Hughie Critz's double in the bottom of the ninth inning scored Ethan Allen with the winning run. Joe Cronin made three throwing errors in the sixth inning, which led to three Cincinnati runs. Cronin would be demoted to the minors not long afterward. He would be acquired by Washington in 1928 and go on to have a Hall-of-Fame career at shortstop with the Senators and Red Sox. Cronin would later serve capably as the American League's president from 1959 to 1973.

- The Brooklyn Robins swept a doubleheader from the Philadelphia Phillies before a delighted home crowd at Ebbets Field, winning the first game 6–1 and the second contest 6–5 in 11 innings. Cy Williams hit a home run in each game for Philadelphia. Harvey Hendrick led the Brooklyn offense, getting five hits in ten at-bats.

- A late Detroit rally fell short as the Cleveland Indians beat the Tigers 10–9 at Navin Field to end Detroit's seven-game winning streak. When pitcher Rip Collins was relieved in the top of the sixth, it marked the first time in eight games that a Detroit hurler had failed to last the full nine innings.

♪ 27 July 8
Yankees at Tigers

Yankees	ab	r	h	po	a
Combs, cf	4	3	2	3	0
Morehart, 2b	4	2	1	2	6
Ruth, lf	3	1	2	2	0
Gehrig, 1b	5	0	1	12	1
Meusel, rf	5	0	0	2	0
Lazzeri, ss	5	1	2	1	4
Dugan, 3b	5	1	1	2	2
Collins, c	4	0	1	2	1
Pipgras, p	0	0	0	1	1
Moore, p	3	2	2	0	0
Pennock, p	0	0	0	0	1
Totals	**38**	**10**	**12**	**27**	**16**

Tigers	ab	r	h	po	a
Warner, 3b	3	1	1	1	3
Gehringer, 2b	5	1	1	3	3
Manush, cf	5	1	2	1	0
Fothergill, lf	2	1	0	1	0
Ruble, lf	3	0	0	1	0
Heilmann, rf	4	0	1	2	0
Neun, 1b	4	2	1	6	2
Tavener, ss	2	1	2	3	3
Bassler, c	4	0	1	8	1
Woodall, c	1	0	1	0	0
Whitehill, p	0	0	0	0	0
Hankins, p	0	0	0	0	0
Wingo, ph	0	0	0	0	0
Smith, p	2	0	0	1	0
DeViveiros, pr	0	1	0	0	0
McManus, ph	1	0	1	0	0
Carroll, p	1	0	0	0	0
Totals	**37**	**8**	**11**	**27**	**12**

New York	1 5 0 2 0 0 0 2 0 -	10
Detroit	2 0 0 0 0 0 2 3 1 -	8

New York's July 8 encounter with the Detroit Tigers at Navin Field marked the midway point of the 1927 season. At the conclusion of the doubleheader, the Yankees had played 77 of their 154 scheduled games and had won 55 of them. The only challengers remotely on the horizon were the Washington Senators, yet it would take a drastic Yankee slump plus a continuation of Washington's recent hot streak to bring the Senators within realistic striking distance. In firm possession of first place, the Yankees began a western road trip. In the pre-expansion days, westward travel meant destinations such as Detroit, Cleveland, Chicago and St. Louis.

After all was said and done in the New York–Detroit doubleheader, 37 runs had been scored, and the boys from the Motor City had managed to split a pair of games with the defending champs. In front of an enthusiastic throng of 25,000, the hometown team had almost managed to keep up with the renowned sluggers from New York for two full games. Detroit won the opener by a 10–8 count, but dropped the second game by an 11–8 final score.

The fascinating home run duel between Gehrig and Ruth continued to simmer, with Ruth edging ahead with an inside-the-park job in the seventh inning of the second affair. (Gehrig's bat was silent as far as round-trippers were concerned.) After leaving Ruth's hefty chunk of lumber, the ball rolled deep to the flagpole in center field, but Ruth made it home with plenty of time to spare, behind both Earle Combs and Ray Morehart.

This home run added a measure of security to a day when no lead was truly safe. It capped a five-run Yankee rally that helped preserve the win for pitcher George Pipgras.

Ruth's home run was not the only marvelous example of baserunning on display at Navin Field that afternoon. In the bottom of the eighth inning of the first game, Detroit pulled off a rare triple steal that Richards Vidmer of the *New York Times* described as "beautiful even to these biased eyes." Art (Speedy) Ruble, a Tiger rookie pinch runner, was on third base. Teammates Johnny Neun and Larry Woodall were on second and first base respectively. Ruble took his lead and surprised the Yankees by cleanly sliding across home plate before Wilcy Moore's pitch arrived. Neun and Woodall also advanced on the play to record the triple steal. Ruble would play just 75 games in the major leagues and would steal a grand total of two bases.

Another player also stole a base during the doubleheader—George Herman Ruth! Ruth accomplished his theft in the second game. Many contemporary fans picture the Babe as a lumbering slugger encumbered with a beer belly. Certainly by 1927 Ruth was not as svelte as he had been during his early days with the Red Sox. Nevertheless even with his increasing girth (which the Yankee pinstripes were supposed to disguise), Ruth always maintained a degree of quickness. The fact that he could leg out an inside-the-park homer and score with relative ease should indicate that Ruth was no liability on the basepaths. During his spectacular 1927 season the Babe would steal seven bases. By the time his playing days ended in 1935, Ruth had pilfered 123 bases, all but six of them for the Yankees. (Joe DiMaggio, in contrast, had but 30 steals in his entire career.)

New York's split in the doubleheader put their record at 55 wins and 22 losses, giving the Yankees an 11½ game lead over Washington. The Senators actually edged a game closer to New York by sweeping Cleveland in a doubleheader of their own.

Other Baseball News

- Ban Johnson, founder of the American League, who was embroiled in a bitter feud with the eight club owners, offered his resignation as league president effective the end of the 1927 season. His statement was tersely worded, as was the owners' acceptance. Publicly the owners expressed their regrets over Johnson's decision, but privately they were pleased to see his heavy-handed method of leadership come to an end. In more cordial times, Charles Comiskey, owner of the Chicago White Sox, had declared, "Ban Johnson is the American League!"

- Charlie Root of the Chicago Cubs allowed just one hit, a two-out single in the eighth to Pirate catcher Johnny Gooch, as the Cubs beat Pittsburgh 1–0 at Forbes Field. The only run of the game was unearned as it was scored on Pie Traynor's throwing error in the second inning.

- Al Simmons was becoming a potent offensive force in Philadelphia. He connected for a triple and a homer as the A's upended the St. Louis Browns 7–5. Browns pitcher Sad Sam Jones was pounded for 13 hits. Ty Cobb drove in two critical runs for the A's with a seventh-inning double.

♪ 28 & 29 July 9
Yankees at Tigers

Yankees	ab	r	h	po	a		Tigers	ab	r	h	po	a
Combs, cf	6	3	1	2	0		Warner, 3b	5	0	2	0	2
Morehart, 2b	4	3	1	3	6		Gehringer, 2b	4	2	2	3	6
Ruth, lf	6	3	5	3	0		Manush, cf	5	2	3	1	0
Gehrig, 1b	5	2	1	12	1		Wingo, lf	1	2	1	1	1
Meusel, rf	5	4	3	2	0		Heilmann, rf	4	1	1	2	0
Lazzeri, ss	5	1	4	2	5		Neun, 1b	4	0	2	10	0
Dugan, 3b	5	2	4	0	2		Tavener, ss	5	0	0	4	5
Grabowski, c	2	0	0	0	0		Woodall, c	4	0	0	6	2
Collins, c	1	1	0	2	0		Holloway, p	1	0	0	0	0
Pipgras, p	3	0	1	0	1		Carroll, p	3	0	0	0	1

Yankees	ab	r	h	po	a		Tigers	ab	r	h	po	a
Moore, p	3	0	0	1	1							
Durst, ph	0	0	0	0	0							
Totals	45	19	20	27	16		Totals	36	7	11	27	17

New York   3 1 0 4 0 2 3 3 3 - 19
Detroit   0 0 3 0 4 0 0 0 0 - 7

When Roger Maris and Mickey Mantle were in the midst of their tremendous home run duel in 1961, members of New York City's media were accused, with some justification, of rooting for Mantle at the expense of Maris. Those sympathetic to Maris, a relative newcomer to Yankee pinstripes, claimed that New York's baseball writers unabashedly praised Mantle whereas Maris received hardly anything but thinly veiled criticism.

The New York writers who covered the Yankees certainly had their favorites in the 1927 home run race as well, and they did little to hide their bias. Like Maris 34 years later, Lou Gehrig was generally considered an unworthy challenger. Within a few seasons, however, Gehrig would be admired as much as any player in the sport.

But in 1927, sportswriters described fans as jubilant when Ruth, on July 9, retook the American League lead in homers. In the process, the Yankees split an abbreviated doubleheader from the Detroit Tigers. New York won the opener by a lopsided 19–7 score. The Tigers took the second game 14–4.

Both of Ruth's homers came in the first game off the generous pitching of Ken Holloway. The two home runs each sailed into the center field seats, but the second one was the more impressive of the two. Despite the output, Ruth was still marginally behind the record pace he had set for round-trippers six seasons earlier. That year he got his twenty-ninth homer in game number 71. After the action of July 9, the Yankees had played 78 contests in 1927.

The first game of the doubleheader was Ruth's finest of the season from an offensive standpoint. The Babe got five hits in six trips to the plate, including a pair of doubles to complement his two home runs.

An overflow crowd was present at Navin Field to witness Ruth's batting exhibition. When the seating capacity of the Tigers' park proved insufficient to handle the patrons, spectators were permitted onto the field provided they stayed behind some hastily strung restraining ropes. The hemp barriers proved inadequate for the task. Restless fans were constantly slipping underneath the ropes in an attempt to get a better view of the action. When Ruth appealed to a group of children to stay where they were supposed to, more youngsters swarmed into the area to be near baseball's greatest star. With all the interruptions, it took 55 minutes to play the first two innings, after which the crowd settled down.

The clubs managed to play only seven innings of the second game before darkness set in. No one griped when plate umpire Emmett (Red) Ormsby terminated the proceedings. Detroit had jumped out to a 9–0 lead after four innings and was well in control when the game was called.

Ormsby was a rare commodity in the big leagues: an umpire who was well liked by the players. During the First World War, he was exposed to a German gas attack. Occasionally, he suffered lingering effects, which included light-headedness. Whenever Ormsby felt such a spell coming on, he would ask the catcher to assist him in calling balls and strikes. Ormsby commanded so much respect that the catcher would dutifully relay his honest opinion.

New York now sported a 56–23 record, but the onrushing Washington Senators chipped away at the Yankee lead in the American League standings by sweeping another doubleheader.

Other Baseball News

• The Philadelphia Phillies beat the Cincinnati Reds 12–11 in a wild game at the Baker Bowl. Philadelphia broke out to a 7–0 lead after two innings. Cincinnati rallied and led 9–8 going into the bottom of the eighth. The Phillies responded with four runs. The Reds got two back in the top of the ninth but fell one run short. Despite the plentiful scoring, the game took just one hour and 58 minutes to play.

• Washington narrowed the Yankees' lead in the American League standings to 10½ games by beating Cleveland twice at Dunn Field. The first game went 13 innings before the Senators won 6–5. Washington won the second game 3–2 as Walter Johnson went the distance and struck out eight Indians.

• Milt Gaston was the winning pitcher as the St. Louis Browns beat the Philadelphia Athletics 7–5 at Sportsman's Park. Gaston helped his own cause by hitting a home run. Harry Rice also homered for the Browns. Al Simmons hit the only homer for the visitors.

⚐ 30 July 12
Yankees at Indians

Yankees	ab	r	h	po	a		Indians	ab	r	h	po	a
Combs, cf	5	1	2	1	0		Jamieson, lf	4	0	0	2	0
Morehart, 2b	5	2	3	3	2		Spurgeon, 2b	3	0	2	1	5
Ruth, rf	4	1	1	6	0		Summa, cf	4	0	0	1	0
Gehrig, 1b	5	1	2	11	2		Burns, 1b	3	0	1	9	3
Meusel, lf	4	0	2	1	0		J. Sewell, ss	4	0	1	4	1
Lazzeri, ss	4	0	0	1	6		L. Sewell, c	4	0	1	5	1

Yankees	ab	r	h	po	a
Dugan, 3b	4	0	2	3	0
Grabowski, c	4	2	2	1	1
Shocker, p	1	0	0	0	3
Totals	36	7	14	27	14

Indians	ab	r	h	po	a
Eichrodt, cf	4	0	0	2	1
Lutzke, 3b	2	0	0	0	3
Hodapp, 3b	1	0	1	0	2
Shaute, p	3	0	1	3	3
Myatt, ph	1	0	0	0	0
Burnett, ph	1	0	0	0	0
Totals	34	0	7	27	19

New York   0 0 3 0 0 0 1 0 3 - 7
Cleveland   0 0 0 0 0 0 0 0 0 - 0

Occasionally Babe Ruth hit rough spots during the 1927 season. For Ruth, a slump meant that he was enduring an abnormal length of time without adding another home run to his impressive total. Even when his hits were not sailing over fences in American League ballparks, he could be counted on to contribute to the Yankee cause with frequent hits.

Nevertheless, Ruth did enter into the game on July 12 at Cleveland's Dunn Field the victim of a genuine decline. Before he knocked a pitch by Joe Shaute solidly into the bleachers, Ruth had suffered a prolonged spell of hitlessness.

Of course, for an average ballplayer, a streak of 14 consecutive trips to the plate without a hit is dismal, but not unexpected. But when your name is George Herman Ruth, it is quite an awful slump indeed.

But the Babe rose from his doldrums at Dunn Field and smacked his thirtieth home run of the season high over the right field fence. This belt not only got the Babe back on track offensively, it also nudged him ahead of Gehrig for major league baseball's home run honors.

The home run did not factor in the outcome of the game, as the New York Yankees cruised to a very comfortable 7–0 win over the languishing Clevelanders. Nevertheless, it was a fine sight to behold. It was one of Babe's specials—a high arching blast that immediately captured the attention of everyone in the ballyard from the peanut vendors to the scrubs riding the bench.

Ray Morehart benefited from the Bambino's clout as he got a free trip home from second base. Joe Shaute was pitching for the Tribe but was having little success. He had given up 13 Yankee hits before Ruth took him deep, and all 13 had been singles. Ruth changed that statistic with one mighty swing.

Having a wonderful time on the mound was Yankees starter Urban Shocker. Shocker recorded a shutout with the aid of a splendid catch by George Ruth, a graceful snag by Lou Gehrig, and general all-around brilliance by Tony Lazzeri. Over the course of the afternoon, Shocker allowed but seven Cleveland hits, none of which did any significant damage. The loss was Cleveland's seventh straight setback.

The afternoon came to a less than satisfactory finish for Shocker, however, when he awkwardly twisted an ankle covering first base for the final out of the game. Thus the shutout pitcher had to be assisted from the field by an assortment of concerned Yankee teammates. Hardly a triumphal procession.

New York surged into the lead in the top of the third inning when they accounted for three of their seven runs. One more New York score occurred in the seventh inning, and three more came in the ninth to put the game well out of reach.

Joe Shaute, who was badly rocked on this afternoon, likely had a special place in his heart for Ruth. When Shaute made his major league debut with the Indians in 1922, the Babe was the first batter he ever faced. Although Ruth would strike out against Shaute more than 30 times over the course of his career, the Babe would hit three homers off the Cleveland lefty during the 1927 season.

Three years earlier, in 1924, Shaute won 20 games for the only time in his career—but still he managed to lead the American League in losses with 17.

The easy win lifted New York's record to 58–24, 9½ games ahead of the Washington Senators.

Other Baseball News

- Sheriff Blake pitched a magnificent two-hitter in Boston as the Chicago Cubs beat the Braves 6–2 in Boston. Although the oppressive heat sapped the energy from the two teams, Boston's Edward (Doc) Farrell, who had been acquired from the Giants earlier in the season, made a spectacular defensive play in the top of the ninth inning. Farrell dived to smother a hot grounder and threw the runner out while lying flat on his back.

- The Chicago White Sox defeated the Philadelphia Athletics 8–5 at Comiskey Park. The bottom of the sixth inning was the turning point in the game as the home team tallied six runs. Winning pitcher Sarge Connally allowed 15 Philadelphia hits, but was saved on several occasions by double plays turned by his teammates. Connally provided some offensive punch himself. He went 4 for 4 at the plate before leaving the game in the eighth inning.

- The Washington Senators, still with high hopes of catching the Yankees, extended their winning streak to seven straight games as they downed the Detroit Tigers 9–6 at Navin Field. Key doubles by Washington's Bobby Reeves and Sam Rice in the top of the eighth provided the margin of victory.

♪ 31 July 24
Yankees at White Sox

Yankees	ab	r	h	po	a
Combs, cf	5	0	0	3	0
Koenig, ss	5	0	2	5	5
Ruth, lf	3	2	2	4	0
Gehrig, 1b	4	0	1	10	0
Meusel, rf	4	0	1	1	0
Lazzeri, 2b	4	0	1	2	1
Gazella, 3b	2	0	0	0	0
Collins, c	2	1	0	2	2
Wera, pr	0	0	0	0	0
Grabowski, c	0	0	0	0	0
Pipgras, p	3	0	0	0	4
Moore, p	0	0	0	0	1
Totals	32	3	7	27	13

White Sox	ab	r	h	po	a
Kamm, 3b	4	0	0	3	1
Hunnefield, 2b	4	0	0	1	1
Metzler, cf	3	1	1	1	0
Barrett, rf	4	1	1	3	0
Falk, lf	4	0	3	3	0
Clancy, 1b	3	0	1	8	1
Peck, ss	4	0	2	0	1
McCurdy, c	2	0	0	8	0
Nels, ph	1	0	0	0	0
Thomas, p	2	0	0	0	1
Totals	31	2	8	27	5

New York	1 0 1 0 0 0 1 0 0 - 3	
Chicago	0 0 0 1 0 1 0 0 0 - 2	

Going into the final week in July, Babe Ruth had managed to hit home runs in every American League city but one: Chicago. Over the course of the long season, the White Sox would prove to be the stingiest club in surrendering home runs to Ruth. Therefore it stood to reason that Comiskey Park was to be the final road stadium to withstand the Babe's 1927 home run barrage. Nevertheless, Ruth finally connected for a homer in front of a large, boisterous gathering of paying customers in Chicago to break the Comiskey hex.

Oddly enough, the blow was well received by the 50,000 souls who had filled Comiskey Park. Apparently, Ruth's popularity extended well into Illinois. The Babe's wallop accomplished several other feats too. It was the deciding margin in the Yankees' narrow 3–2 victory over the Chisox, and it put Ruth back into a tie with Gehrig for American League home run laurels.

There was nothing special or extravagant about the homer. It came in the third inning with two out and established a 2–0 edge for the visitors. The ball screamed into the distant right field seats where many of Ruth's homers had come to rest before. The only person visibly upset when Ruth single-handedly created a run was Alphonse (Tommy) Thomas, the unfortunate Chicago hurler. Up until Ruth's fateful blow, Thomas had been doing a fine job in keeping the great New York lineup reasonably at bay.

Richards Vidmer of the *New York Times* showed considerable foresight by concluding his account of Ruth's homer with this thought: "It was just such a home run as the Babe has hit hundreds of times before and just such a blow as he will belt 29 more times this season. That is, if he is going to break his record."

Ruth's home run was not his only major contribution to New York's offense on this afternoon. In the first inning Ruth provided the Yankees' first run by tripling off Thomas and coming home on Lou Gehrig's solid single. "The Babe's homer," Vidmer continued, "which was hurled high and handsomely into the right field seats in the third with two out, put [New York] another run in the velvet."

Despite falling behind 2–0 after three innings, Chicago had rallied to tie the game by the bottom of the sixth inning. However, the Yankees produced the go-ahead run in the top of the seventh when Mark Koenig's single drove home Pat Collins. The 3–2 lead would hold up through the bottom of the ninth.

Earle Combs, known to baseball fans in the 1920s as "the Kentucky Colonel," returned to the New York lineup after being struck on the temple with a wild throw on July 22. Combs, as usual, took his place in center field, a position he played so capably that he earned himself a coveted spot in the Hall of Fame. (It was late in his life when Combs, a native of Pebworth, Kentucky, was finally elected by the Veterans Committee. Combs received his bronze plaque in 1970, two months after his seventy-first birthday.) Two other Yankee center fielders, Joe DiMaggio and Mickey Mantle, are also enshrined in Cooperstown. With the exception of the war years, when DiMaggio was away in the armed forces, center field at Yankee Stadium was patrolled by Hall-of-Famers from 1924 to 1968. No other franchise has equaled such a sustained period of excellence at this position.

New York's 3–2 victory on July 24 raised the team's seasonal record to 67–26, 13 full games ahead of second-place Washington.

Other Baseball News

- The last-place Boston Red Sox broke out to a 4–0 lead after the top of the second inning but then had to hang on to narrowly beat Detroit 8–7 at Navin Field. The loss ended Detroit's five-game winning streak, but the Tigers' Harry Heilmann, the American League batting champion in 1923 and 1925, extended his personal hitting streak to nine straight contests.

- Reds outfielder Raymond (Rube) Bressler had two triples and a single in Cincinnati's 9–4 victory over the St. Louis Cardinals at Crosley Field.

- Washington exploded for nine runs in the top of the seventh inning to beat the Browns 14–6 at Sportsman's Park in St. Louis. Each team got 15 hits, but the Senators bunched theirs together to great effect. Twelve of them came in the top of the sixth and seventh. Bucky Harris got five hits for the winners.

♪ 32 & 33 July 26
Browns at Yankees

Browns	ab	r	h	po	a		Yankees	ab	r	h	po	a
O'Rourke, 2b	4	0	0	6	7		Combs, cf	5	1	1	6	0
Bennett, rf	4	1	2	0	0		Koenig, ss	5	2	2	3	2
Sisler, 1b	4	0	2	9	1		Ruth, rf	4	4	4	1	0
E. Miller, lf	3	0	1	1	0		Gehrig, 1b	4	2	2	8	0
Rice, cf	4	0	0	3	0		Meusel, lf	4	2	2	2	0
O. Miller, 3b	3	0	0	0	2		Lazzeri, 2b	3	1	0	0	4
O'Neill, cf	4	0	0	2	0		Morehart, 2b	0	0	0	0	0
Gerber, ss	4	0	1	2	5		Gazella, 3b	3	1	0	1	1
Gaston, p	3	0	0	1	0		Grabowski, c	4	1	2	6	0
							Ruether, p	5	1	1	0	2
Totals	33	1	6	24	15		Totals	37	15	14	27	9

St. Louis	0 0 0 1 0 0 0 0 0 - 1
New York	2 0 3 0 2 1 0 7 x - 15

One trait of a championship team in any sport is the ability to regularly defeat teams that are clearly inferior. There is no letup against a weak foe, and certainly no mercy for the victim. The St. Louis Browns, despite having George Sisler on their roster, were never a threat to make a run for the American League pennant in 1927. Whenever they played the Yankees that season, the Browns were decided underdogs.

To their credit, the Yankees never allowed themselves to be lulled into thinking that any of the games they played against St. Louis would be laughers, even though many indeed were. New York put as much effort into their dates with the Browns as they did against their more threatening opponents.

When the Yankees returned home in late July from their prolonged road trip, Babe Ruth and Lou Gehrig kept the 2,000 or so souls who bought tickets to Yankee Stadium atwitter with their ceaseless home run duel. Entering the doubleheader against the Browns, Gehrig and the Bambino were deadlocked at 31 round-trippers apiece.

When all the tumult had died down, Ruth had flicked two more homers into the right field seats, both of which came in the first one-sided contest. Gehrig, however, remained within striking distance as he himself knocked one in the same general direction.

Really, Ruth provided the only offensive spark needed in the opener. His two homers would have been sufficient to beat the Browns as Dutch Ruether surrendered only six hits and one lone run to the visitors. Nevertheless, the Yankees could not help scoring and won in a rout, 15–1, roughing up Milton Gaston for 14 hits along the way.

The two victories continued New York's flawless record against the

Browns in 1927. For those who keep track of such miscellany, that was 13 wins to zero in favor of Miller Huggins's mighty Yankees. The pair of losses dropped the fading Browns into seventh place; the Cleveland Indians now occupied the lofty heights of sixth place in the eight-team American League standings.

With the results of games versus the Brownies a foregone conclusion this season, the fans' focus clearly centered on New York's home run duo. Their rapt attention was amply rewarded. Ruth drew first blood with a man on in the first inning. His other was a solo shot in the sixth frame. It was struck with two men out.

Milt Gaston, the Browns pitcher who served up both of Ruth's homers in the first game, possessed a wicked forkball. He was one of the few players ever to be elevated to the majors without spending at least some time in the minor leagues. He never lived up to his billing, though. Gaston led the American League in losses in 1926. His specialty pitch was as much a curse as a blessing. It moved so erratically that it often eluded his catcher, resulting in many passed balls and wild pitches.

Ruth was virtually unstoppable at the plate during the two games. He was 4 for 4 in the opener and 3 for 4 in the concluding contest. New York's record now stood at 69–26, and the Yanks remained 13 games ahead of second-place Washington.

Other Baseball News

• Lew Fonseca and Nick (Tomato Face) Cullop combined for seven Cleveland hits as the Indians beat Boston 7–2 at Fenway Park. Cleveland scored all seven of their runs in the top of the third inning, and the Indians were never in danger of relinquishing the lead.

• The Cincinnati Reds won their sixth straight game, defeating the St. Louis Cardinals 11–10 at Crosley Field. The Reds' win also capped a four-game sweep of the Cards. Cincinnati led 11–4 after the seventh inning, but St. Louis made things interesting by scoring five times in the eighth and once more in the ninth.

• Former Pirate Max Carey got three hits, scored three runs, stole third base and home; yet his Brooklyn Robins lost 6–5 in Pittsburgh. The Pirates scored two runs in the bottom of the eighth to snatch the victory. Carey's extraordinary efforts did not go unnoticed. He received a rousing ovation from the Pittsburgh fans.

⚡34 July 28
Browns at Yankees

Browns	ab	r	h	po	a		Yankees	ab	r	h	po	a
O'Rourke, 3b	5	1	3	3	3		Combs, cf	4	2	2	4	0
Bennett, rf	5	1	1	1	0		Koenig, ss	5	1	1	1	3
Sisler, 1b	5	1	1	7	0		Ruth, rf	5	2	3	5	0
Williams, lf	4	0	0	4	0		Gehrig, 1b	3	1	0	8	2
E. Miller, cf	4	0	3	2	0		Meusel, lf	1	2	0	3	1
Melillo, 2b	4	1	1	2	3		Lazzeri, 2b	2	1	1	2	2
Dixon, c	4	0	0	4	1		Gazella, 3b	3	0	3	1	0
Gerber, ss	4	0	1	1	2		Collins, c	3	0	0	1	0
Vanglider, p	0	0	0	0	0		Shocker, p	3	0	0	2	0
Stewart, p	3	0	2	0	1							
Adams, ph	1	0	0	0	0							
Totals	39	4	12	24	10		Totals	29	9	10	27	8

St. Louis   3 0 0 0 0 0 0 0 1 - 4
New York   5 0 0 0 1 0 1 2 x - 9

Displaying his knack for showmanship, Babe Ruth rescued a drowsy Yankee Stadium crowd from their slumber by parking his thirty-fourth home run of the 1927 season in the inexpensive seats.

As usual, the visiting St. Louis Browns were putting up only a token resistance against their all-powerful hosts. The hometown rooters were growing weary of the romp until Ruth decided to revive them with one of his patented thumps.

The grand event occurred in the home half of the eighth inning—almost certainly the last time Mr. Ruth would wield his lumber in this particular game. Walter (Lefty) Stewart of the Browns became just another notch on Ruth's belt after seeing one of his best projectiles suddenly reverse directions and soar to the deepest reaches of the right field bleachers. Greatly appreciative, the 10,000 paying customers roared their collective approval as Ruth circled the bases.

Suddenly invigorated, the crowd buzzed as Lou Gehrig stepped into the left-handed hitter's batter's box. But Lou was not up to matching the Babe on this day. He weakly went down on strikes and took the enthusiasm right out of the previously excited throng. Ruth now held a slim 34–33 edge in the 1927 home run chase that everyone was talking about.

With the Ruth-versus-Gehrig home run derby becoming more interesting than the American League pennant race, everyone was willing to engage in comparisons. Yankee manager Miller Huggins said Gehrig "lacked the grace of the Babe at bat. The Babe swings with a free motion of his wrists, and the swing comes right out of his powerful shoulders. Lou, on the other hand, hits with a rigid wrist. Since he is somewhat flat-footed at the plate, he's in a position to get more direct power from his drives—and to get more

hits off good balls. Lou's stance is less flexible than Babe's. It's more dug in."
The contrasting styles of their swings produced different types of home runs.
Many of Ruth's homers, launched with high, majestic arcs, were aesthetically
pleasing. Gehrig's blows tended to be hard-hit line drives that did not elicit
the same degree of awe.

The Browns put a scare into the Yankees in the first inning, but only
momentarily. St. Louis scored three runs in the top of the first, but New York
quickly replied with five of their own in the bottom of the inning. In the 22
games the Browns played against the Yankees in 1927, St. Louis would win
just one. Utility infielder Mike Gazella had a perfect day at the plate for the
Yankees, going 3 for 3.

St. Louis manager Dan Howley was not used to experiencing failure.
Although 1927 was his first season piloting a major league club, he had earned
the reputation as a giant killer while managing Toronto in the International
League. Howley managed the Maple Leafs to the International League pennant in 1918 and then took a coaching job with the Detroit Tigers. He made
a triumphant return to Toronto in 1926. His club won the pennant once again
to break the Baltimore Orioles' seven-year grip on the championship. In 1928
the Browns would come in third, the highest finish Howley would enjoy in
his six seasons as a major league manager.

The Yankees' 9–4 victory raised their record to 71–26, giving them a
huge 14-game lead over Washington.

Other Baseball News

- Rogers Hornsby hit his seventeenth home run of the season as the New
York Giants edged the Chicago Cubs 6–5 at Wrigley Field. The loss was
costly for the Cubs, as it prevented them from gaining a share of first place
in the National League standings.

- Walter Johnson struck out only one batter, but the Chicago White Sox got
just six hits off him as the Washington Senators romped to a 12–2 victory
at Griffith Stadium. Player-manager Bucky Harris got four of the Senators' 16 hits.

- The last-place Boston Red Sox embarrassed the Cleveland Indians by
sweeping a doubleheader at Fenway Park. Danny McFayden pitched a
shutout in the first game, a 3–0 Boston victory. The Red Sox manufactured a run in the bottom of the ninth in the second game to win 4–3. Earlier in the ninth inning, three Indians, including manager Jack McCallister,
were ejected by umpire Van Graflan after a lengthy dispute at home plate.
For McCallister, 1927 would be his only season as a big league manager.

♪ 35 August 5
Tigers at Yankees

Tigers	ab	r	h	po	a
Warner, 2b	4	0	0	1	2
Gehringer, 2b	4	1	2	3	4
Manush, cf	4	1	1	3	0
Fothergill, lf	4	0	2	3	0
Heilmann, rf	2	0	1	0	0
Wingo, rf	1	0	1	0	0
Neun, 1b	4	0	1	8	2
Woodall, c	4	0	0	3	0
DeViveiros, ss	2	0	0	1	0
McManus, ss	2	0	0	0	2
Holloway, p	1	0	0	0	0
Smith, p	2	0	1	2	1
Bassler, ph	1	0	0	0	0
Totals	35	2	9	24	11

Yankees	ab	r	h	po	a
Combs, cf	4	0	1	3	0
Koenig, ss	4	0	1	1	4
Ruth, rf	4	3	2	3	0
Gehrig, 1b	3	1	1	9	3
Meusel, lf	4	1	1	3	0
Lazzeri, 2b	2	0	2	2	1
Gazella, 3b	3	0	0	1	2
Collins, c	4	0	0	3	0
Hoyt, p	3	0	0	2	3
Totals	31	5	8	27	13

Detroit   2 0 0 0 0 0 0 0 0 - 2
New York 3 0 1 0 0 0 0 1 x - 5

Although Yankee Stadium was dubbed "The House That Ruth Built," the park's dimensions favored Ruth only if he pulled the ball toward the short right-field fence. Of course, that's what he often did. The rest of the stadium, however, was so cavernous that many long hits—hits that would have been home runs elsewhere—stayed inside the enclosure. (It should not come as a surprise that of Ruth's 1927 homers, the majority, albeit a slim one, came on the road.) On this afternoon both Ruth and Lou Gehrig hit deep drives that just missed clearing distant fences. For his plucky effect, Ruth was awarded with just a two-base hit. Not until his final turn at bat would he add another homer to his tally with a much weaker shot.

The Bambino's more spectacular blow was struck in the third inning of the August 5 Detroit–New York game. It was a beauty, and the crowd rose expectantly. But it was deceiving. The sheer vastness of the Stadium's center field kept the ball in play. In fact, the ball smacked smartly off the barrier between the bleacher seats and the outfield greensward and bounced back into the grateful hands of a Tiger outfielder.

Realizing his best home run chances came from pulling the ball, Ruth yanked one considerably towards the shorter right field fence in the bottom of the eighth inning. This hit lacked the grandeur of the one five innings earlier, but it traveled far enough to plop over the wire barrier and count as a four-bagger. As Lou Gehrig failed to achieve a similar feat versus the visitors from the Motor City, Ruth gained a bit of ground on the young slugger. Still, Gehrig holds a 37–35 lead in that fascinating department.

Ruth's home run seemed to enliven the Yankees. Their 5–2 victory ended what hard-to-please manager Miller Huggins had termed a "slump" and earned the home team a series split with the Tigers.

Let it not be said that Gehrig did not try to duplicate the Babe's homer—he did. Immediately following Ruth's swat, Gehrig flailed one solidly to left field. By a tiny margin, the ball failed to negotiate its way into the seats and Lou had to settle for a lowly triple. It was his only offensive contribution to his club's three-run win.

Yankee Pitcher Waite Hoyt suffered through a shaky first inning, allowing two Tiger runs, but managed to hold Detroit scoreless from that point onward. New York quickly erased the early two-run deficit by scoring three times in the bottom of the first. Detroit's starting pitcher, Ken Holloway, was removed in the third inning immediately after surrendering Ruth's double and Gehrig's triple. Holloway was replaced by George Smith, who allowed Ruth's home run in the eighth. Smith was a rarity in 1927–: a pitcher who specialized in relief appearances. In his five-year major league career, Smith pitched in 132 games but started just seven. Smith's most productive year was 1927, when he compiled a 4–1 record and a 3.91 ERA.

Waite Hoyt was one of the first baseball players to turn his attention to broadcasting once his playing days had ended. He was the voice of the Cincinnati Reds from 1941 until his retirement in 1965. He was elected to the Hall of Fame—as a player—in 1969. Hoyt was a teammate of Ruth's from 1921 to 1930. Despite working with one another for a decade, Ruth never bothered to learn Hoyt's first name. When Hoyt was traded to the Tigers in 1930, the Babe sadly shook his hand and said, "So long, Walter."

The win lifted the Yankees' seasonal record to 75–30, putting them 11½ games ahead of the second-place Washington Senators.

Other Baseball News

• The Chicago Cubs beat the Boston Braves 5–2 at Wrigley Field. Cubs pitcher Percy Jones starred, allowing just eight hits and getting four hits himself. Jones would get just 14 hits all season. A crowd of 32,000 watched the game, including 17, 247 women who took advantage of Ladies' Day at the ballpark.

• Dolph Luque, the Reds' Cuban-born pitcher, allowed the New York Giants only five hits as Cincinnati won 3–0 at Crosley Field. Only one Giant managed to reach third base. There were no extra-base hits in the game, which took just 94 minutes to play.

• Former major leaguer Ed Konetchy scored a rare victory against the professional baseball establishment when his three-year-old claim against the minor league Petersburg, Virginia, club was upheld by Commissioner Kenesaw Landis. The team was ordered to pay Konetchy his entire 1924 salary—the sum of $1,050—which had been in dispute. The club believed that Konetchy had waived his back salary in exchange for free agency. Landis disagreed, citing a National Association rule that stated no club could hold a player on its reserve list who was due back salary. Konetchy was a first baseman for six major league clubs from 1907 to 1921.

♪ 36 August 10
Yankees at Senators

Yankees	ab	r	h	po	a		Senators	ab	r	h	po	a
Combs, cf	5	2	3	3	0		Rice, rf	4	0	2	3	0
Koenig, ss	5	1	1	2	2		Harris, 2b	2	0	0	3	1
Ruth, rf	4	1	3	1	0		Stewart, 2b	2	0	0	0	2
Gehrig, 1b	4	0	1	11	0		Speaker, cf	4	0	0	3	0
Meusel, lf	4	0	0	0	1		Judge, 1b	4	1	1	8	0
Lazzeri, 2b	4	0	0	0	5		Goslin, lf	4	0	2	3	0
Dugan, 3b	4	0	0	2	2		Ruel, c	3	1	2	2	1
Collins, c	1	0	1	8	0		Bluege, 3b	4	1	1	1	3
Hoyt, p	3	0	0	0	2		Reeves, ss	4	0	0	3	4
Moore, p	1	0	0	0	1		Zachary, p	1	0	0	0	0
							Marberry, p	1	0	0	1	0
							Tate, ph	1	0	0	0	0
Totals	**35**	**4**	**9**	**27**	**13**		**Totals**	**34**	**3**	**8**	**27**	**11**

New York   1 0 3 0 0 0 0 0 0 - 4
Washington   0 1 0 0 2 0 0 0 0 - 3

Umpiring in the major leagues during the 1920s was a little different from how it is today. Instead of the familiar four-man crew contemporary fans are used to, just two arbiters were in charge of games during Ruth's heyday. Making life somewhat hazardous for the twosome in blue was the fact that fans often exited stadiums via the playing field. Unruly spectators often caused trouble by confronting unpopular umpires outside their dressing rooms. On August 10 umpire Clarence Rowland was caught in a phalanx of irate Washington baseball fans after a clash between the American League's top two teams.

While some observers might have argued that the fan's frustration was justified, the real cause of Washington's troubles was a muscular fellow in a New York uniform named George Herman Ruth who single-handedly accounted for all his team's scoring. The locals, however, preferred to place the blame on Mr. Rowland. The harried arbiter needed a police escort to exit Griffith Stadium. How he actually got out remains something of a mystery.

There were two points of contention that the patrons of the ballpark wished to discuss with the aforementioned Mr. Rowland. One third strike he called against Bobby Reeves seemed to be a trifle wide of the prescribed strike zone. Secondly, he refused to acknowledge that Ossie Bluege was hit by a pitched ball, while Bluege and his Senator teammates insist the ball nicked at least a thread on his uniform.

Still, it was Mr. Ruth who provided the true woes to the Senators and their faithful supporters, who were apparently under the delusion that they could make up the dozen or so victories that separated the Washington club from the New Yorkers.

Ruth's contribution to the victory was a three-run homer when the score was level at 1–1. Oddly enough, the Babe was unmolested and greeted with cheers and numerous autograph requests when the game concluded. The same could not be said for Mr. Rowland.

At the end of the game, a sizable collection of miffed baseball fanciers waited for Rowland outside the clubhouse doors. They obviously were an angry lot and had to be dispersed forcibly by the local gendarmes. By that time, however, Rowland was safely in hiding, although no one could say precisely where.

Babe Ruth's home run, which should rightfully have been the main topic of conversation, was his thirty-sixth of 1927. The victimized hurler was Tom Zachary, whom Babe had dented earlier in the season when Mr. Zachary had a different signature on his pay check. Ruth's drive was a little different from his customary blows. It landed amongst the customers in the left-center field stands. Despite this important clout, Babe trailed Lou Gehrig by two in the race for home run honors.

The Senators rallied with two runs in the bottom of the fifth to get within one run of the Yankees, but could get no closer. Waite Hoyt started for the Yankees and was removed from the mound in the bottom of the sixth inning after allowing two Washington hits. Wilcy Moore was summoned from the bullpen, quelled the Senators' threat, and kept the home team off the scoreboard for the remainder of the game.

Ruth's home run was the second he had hit off Tom Zachary in 1927. The first one had occurred on June 16 when Zachary was a member of the St. Louis Browns. On July 7 Zachary was dealt to the Washington Senators in exchange for another pitcher, Alvin (General) Crowder.

Clarence Rowland, the besieged umpire, had managed the Chicago White Sox from 1915 through 1918, leading his club to the World Series in 1917. He became an American League umpire in 1923. The 1927 season would be his last in that capacity. (Perhaps the angry mob at Griffith Stadium on August 10 caused him to examine his means of employment.) Rowland would later become president of the Pacific Coast League and executive vice president of the Chicago Cubs.

Ruth, on this day, was responsible for driving in all four of New York's runs. Apart from the three-run homer, he had singled home Earle Combs in the top of the first inning. That hit broke a personal slump for Ruth in which he had gone hitless in 14 trips to the plate. The Yankees' 4–3 victory raised the team's record to 77–32 and increased their lead to 12 full games over the defeated Senators.

Other Baseball News

• The Boston Red Sox, who had been enjoying recent success, were walloped by the Athletics 12–2 in Philadelphia. Lefty Grove struck out nine Red Sox. Ty Cobb had a triple, a double, and a single for the A's.

• Owen Carroll of the Tigers outdueled Milt Gaston of the St. Louis Browns in a 2–1 pitchers' battle in Detroit. Defense was the difference: the Tigers turned three double plays, and the Browns committed three errors.

• The New York Giants sent ten batters to the plate and scored six runs in the top of the eighth inning to beat the Pirates 8–3 in Pittsburgh. The Pirates had scored three runs in the bottom of the seventh to take a 3–2 lead. Travis Jackson and Freddie Lindstrom got two hits apiece for the Giants. Paul Waner and his brother Lloyd each got three hits for Pittsburgh.

37 August 16
Yankees at White Sox

Yankees	ab	r	h	po	a		White Sox	ab	r	h	po	a
Combs, cf	5	2	2	2	0		Flaskamper, ss	3	0	1	3	4
Koenig, ss	5	2	1	2	2		Kamm, 3b	4	0	1	2	2
Ruth, lf	3	2	2	3	1		Metzler, cf	3	0	0	1	0
Gehrig, 1b	4	1	1	10	0		Barrett, rf	3	0	0	3	0
Meusel, rf	4	0	4	1	0		Falk, lf	2	0	0	4	0
Lazzeri, 2b	4	0	0	5	1		Cole, p	2	0	0	0	1
Dugan, 3b	4	0	1	1	5		Ward, 2b	4	1	3	2	4
Collins, c	4	1	2	3	1		Clancy, 1b	4	0	1	11	0
Pennock, p	2	0	0	0	4		Berg, c	4	0	2	1	1
							Thomas, p	1	0	0	0	2
							Nels, lf	3	0	1	0	0
Totals	35	8	13	27	14		Totals	33	1	9	27	14

New York	2 0 2 0 1 0 0 3 0	– 8
Chicago	0 0 0 0 0 0 1 0 0	– 1

On August 16 at Chicago's Comiskey Park, Babe Ruth set a precedent by launching a baseball completely out of the spacious stadium. No batter had ever accomplished this feat before, and few did it afterward in the six and a half decades the park remained the home of the White Sox. Even though Ruth's solo home run had virtually no effect on the game's 8–1 outcome in favor of the Yankees, it was the most noteworthy event of the afternoon, utterly overshadowing Bob Meusel's perfect day at the plate.

Ruth's homer came in the fifth inning with none of his fellow teammates on base to profit by it. Alphonse (Tommy) Thomas tossed the Bambino a high fastball, which the Babe made disappear as if he were an amateur magician.

There was no doubt it was a home run; the only speculation was whether Charles Comiskey's concrete ballpark could contain it. Witnesses to Ruth's monumental blast last saw it sailing serenely over the double-decked right field stands with plenty of gusto behind it. As no one had ever accomplished a similar feat in the 17-year-old stadium, onlookers were generally dumbfounded.

To show there were no hard feelings, an uncontrollable mob of youthful well-wishers, estimated by some to number 5,000 or more, descended on the field to slap Ruth on the back once the final out was registered in the ledgers. Such was their unbridled enthusiasm that a few of Chicago's finest officers were needed to save Ruth from excessive bruises given by these backslappers. The Babe was delayed five whole minutes before he made it to the safety of the Yankee clubhouse.

Along with his mammoth home run, Ruth also chipped in with a double and two bases on balls. Lou Gehrig, who now led Ruth by just one home run in the round-tripper chase, could only summon a double from his athletic biceps. Bob Meusel was the most consistent Yankee hitter of the bunch, going 4 for 4 at the plate. Herb Pennock went the distance on the mound for New York and was well in control from his first pitch of the afternoon to his last.

New York had opened up a 4–0 lead after the top of the third inning. Three more runs in the top of the eighth eliminated any chance that the White Sox might stage a comeback. Ruth also starred defensively in right field. He personally squelched a Chicago rally in the bottom of the first inning with a dazzling throw. The White Sox had the bases loaded with one out. After Bibb Falk flied out to Ruth, Ray (Flash) Flaskamper tagged up and attempted to score from third base on the play. Ruth's subsequent throw, described by *New York Times* correspondent Richards Vidmer as "a perfect strike over the plate," arrived well ahead of the White Sox shortstop. Flaskamper was easily tagged out to end Chicago's most dangerous threat of the day.

Bob Meusel, who went 4 for 4 at the plate, was the largest of the 1927 Yankees by height, standing 6'3" tall. Meusel was the younger brother of Emil (Irish) Meusel, a star on the New York Giants, and possessed one of the best arms in the American League. On September 5, 1921, he recorded four out-field assists in a game to equal a major league record. He also hit for the cycle three times in his career. Nevertheless, Meusel was considered an under-achiever by manager Miller Huggins and many of New York City's baseball writers. Because of his grim, surly temperament, he also ranked among the most unpopular players of his era. During an infamous 1924 game versus Detroit, Meusel charged Tiger pitcher Leonard (King) Cole and attempted to pound him with his bat. The umpires, helpless to control the ensuing riot, called off the game and charged the Yankees with a rare forfeit loss.

The 8–1 victory over the White Sox lifted New York's seasonal record to 80–33, putting them 13½ games ahead of Washington.

Other Baseball News

• The Detroit Tigers overcame a 6–1 deficit to defeat Boston 10–7 at Navin Field. Harry Heilmann and Charlie Gehringer both homered for Detroit. Fred Hoffman, Boston's catcher, was carried off the field unconscious after Johnny Neun crashed into him during a play at home. Hoffman suffered a broken nose in the collision.

• Bob O'Farrell had five hits for the St. Louis Cardinals, but his team needed 11 innings to beat the Braves 5–3 in Boston. Grover Cleveland Alexander pitched a complete game for the Cardinals and got two hits himself.

• The Philadelphia Athletics swept a doubleheader in Cleveland. Sammy Hale's three-run triple in the first game was the telling blow in the A's 6–3 victory. A five-run ninth inning locked up an 8–0 win in the second game, which took just 96 minutes to play. Jack Quinn recorded the shutout.

♩38 August 17
Yankees at White Sox

Yankees	ab	r	h	po	a		White Sox	ab	r	h	po	a
Combs, cf	5	0	1	2	0		Hunnefield, ss	4	1	1	1	1
Koenig, ss	4	0	0	1	4		Kamm, 3b	5	1	1	1	1
Ruth, lf	4	1	1	3	0		Metzler, cf	4	0	1	2	0
Gehrig, 1b	4	1	1	18	1		Barrett, rf	4	0	0	4	0
Meusel, rf	4	0	0	2	0		Nels, ph	1	0	0	0	0
Lazzeri, 2b	3	0	0	3	6		Falk, lf	4	0	1	4	1
Dugan, 3b	2	0	0	1	0		Ward, 2b	4	0	0	1	4
Durst, ph	1	0	0	0	0		Clancy, 1b	4	0	1	13	0
Gazella, 3b	1	0	1	0	2		Crouse, c	3	0	1	7	1
Bengough, c	2	0	0	2	0		Connally, p	3	0	0	0	3

Yankees	ab	r	h	po	a
Ruether, ph	1	0	1	0	0
Wera, pr	0	1	0	0	0
Collins, c	1	0	0	1	0
Pipgras, p	2	0	0	0	2
Morehart, ph	1	0	0	0	0
Moore, p	0	0	0	0	2
Totals	35	3	5	33	17

White Sox	ab	r	h	po	a
Totals	36	2	6	33	11

New York   0 0 0 0 1 0 0 1 0 0 1 - 3
Chicago   2 0 0 0 0 0 0 0 0 0 0 - 2

Babe Ruth's unquestioned status as baseball's most famous ambassador could often produce unexpected reactions from spectators in the seven other American League cities. Take the near riotous situation in Washington's Griffith Stadium on August 10, when Senators fans were intent on mobbing umpire Clarence Rowland. Yet the very same people were happy to give Ruth a pat on the back, even though he had almost singlehandedly defeated their home team.

In Chicago on August 17, Ruth hit an extra-inning home run to give the Yankees a 3–2 win, yet he received a tremendous ovation. Earlier in the game Ruth had struck out twice and had been soundly heckled. Whether the Chicago fans, saturated by stories of Ruth's fabulous exploits, had been berating the Babe for not living up to his advanced billing is not clear. However, Ruth was often welcomed much like a visiting dignitary into what should have been "hostile" surroundings. Many patrons had likely paid their admission fees solely for the privilege of witnessing Ruth in action. This "star" treatment undoubtedly irked home teams' managers and players alike.

The pitcher who served up the Bambino's thirty-eighth circuit swat of 1927 was also christened George. Like Ruth though, he answered to a nickname—Sarge, in his case—and his last name was Connally.

The man with the military moniker had whiffed Ruth twice in regulation time. His most important strikeout of the reigning home run king came in the eighth inning when the Yankees had two out and the bases filled. This particular embarrassment for the Babe was fodder for the stadium hecklers, who originally seemed delighted that Ruth had come up short when the game was on the line.

The fans' attitude changed abruptly in the fateful eleventh frame, however, when Ruth smote a Connally offering into the left field stands and circled the bases with the decisive tally. Based on the roar of those present when the ball dropped among the outfield spectators, an unbiased observer could be excused for thinking that the game was being contested in front of a ballpark filled solely with New York rooters. In the statistical department, Ruth's four-bagger leveled the score with teammate Lou Gehrig in their ongoing duel for home run supremacy.

The White Sox had jumped out to a quick 2–0 lead in the bottom of the first inning, but the Yankees picked up a run in the top of the fifth and another in the top of the eighth to tie the score. The Yankees used 16 players in the game—an unusually high number for them—including Julian (Julie) Wera and Benny Bengough. During the 1927 season New York often played the full nine innings of many games without enlisting any substitutions. Wera came into the game as a pinch runner in the top of the eighth inning and scored the tying run on Earle Combs's single. It was one of only seven runs he would score all season.

Benny Bengough was one of baseball's truly unique characters. Born in Liverpool, England, in 1898, Bengough nearly became a Catholic priest. Upon immigrating to America, however, he put his religious aspirations aside and concentrated on a career in baseball. He was signed as a catcher by a minor league club in Buffalo but saw very little playing time. Before an exhibition game between Buffalo and the St. Louis Browns, Bengough's feisty mother approached her son's manager and demanded that Benny be allowed to catch the game. With nothing at stake, the manager acquiesced. Benny responded by throwing out four would-be base stealers. His career quickly advanced from that point onward.

Although Bengough was never more than a backup major leaguer, he was remembered for his quirky behavior behind the plate. He attempted to distract opposing batters by running his fingers through his long hair—flowing locks that existed only in his fertile imagination.

Ruth's home run was the second and last he would hit in extra innings during the 1927 season. (The other one had also come in the eleventh inning, hit off Rube Walberg on May 30 against the A's in Philadelphia's Shibe Park.)

New York's 3–2 victory put their seasonal record at 81–33, 14 games ahead of second-place Washington.

Other Baseball News

- Chuck Dressen's eighth-inning home run gave the Cincinnati Reds a 2–1 victory over the Phillies in Philadelphia's Baker Bowl. Dolph Luque was the winning pitcher; Frank Ulrich was the tough-luck loser. The fast-moving game was over in 86 minutes.

- Former Brown University pitcher Haskell Billings made an impressive major league debut for Detroit, holding the Boston Red Sox to just two runs in the Tigers' 6–2 win at Navin Field. Billings struck out five Boston hitters, but issued seven bases on balls. The victory was Detroit's seventh straight.

- The New York Giants' six–game winning streak came to a halt with a 4–1 loss to Pittsburgh at the Polo Grounds. Paul and Lloyd Waner accounted for most of Pittsburgh's offense, scoring three of the Pirates' runs.

⚐ 39 August 20
Yankees at Indians

Yankees	ab	r	h	po	a		Indians	ab	r	h	po	a
Combs, cf	5	0	3	3	0		Jamieson, lf	4	0	0	4	1
Koenig, ss	3	1	1	4	3		Fonseca, 2b	5	3	3	2	1
Ruth, rf	3	1	1	1	0		Summa, rf	4	3	3	1	0
Gehrig, 1b	3	1	0	8	0		Burns, 1b	4	3	4	4	1
Paschal, lf	5	0	1	4	0		J. Sewell, ss	5	3	3	1	2
Lazzeri, 2b	4	1	1	0	6		L. Sewell, c	5	2	4	10	0
Dugan, 3b	3	1	1	2	1		Eichrodt, cf	3	0	2	3	1
Wera, 3b	2	0	2	0	0		Lutzke, 3b	3	0	0	1	2
Collins, c	3	2	0	2	1		Miller, p	0	0	0	0	0
Grabowski, c	1	1	1	0	0		Grant, p	4	0	0	1	0
Ruether, p	2	0	1	0	0		Uhle, ph	1	0	0	0	0
Shawkey, p	0	0	0	0	0							
Thomas, p	0	0	0	0	0							
Giard, p	0	0	0	0	0							
Morehart, p	1	0	0	0	0							
Durst, rf	2	0	0	0	0							
Meusel, ph	1	0	1	0	0							
Totals	38	8	13	24	11		Totals	38	14	19	27	8

New York   2 2 0 1 0 0 0 0 3 - 8
Cleveland 1 0 3 0 4 4 2 0 x - 14

The Yankees arrived in Cleveland for a three-game stop comfortably ahead of their rivals in the American League standings. However, their visit to tiny Dunn Field would prove to be remarkably unproductive. For the first time in 1927, New York would find itself mired in an uncharacteristic slump. An early offensive push in the first game seemed to indicate that the Indians would be pushovers for the Yankees, just as they were when the Babe and his teammates first played in Cleveland in late May. But Jack McCallister's Cleveland club displayed unexpected resilience, showing the Yankees that the Indians were capable of equaling New York's batting prowess, at least for the duration of this one series.

Richards Vidmer, always searching for a catchy new approach to his *New York Times* stories, began his account of the August 20 Cleveland–New York game with a wonderfully creative allusion to the Civil War. "Ulysses S. Grant got a lot of credit for taking Richmond, and Richmond is only a Class B club," he wrote. "Today, George Grant of the Indians took New York, which happens to be leading the American League. A history or two could be written about that also."

George Grant picked up the shattered pieces left to him by starter Jake Miller and put forth a stellar effort in defeating the Yankees. The only bright spots, from a New Yorker's perspective, were matching home runs by Gehrig and Ruth, which kept their individual homer duel tied at 39 apiece.

Ruth's home run flew over Dunn Field's right field wall, but did little to help the Yankees' cause. The Indians had a grand time of it, trouncing the defending American League champions by the unflattering score of 14–8.

Cleveland's lively hitters touched four different Yankee hurlers for 19 hits. The first Cleveland pitcher, Jake Miller, was equally generous with his offerings and lasted but two innings. He was the fellow who served up homer number 39 to the Bambino.

Arriving on the scene then was Grant, the one-man clean-up crew, who proceeded to stifle Yankee aspirations with eight strikeouts and generally good pitching. The Yankees attempted a late flurry, but their aborted comeback fell well short of the mark.

Five Cleveland batters accounted for most of the offensive damage during this game. George Burns and Luke Sewell each managed four hits, and Lew Fonseca, Homer Summa and Joe Sewell had three apiece. Although Jake Miller was ineffective on the mound this day, he was Cleveland's best pitcher during the 1927 season, posting a 10–8 record and a 3.21 earned-run average, respectable figures on a sixth-place club that finished the season with a 66–87 record.

The victory credited to George Grant was just one of four he would notch in 1927. Grant, a native of Alabama (who probably would not have appreciated being compared to the famous Union general), easily had his best season the following year when he recorded ten victories. After 1928 he would not win another game in the majors. Grant's big-league career ended in 1931 with the Pittsburgh Pirates. His lifetime record was an unimpressive 15–20.

Despite the loss, New York, with a record of 82–35, still held a 15-game lead over the surprising Detroit Tigers, who had vaulted into second place with a splendid winning streak.

Other Baseball News

• The Detroit Tigers suddenly found themselves in second place in the American League standings after playing a doubleheader against Washington at Navin Field. Detroit won the first game 5–0 as Earl Whitehill pitched a shutout. The second game ended in a 15-inning, 6–6 tie when the onset of darkness prevented the superb contest from continuing. Harry Heilmann got five hits for Detroit in the second game.

• Grover Cleveland Alexander's rejuvenation as a member of the St. Louis Cardinals continued. Alexander recorded his seventeenth victory of the season as his club defeated the Phillies 8–2 in Philadelphia. St. Louis got 17 hits, five of them in the top of the eighth inning when they scored four runs to clinch the game.

• The Philadelphia Athletics scored four key runs in the top of the ninth inning to record a 5–2 comeback win against the White Sox in Chicago. Howard Ehmke was credited with the win, but Connie Mack needed the services of two other pitchers, Sam Gray and Lefty Grove, to quell a potential Chicago rally in the bottom of the ninth.

40 August 22

Yankees at Indians

Yankees	ab	r	h	po	a		Indians	ab	r	h	po	a
Combs, cf	5	0	0	2	0		Jamieson, lf	4	0	0	4	0
Koenig, ss	5	0	0	1	4		Fonseca, 2b	5	1	2	2	4
Ruth, rf	3	1	1	0	0		Summa, rf	5	2	2	0	0
Gehrig, 1b	3	0	0	12	1		Burns, 1b	5	2	3	9	1
Meusel, lf	4	1	2	0	1		J. Sewell, ss	4	1	4	1	4
Lazzeri, 2b	4	0	1	3	6		L. Sewell, c	5	2	2	5	0
Dugan, 3b	4	2	2	1	5		Eichrodt, cf	5	0	1	4	0
Collins, c	3	0	1	5	0		Lutzke, 3b	4	1	2	1	2
Grabowski, c	0	0	0	0	0		Shaute, p	4	0	3	1	0
Moore, p	2	0	0	0	1							
Shocker, p	0	0	0	0	0							
Pennock, p	0	0	0	0	0							
Wera, ph	1	0	0	0	0							
Paschal, ph	1	0	1	0	0							
Totals	35	4	8	24	18		Totals	41	9	19	27	11

New York	0 0 1 0 0 1 0 0 2 - 4
Cleveland	2 0 2 0 1 0 4 0 x - 9

The New York Yankees' uncontested waltz to the 1927 American League pennant was starting to be contested. No, the challengers were not the suddenly hot Detroit Tigers who had recently been surging up the standings. The Yankees had more pressing concerns with the pesky Cleveland Indians, who were nowhere near the front-runners of the junior circuit.

Cleveland gleefully made it three straight victories at home—the first team to sweep the vaunted maulers from the Bronx in the 1927—with a 9–4 thumping of Miller Huggins's complacent crew. Huggins was not a happy man about what transpired on the shores of Lake Erie and vowed to correct whatever he perceived as the problem. Generally speaking, Huggins thought his team should always score more runs than the opposition.

Joe Ben Shaute, the Cleveland hurler, was the primary thorn in the Yankees' collective side. He scattered eight hits thinly enough throughout the course of the game so that they did not really matter. An exception, perhaps, was Babe Ruth's fortieth home run of the season. This one pushed the Bambino into the American League lead over teammate Lou Gehrig by a scant margin of one.

For practical purposes, however, Ruth's sixth-inning home run was a meaningless blow as no Yankees were aboard to be driven home. It narrowed Cleveland's lead to 5–2, but four runs by the Indians in the bottom of the seventh put the game out of reach. New York responded with two scores in the top of the ninth but fell well short of mounting a meaningful comeback. "Jumping Joe" Dugan got two doubles for the Yankees. Joe Sewell did the same for Cleveland. "This was the Yankees' last appearance at Dunn Field this season," wrote Richards Vidmer in the *New York Times*, "and they are happy to be leaving." Among those in attendance at the ballpark to witness the final game of Cleveland's sweep was Mickey Walker, the reigning world middleweight champion.

"Jumping Joe" Dugan, according to the 1992 movie *The Babe*, was notable for being Ruth's first roommate when Babe broke into the American League with Boston in 1914. The film, like others before it, did not allow facts to interfere with a good story; Hollywood's most recent attempt to portray Ruth's life story is riddled with glaring inaccuracies. Ruth's supposed longtime friendship with Dugan is probably the movie's most flagrant error. Ruth and Dugan were not teammates until Dugan joined the Yankees in 1922. "Jumping Joe" did not even play in the big leagues until 1917. During the period when Ruth was a member of the Red Sox, Dugan was either out of the majors or playing for the Philadelphia A's.

Wilcy Moore, whose dismal batting skills were the constant inspiration for jokes, was the losing pitcher for New York on this day. His woeful lack of hitting ability was widely known and was often discussed by mirthful sports reporters even though Moore was just a rookie pitcher on the team. In 1927, Moore, a native of Bonita, Texas, got six hits (including one home run) in 75 times at bat for a batting average of .080. Over the course of his career, Moore's hitting statistics did not improve very much. When he retired after the 1933 season, he had racked up just 21 hits for a batting average of .102.

The loss dropped New York's record to 82–37, 12½ games ahead of the surging Detroit Tigers.

Other Baseball News

- Chick Hafey's second-inning homer accounted for the game's only run as the St. Louis Cardinals upended the Phillies 1–0 in Philadelphia. Jesse Haines got the shutout, allowing eight hits. Frank Ulrich was unlucky to be tagged with the loss. He gave up just four hits to the Cards.

- The Chicago Cubs, leaders in the National League, suffered their third straight loss to Boston at Braves Field. In Boston's 5–3 victory, Braves outfielder Eddie Brown played in his 534th consecutive game, establishing a new National League record. The previous mark had been set by Philadelphia's Fred Luderus from 1911 to 1913.

- The Detroit Tigers extended their winning streak to 13 with a doubleheader sweep of the Washington Senators at Navin Field. Sam Gibson allowed just five Washington hits as the Tigers won the first game 4–2. Fourth-inning homers by Harry Heilmann and Marty McManus off Walter Johnson propelled Detroit to a 7–3 victory in the second game.

♫41 August 27
Yankees at Browns

Yankees	ab	r	h	po	a		Browns	ab	r	h	po	a
Combs, cf	6	3	4	4	0		O'Rourke, 3b	4	1	1	1	3
Koenig, ss	5	3	3	2	4		Rice, rf	4	0	1	1	0
Ruth, lf	4	3	2	4	0		Sisler, 1b	5	0	1	10	2
Gehrig, 1b	4	1	1	10	1		Williams, lf	3	1	2	3	0
Meusel, rf	4	1	2	3	0		E. Miller, cf	5	1	2	1	0
Lazzeri, 2b	4	1	1	2	4		Melillo, 2b	3	1	1	4	6
Dugan, 3b	3	0	0	0	1		Dixon, c	2	0	1	3	1
Wera, 3b	1	0	0	0	0		Gerber, ss	2	0	1	3	3
Collins, c	3	0	1	2	0		O. Miller, ss	2	0	0	0	2
Hoyt, p	5	2	1	0	3		Jones, p	1	0	0	1	0
							Nevers, p	1	0	0	0	0
							Ballou, p	0	0	0	0	0
							Stewart, p	0	0	0	0	0
							Bennett, ph	1	0	0	0	0
							Schang, ph	1	0	0	0	0
Totals	39	14	15	27	13		**Totals**	34	4	10	27	17

New York	0 0 3 2 1 3 1 4 0 - 14
St. Louis	1 0 0 0 0 0 0 3 0 - 4

After suffering through a prolonged losing spell, the Yankees regained their winning ways by sweeping a key series in Detroit. Their three victories at Navin Field virtually assured New York that the 1927 American League pennant would fly in Yankee Stadium. The Tigers, who had accumulated an impressive winning streak before Ruth and company came to town, had optimistic visions of threatening the Yankees' all-but-certain romp to the league title. With the Tigers subdued, New York moved on to Sportsman's Park in St. Louis where thus far that season they had enjoyed unchecked success against the Browns.

Sure enough the Yankees continued their utter mastery over ever-obliging St. Louis by rolling to their sixteenth consecutive triumph over Dan Howley's lackluster troops with a score of 14–4. It began to seem as if St. Louis were capable of dropping all 22 of their scheduled encounters with New York in 1927.

Leading the Yankees' attack this afternoon were Babe Ruth, Bob Meusel and Earle Combs, who all managed to circle the bases with home runs. Ruth's homer was especially noteworthy. First of all, it was his forty-first of the campaign, allowing him to retake the lead in his constantly shifting home run duel with Lou Gehrig. Secondly, Ruth had now surpassed the 40-homer mark for the fifth time in his career. No one else in baseball history to that point had ever done it even twice; Rogers Hornsby and Cy Williams had done it once each.

The long home run was not the only offensive contribution by Ruth. He also belted a triple. St. Louis actually led 1–0 after the first inning, but New York scored 14 unanswered runs to assume a 14–1 lead after the top of the eighth. The Browns used four pitchers in their futile attempt to halt the Yankee onslaught: Sad Sam Jones, Ernie Nevers, Win Ballou and Lefty Stewart. It was Nevers who surrendered Ruth's home run, the second one the Babe hit off the football star in 1927.

St. Louis's American League team engaged in an annual struggle to attract paying customers through the turnstiles. Richards Vidmer of the *New York Times*, fully aware of this sad reality, wrote, "The Yankees certainly draw the fans. There were at least 3,000 in Sportsman's Park here today. Don't laugh. That's close to capacity for the Browns." The pitiful attendance at the Brownies' home games spawned more than a few zingers. Those who wore the Browns uniform liked to say that no one ever dared heckle the home team because the players outnumbered the fans! Another joke had a potential ticket buyer phoning the club's box office to inquire what time the Browns game was starting. "What time can you be here?" was the response. The witty remarks were only slight exaggerations. The Browns always lagged far behind the Cardinals in the battle for the affections of St. Louis baseball fans. During the lean Depression year of 1934, the lowly Browns drew slightly more than 80,000 customers for the entire season!

New York's easy victory raised their seasonal record to 86–37, 16 full games ahead of their newest challenger, the Philadelphia Athletics.

Other Baseball News

- The Philadelphia A's found themselves in second place in the American League standings for the first time since the early days of the season after beating the Detroit Tigers 8–7 at Navin Field. The Tigers' loss, their fourth straight, resulted from the Athletics rallying for three runs in the top of the ninth inning. Three A's, including the ageless Ty Cobb, hit triples. George Smith, a Detroit reliever, hit a solo home run in the bottom of the sixth.

- Chicago's Ted Lyons allowed just four hits as the White Sox defeated the Senators 6–1 at Comiskey Park. An error by shortstop Ray Flaskamper in the top of the ninth helped Washington avoid the shutout. It was the Senators' tenth straight loss.

- Cleveland won its seventh straight game, routing Boston 9–2 at Dunn Field. The Indians outhit the last-place Red Sox 16–6. Four Cleveland runs in the bottom of the seventh inning decided matters.

♪ 42 August 28
Yankees at Browns

Yankees	ab	r	h	po	a
Combs, cf	4	1	1	2	0
Koenig, ss	3	2	2	0	2
Ruth, lf	4	1	1	5	0
Gehrig, 1b	4	1	2	6	1
Meusel, rf	5	0	0	4	0
Lazzeri, 2b	5	2	2	4	2
Dugan, 3b	4	2	2	1	1
Bengough, c	5	1	3	5	0
Ruether, p	2	0	0	0	2
Shocker, p	2	0	0	0	1
Totals	38	10	13	27	9

Browns	ab	r	h	po	a
O'Rourke, 3b	4	0	0	0	1
Rice, rf	5	1	2	1	0
Sisler, 1b	4	0	1	9	0
Williams, lf	4	1	1	1	2
E. Miller, cf	4	1	1	2	0
Melillo, 2b	3	0	1	2	4
Adams, 2b	0	0	0	0	0
Dixon, c	3	1	1	9	0
O'Neill, c	0	0	0	2	1
O. Miller, ss	4	1	2	1	6
Wingard, p	0	0	0	0	1
Vanglider, p	4	1	2	0	0
Bennett, ph	1	0	0	0	0
Schang, ph	1	0	0	0	0
Totals	37	6	11	27	15

New York   2 2 1 1 2 0 0 0 2 - 10
St. Louis   0 0 4 1 1 0 0 0 0 - 6

Again the New York Yankees played the St. Louis Browns at Sportsman's Park, and even those who were not closely following the goings-on in the American League knew what the likely result was. As expected by everyone, the Yankees prevailed. The score of this game was 10–6 which meant that the boys from the Bronx had won all 17 contests they had played against the Browns thus far in the 1927 season. They had also run their present winning streak to five games.

Babe Ruth made the handful of Browns fans in attendance stand up and take notice when he walloped a baseball clear over the right field pavilion's roof. This forty-second circuit clout of 1927 put Ruth two ahead of persistent challenger Lou Gehrig.

The Bambino was not the only ballplayer to strike for four bases today. Both Ken Williams and Mark Koenig hit long balls in the same general direction where Ruth's ball was last seen, but neither of those men came close to duplicating the sheer length of the Ruthian smack.

Ruth's homer came early on—in the top of the first inning, to be precise. Koenig was on first base via a walk and Ruth politely drove him in with his sapient swat. This run broke up a scoreless tie and sent the New Yorkers on a spree of scoring that hardly subsided through the first five innings.

In those first five frames, the Yankees scored at least one run each time. For good measure, they also added two more tallies in the top of the ninth. To give the vanquished Browns their due, the home side did attempt various rallies throughout the middle innings, and at one point had sliced the New Yorkers' lead to one slim run. But, as with all Yankee-Browns clashes in 1927, the Brownies were destined to get no closer.

Ruth's home run came courtesy of pitcher Ernie Wingard, a native of Prattville, Alabama, who was in his fourth and final big-league season. He was 13–12 for the Browns in his rookie year of 1924. After the promising beginning, Wingard never had another winning season. In 1927 he struggled to a horrendous 2–13 mark and vanished thereafter from the majors.

Elam Vangilder, who relieved Wingard, had a productive day at the plate. He smacked two doubles. Vangilder is known to aficionados of minor league history as the pitcher who halted two of professional baseball's most remarkable batting streaks. While pitching for Tulsa of the Western League in 1919, he ended Joe Wilhoit's fantastic 69-game hitting streak. Ten years later, Vangilder, then a member of Montreal's International League club, stopped Joe Quellich's run of 15 straight hits.

Ken Williams, who homered for the Browns, was the American League home run and RBI leader in 1922, the year Ruth missed a good portion of the season due to suspensions. That season, Williams, a native of Grant's Pass, Oregon, belted 39 home runs and had 155 runs batted in. St. Louis and the Yankees engaged in a terrific pennant race in the summer of 1922, which New York eventually won by one game. That was probably the high-water mark in the Browns' sorry history. The club's lone pennant, won in 1944, should almost be accompanied by a footnote explaining that the major league talent pool was severely depleted that year by the Second World War.

New York's win gave the team a mark of 87–37 and a huge 16-game advantage over the second-place Philadelphia Athletics.

Other Baseball News

• The last-place Boston Red Sox put an end to Cleveland's seven-game winning streak with a 6–5 triumph in 11 innings at Dunn Field. Pitcher Red Ruffing was the Boston hero, shutting the Indians down in 3⅔ innings of relief work and making a key sacrifice bunt in the fateful eleventh. The timely bunt moved Fred Hoffman to second base. Hoffman then scored the go-ahead tally on Jack Rothrock's solid single.

- The Philadelphia A's handed the fading Detroit Tigers their fifth consecutive loss, winning 9–5 at Navin Field. Walter French got three hits for the Athletics. Lefty Grove was credited with the win, but he needed relief help from Rube Walberg to secure the victory. Ty Cobb, showing a glimpse of his once-fearsome speed, stole a base for Philadelphia.

- The Chicago White Sox defeated the Washington Senators 4–0 at Comiskey Park. Ted Blankenship notched the shutout for the home team. He allowed six hits to the Senators. Three of them were doubles. Chicago scored all four of their runs in the bottom of the seventh inning. Losing pitcher Tom Zachary made a costly throwing error on Bud Clancy's bunt, which opened the floodgates in the crucial inning.

🏃43 August 31
Red Sox at Yankees

Red Sox	ab	r	h	po	a		Yankees	ab	r	h	po	a
Rothrock, ss	5	1	2	2	1		Combs, cf	5	1	2	3	0
Myer, 3b	4	0	2	1	0		Koenig, ss	5	2	2	4	2
Flagstead, cf	3	0	0	0	0		Ruth, rf	4	3	1	2	0
Tarbert, cf	2	0	0	1	0		Gehrig, 1b	3	1	1	9	2
Regan, 2b	4	0	0	2	2		Meusel, lf	3	1	1	1	0
Tobin, rf	4	1	2	2	0		Lazzeri, 2b	5	2	3	1	2
Shaner, lf	3	0	1	1	0		Dugan, 3b	2	0	0	0	1
Todt, 1b	3	0	0	3	0		Wera, 3b	1	0	1	1	0
Rollings, 1b	1	0	0	2	0		Bengough, c	4	0	2	4	1
Hofmann, c	1	0	0	5	2		Pigras, p	3	0	0	2	2
Moore, c	2	1	2	4	3							
Ruffing, p	1	0	0	1	0							
Rogell, ph	1	0	0	0	0							
Welzer, p	1	0	0	0	0							
Totals	35	3	9	24	8		Totals	35	10	13	27	10

Boston	0 1 0 0 0 0 0 0 2 - 3
New York	0 0 5 4 0 0 0 1 x - 10

With the woeful and last-place Boston Red Sox the visiting attraction at Yankee Stadium on the last day of August, the only real drama in the air was how many of the great Yankee batsmen would fill the bleacher seats with souvenir home runs. True to their 1927 form, the Red Sox lost to their New York hosts by a predictably one-sided 10–3 count. For the amusement of the fans, there were three New York homers to watch with wonderment.

Tony Lazzeri, the forgotten man in the home run derby, got things started with a potent poke to the left field seats in the third inning. Proving his hit was not an aberration, Lazzeri did it again in the fourth inning—this time depositing the official American League baseball into the right field seats. Lazzeri's season count for homers now stood at 18—a pretty respectable total if he were employed by any other big league outfit.

Not wanting to be upstaged by a lesser teammate, Babe Ruth came up to the plate in the home half of the eighth inning and drove the ball into the Stadium's distant center field seats, much to the delight of the paying customers who had shelled out their shekels to watch this specific act. Lou Gehrig's best output was a long triple. This left the all-important Ruth-Gehrig personal home run grudge match at 43–41 in the Bambino's favor.

The lone home run on the Red Sox side of the ledger occurred in the top of the ninth, and it was a gift courtesy of Babe Ruth. With the Yankees comfortably ahead 10–1, catcher Bill Moore was on first base. Jack Rothrock came to bat. Rothrock knocked a line drive over Ruth's head in right field. If Ruth had put forth even a reasonable amount of effort in chasing the ball, Rothrock would likely have been held to a double. However, Ruth, seeing no reason to exert himself, casually sauntered over to the ball while both Boston runners circled the bases. Rothrock had 428 official times at bat in 1927. The Babe's charity on the play provided the Red Sox infielder with his only home run of the season. In 1928 Rothrock managed to play all nine positions over the course of the season, an indication of his versatility—and of how unsettled the Red Sox lineup was.

The Yankees displayed all their weapons in this game. Mark Koenig and Tony Lazzeri each made an outstanding defensive play to rob Red Sox batters of hits. Although a month remained on the schedule, Lazzeri would not hit another homer in 1927. Still, his 18 home runs would be the third-highest total in the league. Richards Vidmer, well aware that the New Yorkers had the American League championship virtually sewn up, comically concluded his *New York Times* story by noting, "What with hitting, pitching, and fielding all worthy of mention, the Yanks, taken all in all, looked like a pretty fair ball club. They may even win the pennant." New York's seasonal record was now 89–37, 17 games ahead of the Philadelphia Athletics.

Although his home run total was already phenomenal, Ruth's next month would be his most productive. Lou Gehrig, who had surprisingly kept pace with the Babe and had actually led the team in home runs at one point during the year, would falter in September. The battle for individual home run honors would cease, but Ruth would battle the clock and make a run for the incredible total of 60.

Other Baseball News

• Cincinnati's Dolph Luque pitched a shutout, allowing just six hits, as the Reds edged the Braves 1–0 in Boston. Boston's Charlie Robertson hurled a fair game himself, giving up six Cincinnati hits in eight innings before giving way to Guy Morrison in the ninth. The game took just 88 minutes to complete.

- Flint Rhem of the St. Louis Cardinals gave up only four hits to the Brooklyn Robins in the Cards' 3–1 win at Ebbets Field. Ray Blades of the Cardinals was knocked unconscious for five minutes after being struck in the head by a Bill Doak pitch in the first inning. He was revived in the visitors' dressing room and, except for a conspicuous egg-shaped lump, was reportedly none the worse for wear. Doak was one of the few pitchers in organized baseball still allowed to throw a spitball.

- The Pittsburgh Pirates closed to within one game of the league-leading Chicago Cubs by sweeping a doubleheader against the Phillies in Philadelphia. The Pirates won the first game 3–2 in 13 innings and took the second contest 7–2. Clyde Barnhart's winning run in the first game came on a hotly disputed play at the plate. Umpire Charley Moran ejected Phillies manager Stuffy McInnis and second baseman Fresco Thompson for excessive arguing. When each year's baseball season ended, umpire Moran spent his autumns as a football coach. He led the National Football League's Frankford Yellowjackets to a 6–9–3 record in 1927.

♪44 September 2
Yankees at Athletics

Yankees	ab	r	h	po	a		Athletics	ab	r	h	po	a
Combs, cf	6	3	4	4	0		Bishop, 2b	4	0	0	3	3
Koenig, ss	6	1	4	0	6		Hale, 3b	4	0	0	3	2
Ruth, lf	3	1	1	3	0		French, rf	4	0	1	4	1
Gehrig, 1b	5	2	4	10	0		Cobb, cf	3	0	1	2	0
Meusel, rf	4	0	0	3	0		Cochrane, c	1	0	0	3	1
Lazzeri, 2b	4	0	3	4	0		Perkins, c	2	1	1	0	0
Dugan, 3b	5	2	1	0	2		Dykes, 1b	3	1	0	9	1
Collins, c	5	2	2	3	1		Wheat, lf	3	0	1	0	0
Hoyt, p	5	1	1	0	3		Jacobson, lf	0	0	0	1	0
							Boley, ss	3	0	1	2	1
							Walberg, p	0	0	0	0	2
							Gray, p	2	0	0	0	0
							Foxx, ph	1	0	1	0	0
Totals	43	12	20	27	12		Totals	30	2	6	27	11

New York   2 5 3 0 0 0 1 0 1 – 12
Philadelphia   0 0 0 0 0 0 0 0 2 – 2

Although Babe Ruth's quest for home run immortality and the tight National League pennant race had entered September, many of the nation's sports followers were beginning to turn their attention to Soldier Field in Chicago, where Gene Tunney would be making his first defense of the heavyweight title against Jack Dempsey, the man whom he had defeated for the crown one year earlier. With the fight three weeks away, preparations were in full swing. Many of the baseball writers who had been covering Miller Huggins's crew were reassigned to the fight beat. John Drebinger, who had spent most of the 1927 baseball season covering the exploits of the unpredictable Brooklyn Robins for the *New York Times*, was now given the assignment to report on the Yankees during the early days of September. Although the pennant race was all but decided, Drebinger would have the honor of chronicling the start of Babe Ruth's 30 most glorious days in professional baseball.

On September 2 in Philadelphia, Drebinger witnessed home run heroics by both Babe Ruth and Lou Gehrig in their ongoing slugging rivalry. Given the closeness of their five-month battle, few baseball followers in early September would have predicted that Ruth would eventually pull away from Gehrig and romp to the American League home run title by a sizable margin.

The hopelessly optimistic 15,000 fans who were drawn to Shibe Park that day to watch their old favorites attempt to continue their recent winning ways against the almighty New York Yankees were quickly disillusioned. The hometown Philadelphia A's fell behind quickly and were never a threat to pull out a victory. The total damages amounted to ten runs for the New Yorkers and just two for Connie Mack's ancient outfit.

The Athletics had sparked faint hopes of a pennant race revival among the more imaginative of their followers, but the home run power of Babe Ruth and Lou Gehrig shook them out of their fantasies before the game was five minutes old.

The Yankee offense took to the stage in the very first inning. With two out, Ruth blasted a ball over the right field wall that veered toward the scoreboard in center. Impressed by the Bambino's clout but not frightened off, Gehrig followed shortly thereafter with a tremendous blow of his own. It was a Gehrig special: a straight line drive that vanished over the right field wall and was said to have come to a violent landing among the houses across the street.

Before the ball had even landed, the fickle fans of Philly had begun their grand ritual of turning on the home team whenever things did not go their way. Never mind that the A's had won 12 of 14 games on a recent road swing. All was quickly forgotten when the Babe and his young teammate began belting balls skyward. Cheers for the two men continued throughout the game. Conversely, jeers and general derision followed every Philadelphia failure.

Gehrig also connected for a two-run homer in the second inning when

New York scored five times. The Yankees' offense was in high gear throughout the afternoon, battering two A's pitchers for a total of 20 hits. Earle Combs, Lou Gehrig and Mark Koenig had four apiece. Tony Lazzeri had three. New York held a 12–0 lead going into the bottom of the ninth. Philadelphia scored two runs in their final turn at bat to avert the shutout. Both of them came on sacrifice flies. Two of the Athletics' ancient stars, Ty Cobb and Zack Wheat, provided what little offensive spark the A's generated in their lopsided defeat. Cobb showed he still possessed remnants of his tremendous speed. He beat out a bunt single.

Any hopes the other seven American League clubs had that the Yankees would falter in their pursuit of the pennant were now gone. New York's seasonal record now stood at 90–37, 18 games ahead of the second-place Athletics. John Drebinger sarcastically wrote in the *New York Times*, "Only 10 more victories will make the pennant a mathematical certainty [for New York]. The suspense is terrible."

Other Baseball News

- The St. Louis Browns scored twice in the bottom of the ninth to edge the Detroit Tigers 3–2 at Sportsman's Park. St. Louis's late rally comprised a Ken Williams triple, a double by Steve O'Neill and a game-winning single by pitcher Milt Gaston.

- The Pittsburgh Pirates beat the St. Louis Cardinals 5–3 at Forbes Field to move one game ahead of the Chicago Cubs at the top of the National League standings. Ray Kremer outpitched Grover Cleveland Alexander for the victory. Alexander suffered through a rough afternoon, allowing 15 Pittsburgh hits. Four of them went to Paul Waner, three to his brother Lloyd. Walter "Rabbit" Maranville, former star infielder for the Boston Braves, played shortstop for St. Louis, handling four putouts and five assists flawlessly. The Cardinals had recently purchased the 35-year-old Maranville's contract from the Rochester club of the International League.

- The Chicago White Sox used 19 different players but still failed to beat Cleveland, losing 7–6 to the Indians at Comiskey Park. Johnny Mostil got a heartwarming ovation from the crowd when he pinch-ran for Buck Crouse in the bottom of the seventh inning. It was his first appearance of the season. Mostil suffered severe blood loss after he slashed himself more than a dozen times with a razor blade in a Shreveport hotel during spring training. The press reported that Mostil's suicide attempt was linked to neuritis, but widely circulated rumors told a different story: The Chicago outfielder was despondent after teammate Red Faber discovered his wife and Mostil having a torrid affair.

🏃45 & 46 September 6
Yankees at Red Sox

Yankees	ab	r	h	po	a
Combs, cf	4	2	2	2	0
Paschal, cf	1	0	0	1	0
Koenig, ss	6	2	2	1	5
Ruth, lf	6	2	2	4	0
Gehrig, 1b	5	4	4	12	1
Meusel, rf	6	2	4	2	0
Lazzeri, 2b	5	1	3	2	3
Morehart, 2b	0	0	0	0	1
Dugan, 3b	4	1	2	1	0
Bengough, c	4	0	1	2	0
Pennock, p	3	0	0	0	4
Totals	44	14	20	27	14

Red Sox	ab	r	h	po	a
Rothrock, ss	4	1	1	0	0
Myer, 3b	3	0	1	0	1
Rogell, 3b	1	0	1	0	1
Flagstead, cf	1	0	1	1	0
Carlyle, cf	1	0	0	1	0
Regan, 2b	4	0	1	2	5
Tarbert, rf	4	0	0	1	0
Shaner, lf	4	0	0	2	0
Todt, 1b	2	0	0	6	0
Rollings, 1b	2	0	0	6	0
Hofmann, c	2	0	0	7	1
Wm. Moore, c	2	0	1	1	1
Welzer, p	2	1	1	0	1
Ruffing, p	1	0	0	0	0
Cremins, p	0	0	0	0	2
Totals	33	2	7	27	12

New York   0 1 2 1 2 5 2 1 0 - 14
Boston   0 0 2 0 0 0 0 0 0 - 2

🏃47 September 6
Yankees at Red Sox

Yankees	ab	r	h	po	a
Combs, cf	4	0	1	3	0
Koenig, ss	4	0	0	2	2
Ruth, lf	4	1	1	0	0
Gehrig, 1b	4	1	2	11	0
Meusel, rf	4	0	2	1	0
Lazzeri, 2b	3	0	0	1	4
Wera, 3b	4	0	0	3	2
Collins, c	4	0	0	3	1
Ruether, p	2	0	0	0	3
Totals	33	2	6	24	12

Red Sox	ab	r	h	po	a
Rothrock, ss	4	0	0	4	3
Rogell, 3b	3	1	2	1	3
Flagstead, cf	3	1	1	3	0
Regan, 2b	4	1	2	2	4
Tobin, rf	4	0	0	0	0
Shaner, lf	4	0	1	1	0
Todt, 1b	3	0	1	13	0
Hofmann, c	3	1	1	3	0
Russell, p	3	1	0	0	2
Totals	31	5	8	27	12

New York   0 0 0 0 0 0 0 0 2 - 2
Boston   0 0 0 2 2 1 0 0 x - 5

On September 6, in his former home, Fenway Park, Babe Ruth recorded his seventh multiple home run day of the season. It was the only time during 1927 when Ruth managed to connect for three circuit clouts in the space of an afternoon, and he required a doubleheader for him to achieve the feat. The first home run, coming in the midst of a typical Yankee rout, was an awe-inspiring blow, one of the longest Ruth managed to strike in his glorious career. It also launched the impressive spurt that enabled Ruth to pull away from teammate Lou Gehrig.

The "twin thrillers" had entered the afternoon tied at 44 homers apiece. Gehrig briefly took the lead, breaking the deadlock in the fifth inning of the first game with a nifty round-tripper. His edge lasted for all of one inning as the Babe sought to even things in the visitors' half of the sixth. Ruth's sock was one of his most spectacular as it had no trouble clearing Fenway Park's center field wall. Anticipating a slowball from Boston hurler Tony Welzer—which was exactly what the pitcher threw him—Ruth got all of it and sent it on a one-way trip. Reliable witnesses among the 2,000 Beantown observers claimed the home run was the longest ever hit at Boston's American League ballpark.

With his adrenaline still pumping, Ruth overtook Gehrig with his forty-sixth home run of 1927 in the seventh frame. This one merely fell into the waiting hands of a Bostonian in the right field bleachers. To make the day complete, the Bambino rapped his third homer of the set-to in the ninth inning of the second encounter, giving him an edge of two circuit clouts on the fellow who followed him in the batting order.

Ruth's forty-fifth and forty-sixth homers were surrendered by Tony Welzer. Allowing the pair of home runs to Ruth was the most notable "achievement" in Welzer's lackluster career. In two seasons in Boston, the German-born Welzer compiled a 10–14 record with a 4.60 ERA. The 1927 season, in which he went 6–11, would be Welzer's last in the majors.

Despite the laughably easy win the Yankees recorded in the first game of the doubleheader (in which New York got 20 hits), the second contest almost ended in a Boston shutout. Charlie Russell, nursing a 5–0 lead, had stifled much of the New York attack until Ruth hit his forty-seventh homer in the top of the ninth. Gehrig followed with a long triple and scored on Bob Meusel's single. That brief rally ended the scoring as the Red Sox held onto a 5–2 victory. With the split of the two games, the Yankees sported a 92–40 record and a 16-game lead over the second-place Philadelphia A's.

Other Baseball News

• Casey Stengel, the popular manager of the Toledo Mudhens of the American Association, was handed an indefinite suspension by league president Thomas J. Hickey. During a Labor Day doubleheader between the Mudhens and Columbus, enraged Toledo fans invaded the field in an attempt to assault an umpire who had made an unpopular call at first base. Hickey ruled that Stengel had incited the crowd to riot and was responsible for the unsavory incident. For his own protection, the beleaguered umpire took refuge in one of the dugouts and had to be rescued from the angry mob by the police.

• Pittsburgh's Ray Kremer faced just 28 Cincinnati batters as the Pirates shut out the Reds 5–0 at Forbes Field to retain their one-game lead over the onrushing Giants. Kremer allowed just three hits, all singles. No Red runner got past first base. Pie Traynor got three hits for Pittsburgh and stole a base.

• The suddenly hot New York Giants beat the Boston Braves 9–6 at the Polo Grounds to remain within one game of the Pirates. Several New York players had a productive time at the plate. Each of the first six Giants in the batting order had at least two hits in the game.

🏃48 & 49 September 7
Yankees at Red Sox

Yankees	ab	r	h	po	a		Red Sox	ab	r	h	po	a
Combs, cf	3	2	0	3	0		Rothrock, ss	5	0	0	2	3
Koenig, ss	4	1	0	2	3		Rogell, 3b	2	3	1	0	2
Ruth, lf	5	3	4	2	0		Flagstead, cf	4	1	3	2	0
Gehrig, 1b	5	2	2	8	0		Regan, 2b	5	1	3	2	4
Meusel, rf	3	1	1	2	0		Tobin, rf	5	2	2	5	0
Lazzeri, 2b	3	1	0	1	3		Shaner, lf	5	1	3	3	0
Wera, 3b	1	0	0	0	0		Todt, 1b	5	1	0	10	1
Durst, ph	1	0	0	0	0		Hofmann, c	2	1	1	3	1
Gazella, 3b	1	0	1	2	0		Myer, ph	1	0	0	0	0
Bengough, c	5	0	1	7	1		Hartley, c	0	0	0	0	0
Thomas, p	1	0	0	0	0		Rollings, ph	1	0	0	0	0
Giard, p	1	1	0	0	0		McFayden, p	3	0	0	0	0
Shawkey, p	1	1	1	0	1		Harriss, p	0	0	0	0	1
							W. Moore, ph	1	0	0	0	0
							Crimmins, p	0	0	0	0	0
Totals	34	12	10	27	8		Totals	39	10	13	27	12

New York   1 0 0 0 0 6 3 2 0 - 12
Boston   0 0 0 8 0 0 1 1 0 - 10

Babe Ruth continued his impressive slugging streak, establishing a gap of four home runs between himself and Lou Gehrig by socking two more over the outfield fence at Boston's Fenway Park on September 7. In the space of just two afternoons, Ruth had added five homers to his league-leading total. He now stood ten homers shy of his major league record set six years earlier, and his recent power surge had put him in a reasonable position to make a run at that mark. Still, ten home runs was a considerable sum for any player to achieve in the three and a half weeks remaining on the American League schedule.

The Bambino's first clout occurred in the very first inning and established the pace for the high-scoring game that ensued. Danny MacFayden was the unfortunate fellow who served the ball to Ruth. The Babe took a liking to it instantly and sent it on a one-way journey over the high wall in Fenway Park's left field, a place where Ruth home runs seldom came to rest.

Ruth's encore performance occurred in the top of the eighth inning. By this time in the game, Slim Harriss was serving the baseballs for the Bostons, but the Babe saw absolutely no difference between Harriss and MacFayden. This time, Ruth's hit was even more tremendous: It came down with a thud in the distant reaches of the center field seats. It also padded the Yankees' lead and served to take the steam out of a potential Boston comeback. Thus the Yankees managed to eke out a rather hard-fought 12–10 win.

To prove he was a versatile batter and not just a home run slugger, the Babe also gladly contributed a single and a double to the Yankee effort. The two-bagger knocked in a couple of Ruth's playmates to give him five RBIs on the day. Lou Gehrig had to be satisfied with a pair of doubles, one of which just fell a few inches short of clearing the wall in left field.

Ruth's first pitching victim that afternoon, Danny MacFayden, was a quiet chap who somehow managed to pitch in the majors for 17 unproductive seasons. Along with being a member of some truly terrible Red Sox teams, MacFayden also pitched for the Yankees, Reds, Braves, Pirates and Senators. He averaged fewer than eight wins per season. His best results occurred during the 1931 season when he went 16–12 with Boston, leading the Red Sox out of the American League cellar after four consecutive last-place finishes. After his retirement from the majors, MacFayden served as baseball coach at Bowdoin College for many years.

The homer Slim Harriss surrendered to the Babe marked the third time in 1927 that Harriss was so generous to Ruth. Four years earlier, on September 23, 1923, Harriss had played a key role in one of the weirdest no-hitters ever thrown in the major leagues. That afternoon, Harriss was pitching for the Philadelphia A's against the Red Sox. Had it not been for a baserunning gaffe by Harriss, Boston pitcher Howard Ehmke's no-hitter would not have occurred. Here's what happened: In the sixth inning, Harriss hit what should have been a clean double off Ehmke. However, Harriss, a .145 career hitter, was in such a hurry to reach second base that he neglected to touch first. The Red Sox noticed Harriss's blunder and properly appealed the play. Harriss was called out. According to baseball's scoring rules, since Harriss had missed first base, he did not get credit for a base hit. Ehmke then proceeded to retire the rest of the Athletics without permitting a hit.

After their stay in Boston, the Yankees returned to New York for an extended home stand to complete the season. Ruth's two homers at Fenway Park on September 7 were the last of 32 he would hit in visiting stadiums in 1927. It was the only American League contest scheduled that day. The win upped New York's record to 93–40, giving the Yankees a 16½ game lead over the Athletics.

Other Baseball News

- Pittsburgh's lead over the New York Giants in the National League standings was cut to half a game as Cincinnati beat the Pirates 6–5 at Forbes Field. Charlie Dressen's two doubles led the Reds' attack. Cincinnati had opened up a 6–2 lead after the top of the sixth inning. Two late Pirate rallies fell short. Dressen would gain fame as a manager later in life. Despite being just 5'5" and 145 pounds, he was also an NFL quarterback with the long-forgotten Decatur Staleys and Racine Legion.

- Chicago's Hack Wilson connected for a pair of home runs in the second game of a doubleheader versus the St. Louis Cardinals at Sportsman's Park. Wilson now had 25 homers on the season, one fewer than National League leader Cy Williams of the Philadelphia Phillies. St. Louis won the first game 6–2. Wilson's heroics led the Cubs to an 8–4 victory in the second game.

- A letter by a passionate baseball fan to *New York Times* writer James R. Harrison inspired the sports journalist to write a thought-provoking column. A Massachusetts reader informed Harrison that a spirited debate was raging over which player was more valuable to his team—Paul Waner of the Pirates or Lou Gehrig of the Yankees. Harrison replied, "We can conceive of the Yanks losing Gehrig and yet winning the American League pennant. But the Pirates without Paul Waner would probably be battling desperately to stick in fourth place in the National League. To add Gehrig to a team that already has Ruth is to gild the lily, to perfume the violet."

♪50 September 11
Browns at Yankees

Browns	ab	r	h	po	a		Yankees	ab	r	h	po	a
O'Rourke, 3b	3	1	2	2	3		Combs, cf	3	0	1	3	0
Rice, rf	5	1	1	0	0		Koenig, ss	3	0	0	0	1
Sisler, 1b	5	0	3	9	2		Gazella, ss	1	0	0	1	0
Williams, lf	5	0	3	1	0		Ruth, rf	4	1	1	2	0
E. Miller, cf	5	0	0	2	0		Gehrig, 1b	4	0	1	7	1
Schang, c	2	2	1	7	0		Meusel, lf	3	1	0	2	0
Melillo, 2b	4	1	1	3	1		Lazzeri, 2b	4	0	0	1	3
Gerber, ss	4	0	0	1	3		Dugan, 3b	3	0	2	1	1

Browns	ab	r	h	po	a
Gaston, p	4	1	0	2	3
Totals	37	6	11	27	12

Yankees	ab	r	h	po	a
Bengough, c	3	0	0	9	2
Pennock, p	1	0	0	0	1
Shawkey, p	1	0	0	1	1
Durst, ph	1	0	0	0	0
Pipgras, p	0	0	0	0	0
Totals	31	2	5	27	10

St. Louis   1 0 0 4 0 0 0 0 1 - 6
New York   0 1 0 1 0 0 0 0 0 - 2

It took them 22 games to do it, but the St. Louis Browns finally put one in the win column against the Yankees, triumphing 6–2 in the teams' final meeting of the season on September 11 at Yankee Stadium. If New York had defeated the Browns that afternoon, as they had each time in their previous 21 encounters during the 1927 season, it would have been the first instance since major league baseball had adopted a 154-game schedule that one club had recorded a 22–0 sweep against another. One big inning by the Browns prevented them from achieving this dubious note in the history books, and the Yankees had to settle for matching the record set by the 1909 Chicago Cubs, who managed to beat the lowly Boston Braves 21 of 22 times that campaign. More significant, though, was Babe Ruth's fiftieth homer of the year, hit against the backdrop of threatening skies.

With the New York Giants entangled in the tight National League pennant race, and the Dempsey-Tunney fight preparations in full swing, the *New York Times*'s senior sports writers had more pressing business than to follow the Yankees' inevitable march to the American League flag. Incredibly, the assignment to cover Ruth's run at 60 homers was left to someone else—presumably a junior staff reporter, since the article bore no byline.

The capable pitching of Milt Gaston was responsible for the victory. Herb Pennock could not stem the Browns' offensive spurt. His successors, Bob Shawkey and George Pipgras, did not fare much better.

Ruth's fiftieth homer was a tremendous thump that landed in his favorite section of Yankee Stadium—the right field seats. Ruth led off the home half of the fourth inning, and when Gaston fell behind 3–1 in the count, the Babe laced into a high pitch that was likely outside of the strike zone. Putting aside that minor triviality, Ruth powered it over the wall.

A terrific roar rose from the multitudes when the umpires signaled the ball's departure. Thunderous cheers greeted the Bambino as he made the obligatory trot around the sacks. Straw hats by the dozens fluttered onto the field from Ruth's plentiful admirers for several minutes. Such was the display of affection and appreciation that many of the Yankee players and coaches were enlisted to scoop up the chapeaux. Had the shower of headgear lasted much longer, Colonel Ruppert himself would have had to participate in the clean-up.

Lou Gehrig, who once held the lead in the much-ballyhooed home run duel, had nothing more than a single that day, leaving him five home runs behind the reigning king.

This was the fourth home run Ruth managed to hit off Milt Gaston in 1927. Only one other American League hurler, Rube Walberg of the Athletics, was as generous to the Babe. Despite the loss, New York held a huge 17-game lead over second-place Philadelphia. The Yankees' record stood at 96–41.

Other Baseball News

• Many Washington fans at Griffith Stadium missed seeing the Senators defeat the visiting Chicago White Sox 6–5 in 12 innings because they thought their club had won the game two batters earlier. Joe Judge opened the bottom of the twelfth with a triple. Stuffy Stewart pinch-ran for Judge. Bennie Tate hit what appeared to be a game-winning sacrifice fly, which sent many fans out the exits. However, the White Sox appealed that Stewart had left third base too soon. Umpire George Hildebrand agreed and declared Stewart out. The feisty Senators quickly replied. Ossie Bluege doubled and scored on a Jackie Hayes single.

• Fred Frankhouse, a rookie acquired from the Texas League, pitched a four-hit shutout as the St. Louis Cardinals defeated Brooklyn 5–0 at Sportsman's Park. Harvey Hendrick had three of Brooklyn's four hits. St. Louis was now in third place, two games behind league-leading Pittsburgh.

• The Cincinnati Reds swept a home doubleheader from the slumping Boston Braves by scores of 8–4 and 16–5. With the second game completely out of reach, the Braves sent coach Dick Rudolph to the mound to pitch the final 1⅓ innings. He gave up a hit but no earned runs. Rudolph, a key member of the Boston pitching staff back in 1914 when the Braves surprisingly won the World Series, had not pitched since 1923.

♫51 September 13
Indians at Yankees

Indians	ab	r	h	po	a		Yankees	ab	r	h	po	a
Gill, lf	3	0	0	3	1		Combs, cf	5	1	3	2	0
Fonseca, 3b	4	1	1	4	5		Koenig, ss	5	1	2	3	5
Summa, rf	4	0	0	0	0		Ruth, rf	4	1	1	1	0
Burns, 1b	4	0	1	8	0		Gehrig, 1b	2	0	1	8	0
J. Sewell, ss	4	2	2	4	5		Meusel, lf	3	1	1	0	0

Indians	ab	r	h	po	a		Yankees	ab	r	h	po	a
L. Sewell, c	3	0	1	1	2		Lazzeri, 2b	1	0	1	2	3
Langford, cf	3	0	0	1	0		Dugan, 3b	3	0	1	0	1
Lutzke, 3b	3	0	2	3	2		Durst, ph	0	0	0	0	0
Myatt, ph	1	0	0	0	0		Gazella, 3b	0	0	0	0	0
Hudlin, ph	3	0	1	0	3		Bengough, c	4	0	1	11	0
Burnett, ph	1	0	0	0	0		Pipgras, p	3	1	1	0	0
Totals	33	3	8	24	18		Totals	30	5	12	27	9

```
Cleveland    0 1 0 0 0 0 2 0 0 - 3
New York     0 0 1 0 0 0 3 1 x - 5
```

⚾52 September 13
Indians at Yankees

Indians	ab	r	h	po	a		Yankees	ab	r	h	po	a
Gill, lf	5	0	0	1	0		Combs, cf	3	0	1	2	0
Fonseca, 3b	4	1	3	2	2		Koenig, ss	4	0	0	2	2
Summa, rf	3	0	0	2	0		Ruth, rf	4	1	1	2	0
Burns, 1b	4	0	1	8	1		Gehrig, 1b	4	1	1	11	0
J. Sewell, ss	4	0	1	0	5		Meusel, lf	4	0	0	0	0
Myatt, c	4	0	0	7	0		Lazzeri, 2b	4	1	1	1	7
Langford, cf	4	0	1	3	0		Dugan, 3b	3	1	1	2	1
Hodapp, 3b	4	0	2	0	1		Collins, c	3	1	2	7	1
Shaute, p	4	2	2	1	3		Hoyt, p	3	0	0	0	2
Totals	36	3	10	24	12		Totals	32	5	7	27	13

```
Cleveland    0 1 0 0 0 2 0 0 0 - 3
New York     0 0 1 4 0 0 0 0 x - 5
```

To no one's great surprise, the Yankees mathematically wrapped up the championship of the American League with a matching set of 5–3 victories in a doubleheader sweep of the Cleveland Indians on September 13. The pennant had been a foregone conclusion for several weeks, if not the entire season. Since opening day, New York had occupied at least a share of the lead and never once relinquished the top spot despite sporadic challenges from a few different American League rivals. The Yankees' feat of going "wire to wire" would not be matched until the Detroit Tigers did the same in 1984, 16 years after divisional play had relegated to history the quaint concept of one set of standings per league.

This was the fifth gonfalon won by the Yankees in their history. All five of them had been captured since 1921, and all came under the managerial leadership of Miller Huggins, a man small in stature but big in baseball knowledge.

Quite satisfactorily, the great Bambino played a leading role in winning the banner. Babe Ruth connected for two more homers, one in each contest, to up his seasonal total to 52. Some 25,000 New York rooters were on hand to witness both blasts.

Despite the fact that the pennant's clinching culminated the Yankees' first goal of the season, the crowd seemed subdued by the achievement. In other cities, where titles did not come as frequently, an American League crown would have been cause for pandemonium in the aisles followed by dancing in the streets. Perhaps New York's American League baseball followers were not yet satisfied and would not create any revelry until the world's championship was locked up. That minor detail had eluded the grasp of Miller Huggins's boys after a similarly successful American League campaign in 1926.

Despite Ruth's productive bat, he was still somewhat off his record home run pace of 1921. The September 13 games were his 135th and 136th of the season. Back in 1921, when Ruth smacked 59 round-trippers, he had registered his fifty-second homer by his 130th game. The Yankees had 15 games left on their schedule for the Babe to challenge for a new standard.

Cleveland led the first game 3–1 before Ruth tied the score in the bottom of the seventh with a two-run homer to right field. Bob Meusel tallied the go-ahead run in the same inning. Earle Combs tacked on an insurance run in the bottom of the eighth with a solo home run. The Indians held a 2–1 lead in the second game until Ruth's home run in the fourth inning evened the score. Although no one was on base when Ruth connected, the hit started a significant rally. By the time the fourth inning ended, Lou Gehrig, Tony Lazzeri, and Joe Dugan had also scored. Cleveland pitcher Joe Shaute (who allowed Ruth's second homer of the afternoon) doubled in the top of the fifth and scored, but nobody else crossed the plate in the remaining innings. The game—not to mention the American League pennant—was secured in the top of the ninth with a nifty Koenig-to-Lazzeri-to-Gehrig double play.

Ruth's first homer of the day was hit off Willis (Ace) Hudlin, who was in the second year of a very productive career with the Indians. Hudlin's best pitch was a sidearm sinker that enabled him to win 157 games for Cleveland, the seventh-highest total in club history. Hudlin would become a nemesis to the Yankees, defeating them 14 times between 1927 to 1929. In the late 1950s he would serve as a pitching coach for the Detroit Tigers.

The doubleheader sweep lifted New York's record to 98–41. With the pennant now a certainty, the team's 17-game lead over the Athletics was utterly irrelevant.

Other Baseball News

- Sportsman's Park in St. Louis hosted an emotional doubleheader between the two National League teams tied for second place: the Giants and the Cardinals. At the end of the afternoon the clubs were still tied, with 78–56 records, and were three games behind Pittsburgh. A riot almost broke out in the first game when St. Louis's Heinie Schuble tagged New York's Jack Cummings especially hard during a rundown play. Both benches emptied in expectation of a battle, but the umpires managed to maintain order without ejecting anyone.

- Even though the Philadelphia Athletics were officially eliminated from the American League pennant race, they enjoyed a good day at Shibe Park, defeating the Chicago White Sox 15–5. Ty Cobb had two doubles and two singles. Joe Boley had a single, a double and a triple. Starting pitcher Lefty Grove lasted just 5⅓ innings but was credited with the victory.

- The Pittsburgh Pirates picked up a game on both St. Louis and New York by sweeping a doubleheader at Forbes Field against the Boston Braves. The scores were 6–1 and 5–4. Angry Boston manager Dave Bancroft told reporters he was fining Eddie Moore $200 for failing to slide on a crucial play in the top of the ninth. Moore, representing the tying run, was tagged out at the plate by Pirate catcher Johnny Gooch when he attempted to score standing up. Moore had driven in Boston's fourth run with a pinch-hit double.

♣53 September 16
White Sox at Yankees

White Sox	ab	r	h	po	a		Yankees	ab	r	h	po	a
Flaskamper, ss	5	0	1	1	4		Combs, cf	5	0	2	2	0
Kamm, 3b	5	0	0	1	0		Koenig, ss	4	0	2	2	2
Metzler, cf	4	0	1	4	0		Ruth, rf	4	2	1	0	0
Barrett, rf	4	0	0	3	0		Gehrig, 1b	3	1	1	13	0
Falk, lf	4	1	2	2	0		Meusel, lf	4	2	3	1	0
Clancy, 1b	4	0	1	11	1		Lazzeri, 2b	4	1	1	2	7
Berg, 2b	2	1	0	1	2		Dugan, 3b	4	0	1	0	0
Crouse, 2b	4	0	1	1	2		Bengough, c	4	0	0	6	1
Blankenship, p	2	0	0	0	3		Moore, p	4	1	2	1	4
Hunnefield, p	1	0	1	0	0							
Mostil, pr	0	0	0	0	0							
Cole, p	0	0	0	0	0							
Ward, ph	1	0	0	0	0							
Totals	36	2	7	24	12		Totals	36	7	13	27	14

Chicago	0 0 0 1 0 0 1 0 0 - 2
New York	2 0 1 1 1 0 0 2 x - 7

With the pennant firmly in their grasp, the remainder of the Yankees' 1927 schedule would serve two purposes: the powerful club would challenge the 15-year-old American League record for victories in a season, and Babe

Ruth would make a run at a new major league home run mark. The talented 1912 Boston Red Sox had set the league record with 105 wins, and, of course, Ruth was hoping to better his own record of 59 home runs set six years earlier. Ruth managed to connect for homer number 53 on September 16 against Chicago. By defeating the White Sox, the Yankees' win total reached the magical three-digit mark, a feat few teams in baseball history had managed to accomplish. All things considered, it was a highly productive day for a team that could technically play out the remainder of its schedule without having to try very hard. Such was the luxury of clinching a pennant early in September.

The September 16 win was typical in one respect and utterly atypical in another. The normal part was the 7–2 shellacking of the visiting White Sox, who had come to New York City to play five ballgames solely because the American League schedule said they had to. (Given the Babe's proclivity for belting baseballs over fences, one could say a Ruth homer was a normal occurrence too.) As anyone who could read the standings knew, the last few games merely served as warm-ups for the American League champs as they waited to see how things might unfold in the more complicated National League race.

The unusual aspect of the game was the rare hitting frenzy of Yankee pitcher Wilcy Moore. No, that was not a misprint. Wilcy Moore, known mostly for making batters miss baseballs and returning the favor when opposing hurlers threw them at him, came through with not one, but two clean base hits. Not only that, one of them was a home run into the right field stands off Ted Blankenship, who was probably the most embarrassed man in the metropolis that night. Those two hits lifted Moore's 1927 total at Yankee Stadium to two.

Moore was generally a relief pitching specialist, but he was given the starting assignment by manager Miller Huggins in this outing. It was one of 12 starts he would record in 1927. He performed admirably and hurled a complete-game victory.

Ruth's home run came with no runners on in the bottom of the third inning to give New York a 3–0 lead. Bob Meusel accounted for the Yankees' other homer of the afternoon.

Wilcy Moore was indeed the butt of many jokes in the Yankee clubhouse because of his inept batting skills. When the season began, Ruth wagered $300 to Moore's $100 that Wilcy would not get three hits over the course of the entire season. Moore got six hits in 1927 to win the bet. Using the money to buy a pair of mules for his Oklahoma farm, Moore honored his benefactor: He named one of the animals Babe and the other one Ruth.

The Yankees' attention was now focused on the upcoming World Series, even though the identity of their National League opponents was still in doubt. "The game itself was just a romp for the champions and served to keep them in condition for the big test which will come shortly," said the *New York Times*.

The Babe must have been extremely relieved to be a free man that afternoon. Earlier in the day, Ruth had been hauled into court to face an assault charge. A crippled 49-year-old man claimed that Ruth had punched him in the face during an argument on Broadway on the evening of July 4. The presiding magistrate allowed the Babe to walk free when the identity of the assailant could not be absolutely confirmed. Cheers rose from the packed courtroom when the judge announced his decision.

Ted Blankenship, the Chicago pitcher who surrendered the home run to Ruth, had a mediocre big league career, sporting a lifetime record of 77–79 with a 4.32 ERA. Blankenship's greatest day in a White Sox uniform did not even count in official statistics. One afternoon in 1925 he and Grover Cleveland Alexander heroically battled to a 2–2 tie over 19 innings until darkness made further play impossible. Unfortunately, Blankenship's wonderful game was part of the Chicago City Series. This was an annual postseason clash between the Cubs and the White Sox which took place if neither club happened to be in the World Series. This "series for also-rans" happened far too frequently for Chicago's passionate baseball fans.

New York's seasonal record now stood at 100–42. The Yankees held a 16-game lead over the second-place Philadelphia Athletics.

Other Baseball News

• The Pittsburgh Pirates won their ninth straight contest, a 4–3 decision over the Boston Braves at Forbes Field. The loss was Boston's thirteenth in a row, including six consecutive setbacks to the Pirates in this extended series. Pittsburgh led 3–0 after the first inning. Lee Meadows was the winning pitcher, allowing eight Boston hits.

• Ty Cobb went three for four as the Athletics beat the St. Louis Browns 6–3 in Philadelphia's Shibe Park. The aging Cobb was riding a hot batting streak, having gotten 13 hits in his last 18 times at bat. The victory was the A's sixth straight. Jing Johnson was credited with the win. He allowed just six St. Louis hits. Earlier in the day, A's manager Connie Mack filed papers in a Philadelphia court in a drastic attempt to silence the stentorian voice of Harry Donnelly, well known in Shibe Park as an abrasive fan. Mack claimed Donnelly was guilty of disturbing the peace.

• Harry Heilmann had a triple, a double, and a single in Detroit's 4–3 triumph over the Red Sox in Boston. Winning Tiger pitcher Rip Collins lasted until the ninth inning before being relieved by Ken Holloway, who stifled a Boston rally.

✦54 September 18
White Sox at Yankees

White Sox	ab	r	h	po	a
Metzler, cf	3	0	0	4	1
Flaskamper, ss	4	0	1	3	3
Barrett, rf	4	0	1	1	0
Falk, lf	3	1	2	2	0
Kamm, 3b	3	0	1	0	3
Clancy, 1b	4	0	1	9	2
Berg, 2b	4	0	1	2	2
Crouse, c	4	0	1	2	0
Mosil, pr	0	0	0	0	0
Lyons, p	2	0	0	0	1
Nels, ph	0	0	0	0	0
Cole, p	0	0	0	1	0
Hunnefield, ph	1	0	0	0	0
Totals	32	1	8	24	12

Yankees	ab	r	h	po	a
Combs, cf	4	1	3	2	0
Koenig, ss	4	2	2	5	8
Ruth, rf	3	1	2	2	0
Durst, rf	0	0	0	0	0
Gehrig, 1b	4	0	0	10	0
Meusel, lf	4	0	0	1	0
Lazzeri, 2b	4	0	0	4	5
Gazella, 3b	3	0	0	0	0
Bengough, c	3	0	1	2	0
Hoyt, p	4	1	2	1	0
Totals	33	5	10	27	13

```
Chicago    0 0 0 1 0 0 0 0 0 - 1
New York   0 0 3 0 2 0 0 0 x - 5
```

Although their goals were now of the esoteric variety, the New York Yankees did not consider reining in their potent attack. A doubleheader sweep of the Chicago White Sox on September 18 at Yankee Stadium concluded an impressive five-game romp over manager Ray Schalk's charges.

The American League record for wins in a season was 105. It had been set by the Boston Red Sox back in 1912 when the crimson-hosed bunch was a formidable team. That 15-year-old record began to look shaky when the New York Yankees concluded their business with Chicago on September 18. Miller Huggins's array of sluggers had turned in modest scores of 2–1 and 5–1 to bring about seasonal victories 103 and 104.

Of more pressing concern to most of the 45,000 fans on hand was the fact that Babe Ruth connected for home run number 54 of the season. It was only his sixth homer against the White Sox pitching staff in 1927.

This was the third time in his career that Ruth had hit as many as 54 home runs over the course of a season. When he first recorded that sum in 1920, he easily eclipsed the old American League record of 29. Ruth himself had set that mark in 1919, his final season in a Red Sox uniform.

Ruth was a bit of a dud in the first game, disappointing his legion of fanatical followers by failing to hit a home run in four tries at bat. Not until the fifth inning of the second game did the patrons see what they had expectantly paid their money for: a Ruthian sock. When the ball cleared the wall, the Babe was greeted with the usual loud ovation.

The home run produced its share of levity, too. When the inning concluded and the Babe jogged out to his position in right field, a precocious youngster, aged about ten years, decided the time was ripe to seek the great man's autograph. Failing to be restrained by barriers or by social customs, the little fellow simply dashed into right field carrying a ball and waving a pen. His intent was crystal clear, and even the Babe got a chuckle from the youth's brashness. Ruth obligingly signed the boy's ball and most certainly won a fan for life.

Steady George Pipgras pitched the full nine innings in the first game for New York. Waite Hoyt did the same in the second contest, also recording a complete game.

During the second game, the umpires had to make a tricky ruling on a ball hit by Chicago outfielder Bibb Falk. Falk's hit landed just fair inside the right field line, very close to both the outfield wall and the barrier in foul territory. The officials decreed the hit to be a ground-rule double because the ball, after landing fair, swerved right and bounced into the crowd along the right field line. Under 1927 rules, if a fair ball even *bounded* over the outfield wall, a batter was credited with a home run. (This rule stayed on the books until 1931. None of Ruth's 60 homers in 1927 were of this cheap variety.)

Falk was the man who had the unenviable assignment of succeeding Shoeless Joe Jackson as Chicago's left fielder after Jackson had been blacklisted from professional baseball as a result of the 1919 Black Sox scandal. Although Falk was not nearly the ballplayer Jackson was, he was a dependable hitter, averaging .315 in his nine seasons at Comiskey Park. Falk would excel as baseball coach at the University of Texas from 1940 to 1967. In that span, he led the Longhorns to 20 Southwest Conference championships.

Ted Lyons was the first of two eventual Hall-of-Famers victimized by a Ruth home run during 1927. Lyons, who was inducted at Cooperstown in 1955, compiled a respectable 260–230 record with mediocre White Sox teams in his 21-year career. He signed a big league contract without ever pitching an inning in the minors. He prided himself on his control. Lyons was never overpowering, but he was seldom wild. During the 1939 season, he pitched 42 consecutive innings without allowing a base on balls.

The doubleheader sweep lifted New York's record to 104–42. The Philadelphia Athletics were 18 games behind in second place.

Other Baseball News

- The Boston Braves ended an embarrassing 15-game losing streak by defeating the Cubs 11–7 at Wrigley Field in Chicago. When the last Cub was retired, the Braves players let out a rousing cheer. They lifted pitcher Bob Smith to their shoulders and carried him to their clubhouse. The win was Boston's first since Labor Day. Lance Richbourg had four hits, including a double and a triple, for the winners.

- The Cleveland Indians scored twice in the top of the tenth to beat the Washington Senators 6–4 at Griffith Stadium. George Burns's timely double drove in the two crucial runs for the Indians. Bucky Harris and Ossie Bluege each had three hits for Washington.

- The New York Giants split a doubleheader in Cincinnati, thus failing to gain any ground on idle Pittsburgh in the tight National League pennant race. Charles (Red) Lucas only allowed three Giants to reach base in the first game, won 7–0 by the Reds. The Giants rallied to win the second game 4–2.

♪55 September 21
Tigers at Yankees

Tigers	ab	r	h	po	a		Yankees	ab	r	h	po	a
Blue, 1b	3	2	1	11	1		Combs, cf	5	0	1	3	0
Gehringer, 2b	4	1	2	1	2		Koenig, ss	5	0	0	4	2
Manush, cf	4	1	1	1	0		Ruth, rf	5	1	3	4	1
Heilmann, rf	5	1	3	1	0		Gehrig, 1b	4	0	2	9	1
Fothergill, lf	4	0	1	4	0		Meusel, lf	3	0	0	2	0
McManus, 3b	3	1	0	4	1		Lazzeri, 2b	4	0	0	2	4
Tavener, ss	5	0	2	0	4		Dugan, 3b	4	0	0	1	4
Woodall, c	4	0	1	5	0		Collins, c	4	0	1	2	0
Gibson	4	0	0	0	2		Reuther, p	3	0	0	0	3
Totals	**36**	**6**	**11**	**27**	**10**		**Totals**	**37**	**1**	**7**	**27**	**15**

Detroit	1 0 3 0 1 0 1 0 0 - 6	
New York	0 0 0 0 0 0 0 0 1 - 1	

After New York had thoroughly trounced the demoralized Chicago White Sox, the Detroit Tigers were the next out-of-contention club to visit Yankee Stadium. Once the White Sox were vanquished, the Yankees had three days off to prepare for their last series against Detroit in 1927. If anything, the rest hurt Miller Huggins's club. On September 21 the Yankees put on as shabby a defensive performance as they had all season. Even more amazing, the seemingly unstoppable New York offense almost came to a grinding halt.

Luckily for the puzzled but good-natured gathering who made the mistake of paying to watch such an atrociously played affair, George Herman Ruth managed to produce a run—New York's only run of the game—with a ninth-inning solo sock. Otherwise, the much-heralded American League kingpins would have been handed a big goose egg by Detroit hurler Sam Gibson. Ruth's homer, number 55 of 1927, fell into his personal domain—the right field bleachers—and was the lone bright spot in an otherwise dreary day for the club that would be representing the American League in the World Series in less than two weeks.

The game was an ugly one to be sure. There were ten errors in all, six of which fell into the home team's ledger. While the crowd was amused by the lack of polish shown by the Yankees, Dutch Ruether, the New York hurler, was less appreciative of his mates' lackluster defensive play.

Having the pennant locked up freed the assembled throng from concern over piddling things such as errors and miscues. In fact, the hometown crowd seemed to enjoy the parade of errors and laughed heartily at each successive one. It was a parody of baseball not often seen at the stadium.

Detroit's Harry Heilmann, in the midst of a terrific duel with Philadelphia's Al Simmons for the American League batting title, collected three hits. Mark Koenig, the usually reliable Yankee shortstop, committed three glaring errors over the course of the afternoon. New York's woeful defensive play allowed the Tigers to romp to a 4–0 lead after the top of the third inning. Sam Gibson's mastery over the Yankee hitters ensured that the Tiger lead was never in serious jeopardy. Gibson, who won 11 games in 1927, would enjoy only marginal success as a major leaguer. However, he was a terror in the Pacific Coast League. Gibson won the incredible total of 307 minor league games, the last victory coming in 1946 when he was 47 years old.

The unexpectedly easy Detroit win dropped New York's record to 104–43, 17 games ahead of the Athletics.

Other Baseball News

- Hod Lisenbee of the Senators allowed just five hits in Washington's easy 10–0 win over the St. Louis Browns at Griffith Stadium. Foster (Babe) Ganzel, a Washington rookie recently elevated from the minors, enjoyed a perfect day at bat, with four hits in four trips to the plate. The Senators rocked two Browns pitchers for a total of 14 hits. Most came off starter and loser Elam Vangilder.

- Ty Cobb failed to get a hit in three official times at bat in his last game of the 1927 season. His club, the Philadelphia Athletics, lost 6–5 at Shibe Park to Cleveland. The Indians broke a 5–5 deadlock in the top of the ninth when Johnny Hodapp's single drove in Lew Fonseca with the go-ahead run. Cobb had been given permission by manager Connie Mack to leave the team early to go on a hunting trip in Wyoming. The most reliable hitter in baseball history had not decided whether he will return for a twenty-fourth season in 1928. Mack said he was willing to offer Cobb another contract for the following year.

- The Pittsburgh Pirates beat Brooklyn 4–2 at Ebbets Field in the only scheduled National League game. A costly throwing error by Brooklyn pitcher Buzz McWeeny led to a four-run Pirate fourth inning. Among the interested spectators were the New York Giants, who saw Pittsburgh's lead increase to 3½ games in the pennant race. The Giants would travel to Pittsburgh for a critical four-game series at Forbes Field. John Drebinger commented in the *New York Times,* "Only a clean sweep by Rogers Hornsby's galaxy of two-fisted fighters can possibly give New York City its cherished World Series on a five-cent fare."

⚑56 September 22
Tigers at Yankees

Tigers	ab	r	h	po	a		Yankees	ab	r	h	po	a
Blue, 1b	2	2	0	12	2		Combs, cf	4	2	3	2	0
Gehringer, 2b	3	0	3	3	4		Koenig, ss	3	3	2	3	3
Manush, cf	4	1	1	0	1		Ruth, rf	5	2	1	1	1
Heilmann, rf	4	1	1	3	0		Gehrig, 1b	4	1	2	15	1
Fothergill, lf	4	0	0	1	1		Meusel, lf	4	0	1	3	0
McManus, 3b	3	1	1	0	2		Lazzeri, 2b	2	0	1	2	5
Tavener, ss	4	1	1	1	2		Dugan, 3b	4	0	2	0	2
Bassler, c	3	0	1	3	2		Grabowski, c	3	0	0	1	0
Carroll, p	3	0	0	1	1		Moore, p	3	0	0	0	3
Neun, p	1	1	1	0	0		Pennock, p	0	0	0	0	1
Holloway, p	0	0	0	0	0							
Totals	31	7	9	24	15		Totals	32	8	12	27	16

```
Detroit    0 0 1 2 0 0 0 1 3 - 7
New York   1 0 4 0 0 0 1 0 2 - 8
```

In most cases the dramatic moment when a home run is hit occurs when the ball clears the wall and lands safely out of the reach of any fielders. The simple formality of circling the bases is the denouement. Babe Ruth's fifty-sixth home run of the 1927 season was clearly an exception. In one of the strangest scenes ever witnessed at Yankee Stadium, the Babe was accompanied around the bases by a youngster who was determined to leave the stadium with a spectacular souvenir.

Back in a spring training game in 1925 (shortly before Ruth was hospitalized with his infamous "bellyache"), a group of children had been the focus of another one of the Babe's homers. The Yankees were playing Brooklyn in Knoxville, Tennessee, and several dozen black children were sitting in a tree beyond the center field fence to beat the price of admission. During the game Ruth connected solidly with a fastball. The ball cleared the wall, flew into the tree and severed one of its limbs. The tree promptly loosed a torrent of startled children, who dropped from the branches like ripe fruit in a hailstorm.

The Yankees-Tigers game on September 22 was a wild offensive shoot-out. Detroit trailed 5–1 after three innings but rallied to assume a 7–6 lead by scoring three runs in the top of the ninth. Mark Koenig led off the bottom of the ninth with a solid single. Up to the plate stepped Ruth.

Much like the make-believe scene in the celluloid masterpiece the Babe had made during his last off-season, it was the chance to be a baseball hero. With Koenig waiting eagerly to be driven in by the reigning home run king, the Babe cheerfully obliged in the best way he knew how. He walloped the ball, which came to a smashing stop six rows from the very top of the right field bleachers.

But the excitement was just beginning. One of New York City's enthusiastic children decided to circle the bases with the Bambino. But the youngster was more than just an annoying trespasser—he was a potential thief as well.

The Babe, jealously protective of his lumber, always took the precaution of touching the sacks with his bat in tow. The boy thought Babe's bat might make the perfect souvenir to show off to his neighborhood chums—but he soon found out that Ruth's rumored kindness did have its limits. When the boy brazenly tried to swipe Ruth's bat, the Babe steadfastly resisted with all his might.

It was no contest; the boy was no hardier than the average grammar school attendee. Despite persistent tugs from the youth, the bat remained in Ruth's hands. Moreover, the Babe ended up dragging the kid for a good portion of the 360-foot trek around the sacks. The juvenile was still attached to the piece of wood when Babe was last seen heading into the Yankees' clubhouse.

The New Yorkers recorded their 105th victory of 1927 with this 8–7 triumph over the Tigers. They now stood level with the 1912 Boston Red Sox. Lou Gehrig earned a place in the record books all by himself. His two runs driven in gave him 172 for the year and surpassed the standard of 170 set by the Babe in 1921. With six games left in the regular season, the Babe was three homers behind his famous 59 set that same year.

This was the only instance in 1927 when a Ruth homer ended a game. Although he had twice hit extra-inning home runs—on May 30 and August 17—both came when the Yankees were the visiting team, so neither blow actually concluded the action. Detroit's Johnny Neun very nearly was the star of the game. His clutch pinch-hit triple drove in two runs in the top of the ninth to even the score at 6–6. He scored the go-ahead run on Lu Blue's sacrifice fly, but Ruth's dramatics robbed Neun of the headlines.

Neun's triple was just one of seven hit during the game. Earle Combs hit three to tie an individual American League record. Herb Pennock, who pitched just ⅔ of an inning, got the win in relief. New York was now 105–43, 16½ games in front of Philadelphia.

Other Baseball News

- The New York Giants split a doubleheader in Pittsburgh but fell into third place in the National League standings. The Pirates won the opener 5–2. New York took the second game by a 7–1 score. Rogers Hornsby of the Giants homered in each game.

- The St. Louis Cardinals dramatically scored two runs in the bottom of the ninth inning to edge the Boston Braves 6–5 at Sportsman's Park. The win vaulted the Cardinals ahead of New York and into second place. St. Louis had eight hits—each one from a different player.

- Walter Johnson hit a home run in his only time at bat in Washington's 10–7 victory over the St. Louis Browns at Griffith Stadium. Johnson fanned two Browns (raising his career strikeout total to 3,508 over 21 seasons) before being relieved in the fourth inning. It was Johnson's final appearance as a pitcher in the major leagues.

𝄞 57 September 27
Athletics at Yankees

Athletics	ab	r	h	po	a		Yankees	ab	r	h	po	a
Bishop, 2b	5	1	2	6	6		Combs, cf	4	1	0	4	0
Dykes, 3b	4	1	2	0	3		Koenig, ss	4	0	0	1	5
Bates, rf	5	0	0	3	0		Ruth, rf	5	1	2	1	0
Simmons, cf	4	0	0	1	0		Gehrig, 1b	4	2	1	11	1
Cochrane, c	3	0	2	3	0		Meusel, lf	5	0	1	0	0
Perkins, c	1	1	0	1	0		Lazzeri, 2b	4	1	3	4	4
Foxx, 1b	4	0	1	6	0		Dugan, 3b	3	1	3	1	1
French, lf	4	0	1	1	0		Grabowski, c	3	1	0	4	0
Boley, ss	3	1	1	2	5		Pennock, p	1	0	0	0	0
Walberg, p	1	0	0	0	0		Moore, p	1	0	0	1	1
Quinn, p	0	0	0	0	0							
Gray, p	0	0	0	0	0							
Saunders, ph	1	0	0	0	0							
Grove, p	0	0	0	0	0							
E. Collins, ph	1	0	0	0	0							
Powers, p	0	0	0	1	0							
Totals	36	4	9	24	14		**Totals**	34	7	10	27	12

Philadelphia   0 0 0 1 0 0 1 1 1 - 4
New York   0 0 0 1 1 4 1 0 x - 7

Babe Ruth knew what had to be done to challenge his own home run record. Realizing that time and circumstances were against him, on September 27 the Bambino smote one more homer against the Philadelphia Athletics to up his seasonal count to a whopping 57.

To make matters even more delightful, this one came with the bases full of Yankee teammates, and it played a highly significant role in New York's 7–4 win against Connie Mack's squad, who as always put up a valiant battle before succumbing to Miller Huggins's star-studded champs. Joe Dugan, Johnny Grabowski and Mark Koenig were the fortunate trio who were driven home by Ruth's sock.

A hearty gathering of about 15,000 home run watchers were in attendance at Yankee Stadium to see Ruth hit the 57 mark. With the championship of the American League safely locked, there really was no other enticement to come to the ballyard. Robert (Lefty) Grove was Ruth's patsy in the affair. He tossed one to the Babe's liking, and the oft-seen result occurred again: The ball smacked soundly into Ruth's bat and quickly redirected itself into a truly majestic arc. Upon its descent into the right field bleachers, Ruth's favorite target in all of vast Yankee Stadium, the throng roared its approval.

Despite being baseball's all-time home run leader, the Babe had not hit very many with the bases loaded. The September 27 homer off Grove marked only the sixth time in his illustrious career that he achieved such a feat. Moreover, it was just the third time he had done the trick while in the employ of New York City's American League club. The other three had come a few years back when the Babe was still splitting his time between pitching and tormenting his counterparts while wearing a Boston Red Sox uniform.

The game marked the last New York appearance by the Philadelphia A's for the 1927 season. The following day the Washington Senators would arrive for a three-game set that would finish off the Yankees' American League schedule for 1927. Therefore, the Bambino needed to average one home run per afternoon to surpass his six-year-old record—a tall order indeed.

Ruth also hit a towering fly ball in the eighth inning that many hopeful fans expected to see sail over the right field fence. Its height, however, was deceiving. The ball came down well in front of the wall and was misplayed by outfielder Charlie Bates into a two-base error. Bates's brief major league career would consist of just nine games—in which he was charged with three errors.

Lou Gehrig ended a peculiar three-week home run drought when he solidly connected with a Jack Quinn pitch in the fourth inning. It was Gehrig's first homer since his September 6 clout at Boston's Fenway Park, when he briefly took the American League lead in home runs for the last time in 1927.

Ruth's grand-slam home run (his first of the season) was surrendered by Robert Moses (Lefty) Grove, whose name usually appears on most experts' top-ten lists of the all-time greatest pitchers. Nine times he led the American League in earned-run average. No other pitcher has done it more than five times.

Unquestionably, Grove must be considered number one on the list of all-time tantrum throwers. He freely destroyed uniforms and clubhouse paraphernalia when he suffered a disappointment. Grove was fiercely competitive, especially during his prime. He was absolutely unforgiving if a teammate's miscue cost him so much as a run.

His most famous outburst occurred in 1931. Grove was at the peak of his phenomenal career and had amassed a 16-game winning streak, equaling the mark set by both Walter Johnson and Smokey Joe Wood. In his attempt for a record seventeenth consecutive victory, he lost an excruciating 1–0 squeaker to the lowly St. Louis Browns. Grove gave up just one hit, but that runner came in to score after rookie outfielder Jim Moore muffed a routine fly ball. Moore was taking the place of Al Simmons, who had skipped the game to attend a doctor's appointment. Grove recalled his ugly postgame mood: "I went in and tore the clubhouse up. I wrecked the place. I tore those stall lockers off the wall. I threw everything I could get my hands on, giving *Simmons* hell all the while."

Grove would eventually win 300 games and was inducted into the Hall of Fame in 1947.

New York's win was the fourteenth in 22 games versus the A's in 1927. The Yankees' record stood at 107–44. Second-place Philadelphia was well back, 17½ games behind.

Other Baseball News

• Ban Johnson's last official duty as American League president was the nomination of two umpires from his league to work in the upcoming World Series. Johnson selected Red Ormsby and Richard Nallin. Both men were well respected arbiters. Nallin had post-season experience, having umpired in the World Series in 1919 and 1923.

• Pittsburgh defeated the Chicago Cubs 2–1 at Wrigley Field to complete a four-game series sweep. George Grantham hit a home run in the top of the fifth inning with Pie Traynor aboard to account for all of the Pirates' scoring. Pittsburgh starter Lee Meadows was forced to leave the game in the sixth inning for an odd reason: He broke his glasses.

• The St. Louis Cardinals stayed within two games of league-leading Pittsburgh by beating the Cincinnati Reds 4–1 at Crosley Field. Winning pitcher Grover Cleveland Alexander allowed just three hits to the Reds. Chick Hafey's two-run homer in the top of the eighth inning iced the game for the visitors.

♪ 58 & 59 September 29
Senators at Yankees

Senators	ab	r	h	po	a
Rice, rf	3	0	0	0	0
Hopkins, p	1	0	0	0	2
Harris, 2b	4	1	2	1	3
Stewart, 2b	1	0	0	0	1
Ganzel, cf	4	1	0	2	0
Goslin, lf	5	0	1	3	2
Judge, 1b	4	0	2	7	1
Speaker, 1b	0	0	0	2	0
Tate, c	4	0	2	5	0
Bluege, 3b	4	1	0	0	0
Reeves, ss	4	1	1	2	4
Lisenbee, p	1	0	0	0	0
Marberry, p	0	0	0	0	0
Barnes, rf	3	0	0	2	1
Totals	**38**	**4**	**10**	**24**	**14**

Yankees	ab	r	h	po	a
Combs, cf	5	1	1	4	0
Koenig, ss	5	3	3	0	2
Ruth, rf	5	3	3	3	0
Paschal, rf	0	0	0	0	0
Gehrig, 1b	3	2	1	9	0
Durst, 1b	0	0	0	0	1
Meusel, lf	5	2	3	3	0
Lazzeri, 2b	3	1	3	0	1
Morehart, 2b	1	0	1	0	0
Dugan, 3b	3	1	1	1	3
Gazella, 3b	2	0	0	0	1
Collins, c	2	1	2	6	0
Shocker, p	1	0	0	0	0
Ruether, p	2	1	1	0	0
Shawkey, p	1	0	0	1	0
Totals	**38**	**15**	**19**	**27**	**8**

```
Senators    0 2 0 0 2 0 0 0 0 -  4
New York    1 7 0 3 4 0 0 0 x - 15
```

With both momentum and confidence building, Ruth took a giant leap toward breaking his six-year-old major league record for home runs in a season by blasting two off downtrodden Washington pitchers on September 29, thus equaling his previous high of 59. It was a day when Ruth was at his magnificent best at the plate. Although the final score was 15–4 in favor of the home team over the bedraggled Washington Senators, nobody really cared about such trivialities while Ruth's pursuit of history was ongoing.

Two different Washington hurlers, Horace (Hod) Lisenbee and Paul Hopkins, were added to Ruth's list of 1927 home run victims. The Babe got things rolling early. In the bottom of the very first inning with two men out and nobody on base, Ruth flailed one to right field that barely crept into the lower stands. Lisenbee was up 0–2 in the count at the time and tried to baffle the Bambino with one of his curveballs. It did not work.

To say that home run number fifty-nine, which entered the box score in the bottom of the fifth inning, was more pleasing to the eye would be a gross understatement. Compounding its beauty was the cheery fact that three of Ruth's Yankee playmates were on base, making it two consecutive days that the Bambino had stroked grand slam home runs. The ball eventually came to rest well up in the right field bleachers. Even though the paid attendance was only somewhere in the 7,500 range, they made enough clamor to rock the entire stadium. Ruth responded to their cries of affection with a tip of his cap. Upon reaching home plate, the Babe shook the hand of Lou Gehrig. Already it seemed eons ago that Gehrig had held the lead in the home run derby.

Ruth very nearly added two more home runs to his output on this day. In the second inning, he tripled by hitting a ball to deep center field. In the seventh, a fly ball to right field sent Washington outfielder Red Barnes to the base of the wall, where he made the catch.

The outcome of the game was decided in the second inning when New York tallied seven runs to take an 8–2 lead. Altogether, the Yankees rocked the Senators pitchers for 19 hits. Two Washington batters, Babe Ganzel and Bobby Reeves, managed to hit home runs in the lopsided defeat. For each man, it was his only homer of the season.

New York Times correspondent John Drebinger, who chronicled the exploits of the Yankees for much of the latter part of 1927 including this particular game, would not have the privilege of covering the World Series for his newspaper; that honor would fall to James R. Harrison. However, Drebinger, who joined the *Times* staff in 1923, would witness a fair number of Fall Classics. In fact, Drebinger would report on 35 consecutive World Series for the *Times* from 1929 until his retirement in 1963. In 1974 Drebinger was given the prestigious J. G. Taylor Spink Award during the induction ceremonies at the National Baseball Hall of Fame.

Hod Lisenbee, who surrendered home run number 58, was a rookie sensation who had performed admirably early in the season but by September had been "figured out" by American League hitters. Still, Lisenbee could boast that he defeated the mighty Yankees on five occasions in 1927. Along with this homer, Lisenbee had given up another to Ruth on July 3. He would be a journeyman pitcher for the rest of his career, winning just 19 more games.

Paul Hopkins, Ruth's second home run victim of the day, was a raw rookie, one of many elevated by major league clubs at the end of the season when the pennant was out of reach. Hopkins pitched in just two games in 1927 (and in 11 over his two-year career). He would be utterly forgotten had he not been one of the hurlers Ruth placed on his "honor roll."

The victory merely added to the American League record the Yankees had already established. New York now had a mark of 108–44. Second-place Philadelphia was 18½ games behind.

Other Baseball News

• Jack Bradley of the Red Sox (recently elevated from Waterbury of the Eastern League) allowed just five hits to the A's as Boston won 6–1 at Philadelphia. Guy Cantrell gave up 14 hits to the visitors, including three triples.

• Ray Miller of the Philadelphia Phillies gave up 11 hits to the Braves in Boston but still cruised to an easy 7–1 victory. The Phillies scored three runs in the first inning and three in the second to secure the win.

• Even though the Pirates were idle, Pittsburgh was now guaranteed no worse
than a first-place tie in the National League standings after the St. Louis
Cardinals lost 3–2 to Cincinnati at wet Crosley Field. The Reds jumped
out to a 3–0 lead in the bottom of the fourth inning. St. Louis's Frankie
Frisch hit a home run to narrow the gap, but the Reds held onto the win.
Only 340 spectators sat through the drizzle. Among them were the happy
members of the Pirates, who had arrived in Cincinnati to begin a series
with the Reds the following day.

🏃 60 September 30
Senators at Yankees

Senators	ab	r	h	po	a		Yankees	ab	r	h	po	a
Rice, rf	3	0	1	2	0		Combs, cf	4	0	0	3	0
Harris, 2b	3	0	0	3	4		Koenig, ss	4	1	1	3	5
Ganzel, cf	4	0	1	1	0		Ruth, rf	3	3	3	4	0
Goslin, lf	4	1	1	5	0		Gehrig, 1b	4	0	2	10	0
Judge, 1b	4	0	0	8	0		Meusel, lf	3	0	1	3	0
Ruel, c	2	1	1	2	0		Lazzeri, 2b	3	0	0	2	2
Bluege, 2b	3	0	1	1	4		Dugan, 3b	3	0	1	1	1
Gillis, ss	4	0	0	2	1		Bengough, c	3	0	1	1	2
Zachary, p	2	0	0	0	1		Pipgras, p	2	0	0	0	2
Johnson, ph	1	0	0	0	0		Pennock, p	1	0	0	0	1
Totals	30	2	5	24	10		Totals	30	4	9	27	13

Washington	0 0 0 2 0 0 0 0 0 - 2
New York	0 0 0 1 0 1 0 2 x - 4

Many fans of Babe Ruth are under the false impression that Ruth belted
his sixtieth home run of the season in dramatic fashion on the final day of
the season. Numerous scholarly works about baseball have failed to quash this
falsehood and instead have given it a life of its own. One exception was Ken
Burns's acclaimed 1994 PBS television documentary, *Baseball*, which correctly
stated that Ruth broke his record "on the next-to-last day of the season."

The mistake, however, is understandable, because Ruth hit his sixtieth
home run in the Yankees' 154th game of the 1927 season. The misunder-
standing lies in the fact that the Yankees officially played 155 games in 1927!
Miller Huggins's club was involved in a legal tie game—where players' statistics count—earlier in the season, creating this confusion. Look up Lou
Gehrig's statistics for that year. In the "games played" column, you will note
that Gehrig's number for 1927 is 155. Fittingly, though, Ruth's milestone
home run was more than window dressing. It drove in the game-winning
runs against the Washington Senators.

Strangely, fewer than 10,000 fans were on hand in Yankee Stadium for
the momentous event. The identity of the correspondent for the *New York*

Times—who had the privilege of watching this piece of sports history unfold—is unknown. The writer did not get a byline in the next day's newspaper. Perhaps, like journalist Paul Gallico, the baseball fans in New York knew that Ruth would set a new record. Some years afterward Gallico would write, "Once [Ruth] had that 59, that number 60 was as sure as the setting sun. A more determined athlete than George Herman Ruth never lived. He is one of the few utterly dependable news stories in sports." Still, the Bambino's sixtieth clout of 1927 was banner news.

The ground-breaking achievement occurred in the bottom of the eighth inning at Yankee Stadium. Mark Koenig was stationed at third base, having hit a triple. On the mound for the Washington Senators was Tom Zachary, a crafty southpaw. The score was tied 2–2 and the tension was thick.

Zachary's first fling was a fastball that was deemed a strike. His next offering was high for a ball. The third pitch put George Herman Ruth into the record books again. The Babe whacked at it viciously. The crack that followed could be heard in the furthest reaches of the stadium. There was no doubt of a homer from the moment the ball left the Babe's bat, and it fell high into the right field stands.

Predictably, the roar that greeted the home run was thunderous. A shower of hats, paper and miscellaneous debris drifted from all portions of the stadium in an instantaneous and wonderful celebration. The Babe made an especially memorable trot around the basepaths. Each base was touched with great deliberation so there could be no doubt that the home run was valid. Incidentally, it also held up to provide the margin of victory in New York's 4–2 triumph.

The lucky patron who collected home run ball number 60 was later identified as Mr. Joe Forner of 1937 First Avenue in Manhattan. Mr. Forner told the press that he has been a passionate follower of baseball since he was in short pants. He was permitted to enter the Yankee clubhouse afterwards to gleefully show the Babe the treasure he possessed.

On the other hand, poor Zachary was so flummoxed by the occasion that his eyesight failed him. He apparently was the only person in the stadium who questioned the validity of the home run. Believing Ruth's drive had drifted foul, he started a futile argument with the umpires. Ruth would always remember Zachary's beef. Twenty years later, Zachary was one of a select group of old-timers invited to greet the ailing home run king during "Babe Ruth Day" at Yankee Stadium. "You crooked-arm son of a bitch," Ruth whispered to him, "are you still claiming that ball was foul?"

Ruth himself was buoyant about his new record. In the clubhouse after the game, Ruth bellowed, "Sixty! Count 'em, 60! Let's see some other son of a bitch do that!" Later he paid tribute to the man whose own terrific season had pushed him to excel. Ruth declared if anyone had the potential to hit more than 60 homers in a season, it was Lou Gehrig.

Koenig, who scored ahead of Ruth on the famous home run, may have been the last surviving witness to home run number 60. After the death of Waite Hoyt in 1984, Koenig became the sole enduring legacy of the great 1927 Yankee team, and he lived into his ninetieth year. When asked about this honor late in his life, Koenig said, "I'm not really sure. I'm already listed as being dead in some books."

Tom Zachary, whose name has gone down with those of Ralph Branca, Al Downing, Tracy Stallard, Ralph Terry and Mitch Williams as pitchers who surrendered famous home runs, earned another place in baseball lore on September 30, 1927. Late in the game, he was removed for a pinch hitter. The man who replaced Zachary was Walter Johnson. It was Johnson's last appearance in the big leagues as a player. (Note to trivia buffs: Johnson flied out to George Herman Ruth in this final at-bat!) Zachary was acquired by the Yankees in August 1928 and would pitch New York to a 7–3 victory in game three of the 1928 World Series. In 1929 Zachary went 12–0 for the Yankees. It is the highest seasonal win total ever recorded by a pitcher who did not suffer a loss.

The win, almost forgotten in the tumult of Ruth's accomplishment, lifted New York's seasonal record to 109–44. The following afternoon, on the last day of the regular season, Lou Gehrig homered for the forty-seventh time in 1927. Ruth went hitless, but New York won 4–3. The Yankees finished the season at 110–44, 19 full games ahead of the Philadelphia Athletics. Twenty-seven years would pass before another American League club—the 1954 Cleveland Indians—would win more games over the course of a season.

Other Baseball News

- Pittsburgh failed to clinch the National League pennant, losing 2–1 at Cincinnati. Red Lucas allowed just six Pirate hits. Hughie Critz made several stellar defensive plays at second base for Cincinnati.

- Outgoing American League president Ban Johnson assailed the Chicago White Sox and Commissioner Kenesaw Landis, berating them for a lack of cooperation and accusing them of attempting to embarrass his league. Johnson said, "The childish spite and rebellion on the part of the Chicago club has been matched, even outdone, by the petty action of the office of the Commissioner of Baseball." Landis refused to comment on Johnson's remarks.

- The Boston Braves scored seven runs in the first two innings to beat the Philadelphia Phillies 12–2 in Boston. The Braves had 18 hits. Three of them were doubles by Eddie Brown.

The 1927 World Series

🏃 World Series **1** October 7
Pirates at Yankees

Pirates	ab	r	h	po	a
L. Waner, cf	4	0	1	1	1
Rhyne, 2b	4	0	0	0	6
P. Waner, rf	4	0	0	0	0
Wright, ss	3	0	0	3	2
Traynor, 3b	3	1	1	0	3
Barnhart, lf	3	0	1	0	1
Harris, 1b	3	0	0	11	0
Gooch, c	2	0	0	9	0
Spencer, ph, c	1	0	0	0	0
Meadows, p	2	0	0	0	1
Cvengros, p	0	0	0	0	0
Groh, ph	1	0	0	0	0
Totals	**30**	**1**	**3**	**24**	**14**

Yankees	ab	r	h	po	a
Combs, cf	4	2	2	5	0
Koenig, ss	4	2	2	1	2
Ruth, rf	4	1	1	1	0
Gehrig, 1b	3	0	2	12	0
Meusel, lf	4	0	0	2	0
Lazzeri, 2b	4	1	1	1	7
Dugan, 3b	3	1	1	1	2
Grabowski, c	2	0	0	3	0
Bengough, c	1	0	0	0	0
Pennock, p	4	1	0	1	1
Durst, p	1	0	0	0	0
Totals	**34**	**8**	**9**	**27**	**12**

Pittsburgh	0 0 0 0 0 0 0 1 0 - 1
New York	2 0 0 0 0 0 6 0 x - 8

On the final day of the regular season, Pittsburgh clinched a spot in the World Series. After losing the first two games of the Series at Forbes Field to the Yankees, the Pirates must have wondered whether their long struggle to hoist the National League pennant in their ballpark had been worth the effort.

Although the Pittsburgh club had their share of quality hitters—such as the Waner brothers and Harold (Pie) Traynor, to name but three—many of the Pirates were in awe of the reputation of the great Yankee sluggers before Ruth and his mates ever set foot in Pittsburgh. According to a well-circulated story, the Pirates, already undone by fawning newspaper accounts of the Yankees' fearsome power, were completely demoralized after watching the Yankees take their batting practice before Game One. The Yankee hurlers grooved pitches down the heart of the plate, allowing Ruth, Gehrig, Combs, Meusel and Lazzeri to have a feast. "Do these guys always hit like this?" asked one thoroughly intimidated Pirate.

In Game One, played on October 4, Ruth and Gehrig accounted for five of New York's six hits as the Yankees eked out a 5–4 win. The next afternoon, Gehrig hit a timely double in the third inning (in which New York scored three times) and George Pipgras tossed a complete game in the Yankees' easy 6–2 win in Game Two. Now the Pirates, down two games to none, had to travel to the Bronx knowing that the Yankees were virtually invincible at home. The result was worse than they feared: an 8–1 Yankee win that was even more one-sided than the score indicates.

Some 64,000 paying customers contributed $209,665 to the coffers and made this the most lucrative game in the history of the World Series. About 3,000 others—reporters, assorted dignitaries, special guests, and other freeloaders—got to watch the rout for nothing.

The victory gave Miller Huggins's maulers a commanding 3–0 edge in the best-of-seven series. No team in World Series history had ever recovered from such a daunting deficit, and the crew from Pittsburgh seemed an unlikely candidate to set a precedent. After Game Three, the network of illegal bookmakers in New York City were giving long odds, ranging from 15–1 to 20–1, on Pittsburgh winning the World Series. The Yankees were now solid 3–2 betting favorites to sweep the Pirates in four straight games.

Herb Pennock, the Yankee hurler, pitched a masterful game, although a mediocre showing would have still been enough to record a victory in such a shellacking. Not one of the first 22 Pirates to wave a stick in the batter's box so much as reached first base. To make the occasion truly festive, Babe Ruth sent a line drive screaming into the right field bleachers for a home run in the home half of the seventh. Two Yankees preceded the Babe around the sacks on his home run trot.

The game was never in doubt from the first inning onward. In that frame, Lou Gehrig walloped a triple which drove in two teammates. Not long afterward, the Pirates took on the collective look of men walking towards the gallows. The big inning was the seventh, when six of the home team crossed the plate, three of them on the Ruth homer. Still, the Pirates were a game lot, but they were utterly outclassed by the soon-to-be world champions.

"All the Pirates have to do is grab four in a row," commented James R. Harrison in the *New York Times*. "If this happens, we wouldn't be surprised to see water run uphill and the sands of the desert grow cold."

During the Yankees' six-run rally in the seventh inning, which was capped by Ruth's three-run homer off left-hander Mike Cvengros, a heckler seated near the press box taunted the visiting Pirate players. "Take off those Pittsburgh uniforms!" the fan shouted. "We know you. You're the St. Louis Browns!"

Cvengros was only a mediocre major league pitcher at best, but he uncannily seemed to turn up on pennant winners. His first experience in the majors came in 1922 when he appeared in one game for the New York Giants, the team that would eventually win the World Series that season. After playing for the National League champion Pirates in 1927, Cvengros next resurfaced in 1929 as a member of the Chicago Cubs, a team that also captured the pennant.

World Series Notebook

• Pie Traynor finally broke up Pennock's bid for a perfect game. He singled to right field after 22 previous Pirate batters had failed to reach first base. Clyde Barnhart drove in Traynor with a double to right center to score the visitors' only run. Lloyd Waner got the third and final hit for Pittsburgh in the top of the ninth. In contrast, the Yankees had 16 hits. Gehrig, Combs and Koenig had two apiece. Gehrig's hits were a double and a triple.

• Judging by the sparse crowd preparing for an overnight vigil, many rabid New York baseball fans figured the World Series was now in the bag. The *New York Times* reported that 69 fans had slept in front of the Yankee Stadium ticket office before Game Three in order to ensure themselves bleacher seats. On the evening before Game Four, only two stalwart supporters decided to spend the night on the street.

World Series 2 October 8
Pirates at Yankees

Pirates	ab	r	h	po	a		Yankees	ab	r	h	po	a
L. Waner, cf	4	1	3	0	0		Combs, cf	4	3	2	2	0
Barnhart, lf	5	0	1	2	0		Koenig, ss	5	0	3	0	3
P. Waner, rf	4	0	1	0	0		Ruth, rf	4	1	2	1	0
Wright, ss	4	0	1	1	6		Gehrig, 1b	5	0	0	14	2
Traynor, 3b	4	0	0	1	4		Meusel, lf	5	0	0	2	0
Grantham, 2b	4	0	2	0	2		Lazzeri, 2b	3	0	0	5	4
Harris, 1b	4	0	2	11	0		Dugan, 3b	4	0	1	1	4
Smith, c	3	0	0	8	0		Collins, c	3	0	3	2	1
Yde, pr	0	1	0	0	0		Moore, p	4	0	1	0	3
Gooch, c	0	0	0	3	0							
Hill, p	1	0	0	0	0							

Pirates	ab	r	h	po	a		Yankees	ab	r	h	po	a
Brickell, ph	0	1	0	0	0							
Miljus, p	1	0	0	0	0							
Totals	34	3	10	26	12		Totals	37	4	12	27	17

Pittsburgh	1 0 0 0 0 0 2 0 0 - 3	
New York	1 0 0 0 2 0 0 0 1 - 4	

When a team—any team—wraps up a World Series by scoring the winning run in the bottom of the ninth inning, one can imagine a finish of high drama. Considering that the winning club happened to be the fabled 1927 New York Yankees, one might have expected heroics from the bat of either Babe Ruth or Lou Gehrig to put an end to the season. Both men did come to the plate in the final frame. Ruth was intentionally walked, and Gehrig struck out. However, despite their 4–3 win, the Yankees saw their outstanding season end with a terribly unsatisfactory climax.

The score of Game Four was tied 3–3 in the bottom of the ninth. The bases were loaded. Ruth's walk and Gehrig's strikeout were followed by a second strikeout, this one by Bob Meusel. Tony Lazzeri was the next New Yorker to face the nervous relief pitcher, Johnny Miljus, who was not quite up to shutting down the great Yankee power machine. Lazzeri's first swing put a foul ball into the stands.

Then Miljus wound up and threw a pitch so wild that the best that catcher Johnny Gooch could do was barely touch it with his outstretched glove. As the ball trickled to the backstop, in scampered Earle Combs with the run that won the game, the series, and a place in history for Miller Huggins and his talented underlings.

It was a disappointing way to win all the marbles, but after the previous year's stunning World Series disaster at the hands of the St. Louis Cardinals, the Yankees did not quibble over the aesthetics.

Apart from the game-winning run, every other New York run was driven in by George Herman Ruth, a fitting offensive hero in the final baseball game of 1927. He hit another home run, his second in two days, when the score was deadlocked 1–1. It was no fluke. It carried deep into the right field bleachers where many of his record 60 regular-season home runs came crashing down.

Babe's blast came in the bottom of the fifth inning. Earle Combs had started things off with a single and was still at first base when Ruth's turn to bat came up. The home run pitch, thrown by Pittsburgh starter Carmen Hill, was probably too low to be ruled a strike, but when Ruth smells a home run, he is not too finicky about such matters. He simply golfed the ball toward the right field bleachers. Both Waner brothers futilely pursued the ball, but had to watch it sail into the seats along with everyone else. About 60,000 Yankee rooters shrieked with delight at the sight of it scaling the wire screen and falling into the hands of the paying customers.

Costly errors by Wilcy Moore and Tony Lazzeri led to two Pirate runs, which tied the score, in the top of the seventh inning. Miljus entered the game as a relief pitcher in the bottom of the seventh. After no runs were scored in the eighth inning or the top of the ninth, the stage was set for Miljus's catastrophic blunder. Baseball historian A. D. Suehsdorf sympathetically described Miljus, a decorated veteran of the First World War, as "one of those unfortunates whose career compresses to a single play." Indeed, Miljus is largely remembered by baseball scholars for that one errant toss. Few fans recall that Miljus pitched four scoreless innings in Game One and had a 1.35 ERA for the 1927 World Series. No other World Series game, before or since, has ended on a wild pitch.

By allowing Ruth's final homer of 1927, Hill earned a bit of immortality—but he had to wait 56 years for it. A picture of the Babe belting his Game Four home run appeared on a commemorative 20-cent postage stamp in 1983. Hill lived long enough to have received mail bearing the picture. He died on January 1, 1990, at the age of 94.

Ruth had hit the only two homers of the entire 1927 World Series. Wilbert Robinson, Brooklyn's wily and colorful manager, whose views on the series were being printed by the *New York Times*, commented, "Out of fairness, Ruth should only be allowed to play in every second game."

The win gave the Yankees their second World Series title in history. Their first one had come four years earlier, in 1923. (The Yankees had been three-time World Series losers in 1921, 1922 and 1926.) Of the 24 installments of the Fall Classic that had been contested up to that time, the 1927 World Series was just the fourth occasion in which a series had been swept by one team in the minimum possible games. (This includes the unusual 1907 World Series when the Chicago Cubs defeated the Detroit Tigers 4–0 with one game ending in a tie. Similarly the 1922 World Series saw the Giants upend the Yankees 4–0 with one tie game.) The whitewash administered by "Murderers' Row" was the first time an American League club had managed to accomplish the impressive feat.

The Yankees, of course, would continue to dominate the American League through the mid–1960s. In stark contrast, the Pirates fell on hard times. Pittsburgh fans would have to wait patiently for their club's next World Series appearance. It would not come until 1960. That autumn, the Pirates achieved a remarkable seven-game upset to defeat a terrific and dynastic Yankee team that boasted Mickey Mantle, Roger Maris, Whitey Ford and Yogi Berra, among others.

The Pirates' loss in the 1927 World Series was a rare defeat in a professional sports championship for the city of Pittsburgh. The Pirates had played in two previous World Series (1909 and 1925) and won them both. In the 68 years that followed the 1927 World Series, the Pirates were victorious in all three of their subsequent World Series appearances. The Pittsburgh Penguins won the Stanley Cup in their only two trips to the NHL championship series, and the Pittsburgh Steelers won four Super Bowls without a loss. The streak of success for Pittsburgh's pro teams finally ended with the Steelers' loss to the Dallas Cowboys in Super Bowl XXX on January 28, 1996.

World Series Notebook

• News of the Yankee victory was unexpectedly greeted with cheers by many Pittsburgh fans who were engrossed with play-by-play accounts from scoreboards erected outside newspaper offices. The cynical fans had soured on the Pirates after they had dropped the first three games of the World Series.

• Despite the rancorous conclusion to his tenure as American League president, Ban Johnson was elated by the news of New York's series-ending win. Moments after Combs crossed the plate with the winning run, Johnson sent a telegram to Colonel Ruppert, the owner of the Yankees. It said, "Hearty congratulations to you, Manager Huggins, and the players. We like to destroy the enemy in that manner. Four straight victories will have a wholesome effect upon the public mind and will strengthen the position of professional baseball."

• Manager-turned-reporter Wilbert Robinson was a member of the great Baltimore Orioles teams of the 1890s, which dominated the National League at that time. Before the 1927 Yankees were lauded as the greatest array of baseball talent ever assembled, the old Orioles were claimants of that mythical title. (Fans of Connie Mack's 1910–1914 Philadelphia Athletics might wish to argue the point.) The torch, however, had clearly been passed. When asked to compare the 1927 champions to the Baltimore team of 30 years earlier, Robinson candidly admitted, "These Yankees would have wiped the streets with us!"

• Ruth and Gehrig immediately began preparations for an off-season barnstorming tour, hastily rescheduled to begin the very next day. Both men would be part of a team called "The Bustin' Babes," which made a cross-country tour. They did not have far to travel for their first game. It was scheduled for a small ballpark in the Bronx where their opponents were the Lincoln Giants, a leading Negro League outfit.

5

BABE RUTH
AFTER 1927

With his record-smashing 1927 season entered into the record books, Ruth's greatest statistical accomplishments were now behind him, although many wonderful moments were still to come in his eight remaining years as a player. Surprisingly, Ruth did not dwell on his 60-homer season in his autobiography. His chapter on the 1927 season deals mostly with team accomplishments, with the exception of one paragraph:

> Speaking of my 60 home runs in 1927, they were made before many of the parks had been artificially shortened so as to favor the home-run hitter. I hit them in the same parks where, only a decade before, 10 or 12 homers were good enough to win the title. They said they livened up the ball for me, and some of the writers called it the jack-rabbit ball. Well, if they put some of the jack in it around the 1927 period, they put the entire rabbit into it in 1947 and at the same time shortened a lot of fences. But my old record has held up.

There were those who thought that Ruth's output of 60 home runs would never be equaled in the major leagues, and they were in the majority. When Roger Maris did eclipse Ruth's record by one homer in 1961, he had the benefit of an expanded schedule of 162 games. Maris's sixty-first home run was hit during the final game of the regular season, which cast some doubt as to whether Maris had legitimately toppled the Babe. The advantage of the eight extra contests for Maris has been endlessly debated. Even official baseball record books are hard-pressed to declare one man's feat superior to the other's. Maris is listed as the home run king of the 162-game schedule and Ruth is still recognized as the champion of the 154-game campaign.

However, in 1928, Ruth, still basking in the glory of his outstanding season the year before, continued his assault against the pitching staffs of the other seven American League clubs. The Yankees won 50 of their first 66 games and were expected to cruise home as easily as they had in 1927. Suddenly though, the Yankees ran into trouble with their own pitching corps. Wilcy Moore (whom many fans suspected was quite a bit older than he admitted) inexplicably could not get anybody out. Herb Pennock's arm went dead. Urban Shocker died after a bout with pneumonia.

To make matters worse, Ruth began to slump. From July 1 to August 15, he hit but six home runs after having blasted 38 through June. New York's 11-game lead over Philadelphia vanished by early September. The Yankees managed to sweep a critical three-game series against the A's, in which Ty Cobb, Eddie Collins and Tris Speaker all glaringly showed their age. New York hung on to win the pennant by 2½ games. The Athletics had served notice to New York. Connie Mack's fine club would win the next three American League pennants.

The 1928 World Series pitted New York against the St. Louis Cardinals. Only on paper was it a rematch of the closely fought 1926 Series. Instead it turned out to be a showcase series for Ruth. He batted .625 (a mark that stood for 62 years) and swatted three home runs. All of them came in the final contest of the four-game sweep to equal a Series record he had set versus the Cards in 1926. Only Reggie Jackson, who walloped three homers against the Los Angeles Dodgers in the final game of the 1977 World Series, has done it since.

In January 1929 Ruth was saddened by the news that his estranged wife Helen had been killed in a house fire in Watertown, Massachusetts. She had been living with a local dentist and was known as Helen Kinder. The Babe's incessant womanizing had finally driven a wedge between them by 1925. Because they were of the Catholic faith, divorce proceedings were out of the question. Ruth was a pitiful sight at Helen's funeral, but soon afterward he married his longtime mistress, Claire Hodgson. Claire, much to the relief of the Yankee hierarchy, was able to keep her husband under control. She traveled with the club on road trips and shrewdly controlled Ruth's money, giving America's greatest athlete only small amounts to blow. (Ruth never completely gave up his bimbos; he just became more discreet about his frequent rendezvous. His favorite ploy was to borrow the hotel keys of rookie teammates.)

The most interesting occurrence of the 1929 season—one that would start a chain of events that permanently damaged Ruth's relationship with Yankee management—was the stunning death of Miller Huggins. When the season began, the diminutive field pilot appeared even more weather-beaten than usual. Colonel Ruppert urged his manager to see a doctor, but the 49-year-old Huggins insisted he was fine. After leaving Yankee Stadium on September 20, Huggins went home and fell asleep. Five days later he was dead of erysipelas, a strep skin infection. Among the most tearful of mourners at the funeral service was Ruth. Although Huggins had disciplined him often, Ruth liked Huggins because of his generally easygoing managerial style. Art Fletcher, one of the team's coaches, took on the interim managerial duties for the remainder of the season. At the time of Huggins's death, the Athletics held a comfortable lead over New York and eventually cruised to the pennant by 16 games.

When Fletcher surprisingly turned down the offer to continue as Yankee manager in 1930, some writers began to suggest that Ruth would be an ideal candidate. Others close to Ruth laughed at the idea. "How can the Babe be expected to manage a team when he can't even manage himself?" was the common response to refute this suggestion. Back in 1925 at a baseball writers' dinner, a fantasy skit was performed in which Ruth actually was Yankee manager. The uproarious performance had the drunken Babe plotting out managerial strategy to defeat Cleveland during a 3 A.M. poker game—only to discover afterward that his club's upcoming opponents actually were the St. Louis Browns. After Bob Shawkey was named the team's new manager, Ruth did not seem angry at the appointment.

Shawkey lasted at the managerial helm for just one season. His abrasive style and constant criticism did not work well on a team used to playing under the calm leadership of Huggins. Ruth, at the request of his wife, now seriously lobbied for the manager's job. He did not get it. It went to Joe McCarthy, who had been managing the Chicago Cubs with better than average success. McCarthy was an emotionless man who stood for no shenanigans. Quite naturally, he and Ruth did not see eye to eye. Ruth, still under the impression that he might talk his way into managing the team, openly criticized McCarthy in the press. Ruth hit .373 in 1931, a tremendous accomplishment for a 36-year-old who now weighed in the neighborhood of 230 pounds. He also tied Lou Gehrig with 46 home runs to claim his twelfth and final home run title. (Because of the dead heat, both Gehrig and Ruth are credited with winning the 1931 AL home run crown.) Defensively, however, the Babe was now a liability. He could no longer chase down long fly balls. In the era before the designated hitter, his days were numbered. His powerful bat and his potential as a drawing card, however, kept Ruth in the Yankee lineup through 1934.

Throughout his life, Ruth always showed genuine affection for all children—especially those who were ill or orphaned. Amateur psychologists might theorize that Ruth could empathize with these youngsters because of his own loveless childhood. Over the years, Ruth dispatched hundreds of personal letters of encouragement to unfortunate youths all across America. In 1996, the National Baseball Hall of Fame displayed a typical example of this correspondence in its Babe Ruth Room. The Hall's curator had acquired it from the descendants of Freddy Clark, who, as an eight-year-old polio victim, received the hand-written note from the great Bambino. It was reprinted in the Hall of Fame's quarterly newsletter, *Memories and Dreams*, in July 1996. According to the information that accompanied the letter to the Hall of Fame, young Freddy recuperated well enough to be discharged from the hospital. He lived for another 35 years.

The 1932 season provided Ruth with one last great moment of showmanship. New York had ended Philadelphia's three-year grip on the pennant and faced the Chicago Cubs in the World Series. In Game Three at Wrigley Field, Ruth supposedly hit his famous "called shot" home run off Charlie Root. Whether or not the Babe truly signaled that he would deposit one of Root's pitches into the bleachers is very debatable. Root always scoffed at the notion. So did Joe McCarthy. On the other hand, teammates Joe Sewell and Lou Gehrig steadfastly maintained Ruth had indeed done it. (Amateur movies of the incident surfaced in the 1990s and show Ruth waving his arm derisively at the Cub bench—nothing more.) Regardless of the circumstances in which it was hit, the home run was Ruth's fifteenth and final round-tripper in World Series play. The Cubs fell to the Yankees in four straight games.

By 1933 Ruth's home run output had dropped to 34, certainly a respectable total but definitely not the amount the public expected from the great Babe. Lou Gehrig was now unquestionably the best player on the team. Still, Ruth was nominated to play in baseball's first All-Star Game at Comiskey Park. In typical Ruth fashion, he responded by launching a home run in the American League's 4–2 win. The capacity crowd gave the fading Bambino a tremendous ovation. Washington won the pennant that season, which gave Ruth a chance to make one final pitching appearance in a meaningless late-season game at Fenway Park. Joe C. Glenn, the catcher in Ruth's final pitching performance, remembered the circumstances:

> It was the closing day of 1933, and I had just returned to the club [from the minors]. We were in Boston. Washington had already clinched the pennant. The Red Sox were trying to get people to the park, and since Babe had established a reputation there, first as a pitcher, he was advertised as a special attraction. Ruth hadn't pitched in some time, yet he went all the way and won, 6–5. His personal magnetism brought out 30,000 [fans], and everyone enjoyed the game.

As a goodwill gesture, the club asked Ruth if he would be interested in managing the Yankees' top farm team, the Newark Bears, in 1934. Although many aspiring managers would have jumped at such an opportunity, the Babe considered the offer to be degrading. "I'm a big leaguer," Ruth said in declining the position. "Why should I have to go down to the minors first? Cobb and Speaker didn't. Why do I have to?" Ruth instead endured one last unproductive season as a Yankee player.

By 1934 Ruth could no longer frighten opposing pitchers. Many were striking him out on fastballs he would have blasted 500 feet just a few seasons earlier. His relationship with the Yankee front office deteriorated, as did his long friendship with Lou Gehrig, his fishing buddy and barnstorming companion. According to Robert Creamer, who interviewed Ruth's surviving teammates for a 1974 biography, *Babe: The Legend Comes to Life*, the split between the Yankees' greatest heroes began with a petty comment made by Gehrig's mother about Ruth's 12-year-old daughter. Apparently Mama Gehrig remarked that Claire Ruth, in outfitting her 17-year-old girl from her first marriage, spared no expense for the finest clothes, yet Dorothy was constantly dressed like a tomboy. Claire learned about the statement and became infuriated. Her anger spawned a similar sentiment in the Babe, who stopped talking to Gehrig altogether.

There was no question that 1934 would be Ruth's last one in Yankee pinstripes. ("The Babe was fading away in everything but poundage," wrote Ray Robinson in his biography of Gehrig.) With Detroit having clinched the pennant, Ruth made his final appearance as a player at Yankee Stadium on an overcast afternoon before fewer than 2,000 paying customers. The club had planned no special ceremony to honor him.

After the 1934 season was concluded, Ruth traveled to the Far East for an exhibition tour of Japan, Shanghai and the Philippines with a team of all-stars. (It was when Ruth applied for a passport and required a birth certificate that he realized that he was born 364 days later than he had always believed. Nevertheless, he continued to celebrate his birthday on February 7 each year as he always had. "What the hell difference does it make?" Ruth asked.) Lou Gehrig, accompanied by his new bride Eleanor, was part of the team, but Babe and Lou stayed as far away from each other as the ocean liner would allow. Eleanor, to her credit, tried to instigate a truce by having a drink with Ruth, but her efforts were fruitless. In a book she later wrote, Eleanor accurately described the Babe as "a huge man and a small child combined in one runaway personality."

The trip turned out to be a wildly spectacular success. Ruth and the others were accorded celebrity status in Tokyo. (Years later catcher Moe Berg remembered accompanying Ruth to a geisha house for a taste of Oriental entertainment. Ruth assumed he had entered a brothel and began undressing, much to the embarrassment of the worldly Berg.) The geisha house faux pas was the only glitch in Ruth's visit to Japan. He was revered as the great "Babu Ruso" by a public that absolutely adored baseball and its American heroes—folks they had only read about. The Babe recalled the fans' enthusiasm in his autobiography:

> Despite the treacherous attack the Japanese made on us only seven years later, I cannot help but feel the reception which the millions of Japanese

gave us was genuine. They lined the streets of the Ginza, the Broadway of Tokyo, for miles and greeted us as though we were real heroes. Everywhere we went they feted us and tried to make our stay pleasant. No doubt there were plenty of stinkers among them; but looking back at that visit I feel it is another example of how a crackpot government can lead a friendly people into war.

Although the 1934 tour was the Babe's first venture to that part of the globe, Ruth had been approached by Japanese baseball moguls in the early 1920s to make a special postseason visit to their country. He was asked through an interpreter, "Would the honorable Babe Ruth honor the people of Japan by coming to our country to hit an honorable home run?"

"Sure," responded the Babe, "if the honorable price is right."

Towards the end of the tour, Ruth stopped for a few days in Paris. He hated the place. Used to adoring crowds forming around him wherever he went, the Babe found it disconcerting that he could walk all over the French capital city without once being recognized and mobbed by fans. When he returned to New York City after four months abroad, he discovered that his days with the Yankees were nearing an end.

Despite his stature as baseball's greatest ambassador, Ruth was officially released by the Yankees upon returning from the Orient. (Ruth could have stayed in New York if he would have agreed to play for the nominal fee of $1 for the upcoming season. Insulted by the token gesture, Ruth refused.) In an arrangement between Colonel Ruppert and the lowly Boston Braves, Ruth's rights were acquired by the worst club in the National League. The Babe's presence in the Braves' roster was solely for purposes of attracting crowds to the ballpark of a dismal team.

Although Braves owner Emil Fuchs had hinted that Ruth might eventually assume the duties as manager, his stint with the club only lasted until midseason when he was handed his release. "He expected to cash in on me as a player," Ruth said of Fuchs. "And at first people did come out to see me, as a curiosity. But my batting average had fallen to .181 for 28 games. For the first time in my life, baseball was a drudgery."

Being on a club that failed to win even 25 percent of its games did not help Ruth's outlook. The Braves would suffer through a truly terrible season, finishing with a 38–115 mark. In a 1994 book, statistician Harry Hollingsworth ranked the 1935 Braves as the fourth-worst major league team of the twentieth century.

The Babe did go out in sensational style, though. In one of his final games, Ruth smashed three home runs in Pittsburgh to raise his career total to 714. Like his record of 60 homers in 1927, the mark was believed to be unapproachable. Fittingly, Ruth's last shot was a titanic blast that cleared the right field roof at Forbes Field. No batter had ever done that before. Pirate pitcher Guy Bush, who surrendered the Babe's last two homers and thus earned a spot in baseball trivia books, easily recalled the final one years later.

> [Ruth] came up again in the ninth. I was a little mad. I told my catcher he was not good enough to hit my fastball. I came through with a fastball for strike one. I missed with the second. The next pitch I was going to throw the ball past Mr. Ruth. It was on the outside corner.
>
> As he went around third, Ruth gave me the hand sign meaning "to hell with you." He was the best who ever lived.
>
> That big joker hit it clear out of the ball park for his third home run of the game. It was the longest homer I'd ever seen in baseball.

Ruth had once arrogantly predicted that the game would fall into an irreversible decline once he left, but the sport managed to get along quite well without him. New stars took his place in the limelight. When the Babe phoned Yankee Stadium to inquire about passes for Opening Day in 1936, he was tersely told to forward a check to the ticket office. Insulted by the snub, Ruth instead attended the Giants' opener at the Polo Grounds. For the first time since 1913, Ruth was not wearing the uniform of a professional baseball club. "It feels strange," he sadly told a reporter.

His last direct association with the big leagues came in 1938, when he briefly served as a base coach with the Brooklyn Dodgers. It was virtually a repeat of his 1935 experience with the Braves. Ruth's presence on the field infuriated Leo Durocher, who realized Ruth was simply there as a means to lure nostalgic fans to Ebbets Field. Ruth constantly forgot the signals and his employment with the Dodgers was brief.

The remaining decade of his life saw Ruth transformed into a gentleman of leisure. He played round after round of golf. He and Claire spent a great many evenings playing bridge within their small circle of close friends. He was on hand in Cooperstown in 1939 when he was enshrined as one of the first five players in the National Baseball Hall of Fame. (Christy Mathewson, Walter Johnson, Ty Cobb and Honus Wagner were the other four. Incredibly, none of them were unanimous selections.) After expertly playing himself in the 1942 film biography of Lou Gehrig, *The Pride of the Yankees*, a roll that was far from flattering, Ruth twice tried his hand at radio sports commentary with little success. In 1947 an ideal job for Ruth emerged. He was asked to be baseball's elder statesman as a figurehead leader for Little League Baseball. It would have been the perfect opportunity for Ruth to pass along advice to the youth of America to whom he was always regarded with great reverence. However, he was in no condition to take on the task. He was diagnosed with throat cancer. His health declined rapidly.

Ruth's deterioration was a sorry sight. When George Bush was in the White House, he recalled meeting Ruth when the Babe paid a visit to a baseball game at Yale University in 1948:

I was captain of the ball club, so I got to receive him there. He was dying. He was hoarse and could hardly talk. He kind of croaked when they set up the mike by the pitcher's mound. It was tragic. He was hollow. His whole great shape was gaunt and hollowed out. I remember he complimented the Yale ball field. It was like a putting green, it was so beautiful. I don't remember too much more about it.

In June 1948 Ruth's long overdue tribute at Yankee Stadium—in which his uniform number was retired—took place a few weeks before his death. Fans were shocked by his appearance. Ruth bore no resemblance to the impressive physical specimen he had been during his days with the Red Sox. He was thin and pale; his hair was ghostly white. Ruth's voice was now barely a raspy whisper, but he encouraged the boys of America to keep playing the greatest game in the world. He died on August 16, 1948, not long after the release of his autobiography, which predictably did not dwell on some of the slugger's less than wholesome activities. More than 80,000 people filed past his open coffin at Yankee Stadium to pay their last respects to one of the most remarkable figures in American history.

Waite Hoyt, a member of the 1927 Yankees' pitching staff and a pall bearer at Ruth's funeral, was a major source of Ruth lore for Robert Creamer's 1974 autobiography of the Babe. At one point Hoyt sent Creamer a poignant letter that read in part,

> I am almost convinced you will never learn the truth on Ruth. I roomed with Joe Dugan. He was a good friend of Babe's. But he will see Ruth in a different light than I did. Dugan's own opinion will be one in which Dugan revels in Ruth's crudities, and so on. While I can easily recognize all of this and admit it freely, yet there was buried in Ruth humanitarianism beyond belief, an intelligence he was never given credit for, a childish desire to be over-virile, living up to credits given his home-run power—and yet a need for intimate affection and respect and a feverish desire to play baseball, perform, act and live a life he didn't and couldn't take time to understand.

Ruth's grave is located in Gate of Heaven Cemetery in Hawthorne, New York. The words Cardinal Spellman incorporated into his eulogy of George Herman Ruth were inscribed on the Babe's tombstone: "May the Divine Spirit that animated Babe Ruth to win the crucial game of life inspire the youth of America!" Claire Ruth, who died in 1976, would be buried alongside her famous husband.

Hollywood, in its attempt to cash in on Ruth nostalgia, paid tribute to him with a dreadful film version of *The Babe Ruth Story*. Babe lived long enough to attend the premier on July 26, but he left well before the final credits had rolled. "Terrible" was one of the more charitable reviews it received.

Film critic Leonard Maltin has called the film, directed by Roy Del Ruth, "an insult to the famed baseball star." Others scoffed at the story line. "The movie played fast and loose with the truth," wrote Bruce Nash and Allan Zullo in *The Baseball Hall of Shame*, "and relied on maudlin cliches and outright lies."

The Babe was portrayed by the unathletic William Bendix, who wore a fake putty nose that wiggled when he walked. In one of the film's many unbelievable scenes, Ruth saunters into a bar and orders a glass of milk! Dan Daniel, in his review for *The Sporting News*, was struck by another of the movie's ludicrous moments:

> The boy-and-dog sequence ... is very tough to take. Ruth almost kills a pooch on the playing field with a batted ball. The boy owner of the dog is disconsolate. Ruth rushes dog and boy down to a hospital and induces a surgeon to work on the canine. Of course, the dog recovers. But Ruth misses the game, and for that, we are told, he is fined $5,000 by Huggins.

Writer Bob Broeg later wrote, "If cancer hadn't done him in, the Babe certainly would have become ill from the hearts-and-flowers movie based on his life." Like the forgettable silent films of the 1920s in which Ruth starred, *The Babe Ruth Story* flopped badly at the box office.

Ironically, one of the last outsiders to have seen Babe alive was Ford Frick, a sportswriter whom Ruth befriended years earlier after Frick agreed to ghostwrite baseball articles under the Babe's name. Frick, of course, would later become the commissioner of baseball. It was he who made the controversial 1961 "asterisk" ruling that declared Roger Maris had not technically eclipsed Ruth's 1927 record of 60 home runs.

Tributes to the deceased Bambino were numerous, but perhaps the best appeared 37 years after Ruth's death in Donald Honig's *Baseball America*:

> If Babe Ruth had not been born it would have been impossible to invent him. The reality is hard enough to accept... He was a one-man circus, born and molded to entertain, dominate, captivate, and altogether flourish in the imagination.... Everything about Ruth was big, big, big, from the statistics to the personality to the impact. He was Moby Dick in a goldfish bowl. To write about him is to drain your vocabulary of superlatives. To whatever engaged him he was the mightiest: hitter, pitcher, womanizer, drinker, eater. He was the greatest player on the greatest team in the greatest stadium in the greatest city. He was power. He was the Yankees. He was New York. He was baseball.

EPILOGUE

Although more than seven decades have passed since Babe Ruth's fabulous 1927 season in Yankee pinstripes, his accomplishment of hitting 60 regular-season home runs remains one of the most remarkable achievements in all of sports. Even Roger Maris's 1961 feat of 61 homers (achieved, of course, during a 162-game schedule) does not merit the scholarly attention accorded to Ruth's terrific year.

Statistics can often be misleading, but for Ruth in 1927 his numbers are a clear indication of just how dominant the Bambino was. The Yankees, not surprisingly, led the American League in homers, walloping 158 for an average of slightly more than one per game. The second-highest team total belonged to the Philadelphia A's—and they managed just 56! (The anemic bats of the sixth-place Cleveland Indians connected for just 26 homers all season, a total that Ruth, all by himself, had reached by the first week of July. Apparently even the tiny dimensions of Dunn Field were no help to the Indians.) In other words, Ruth—alone—surpassed the home run total of every other AL team! More precisely, the Babe hit nearly one-seventh (13.7 percent) of the 439 AL homers in 1927. Together, Ruth and Gehrig accounted for 24.4 percent of the American League's home runs.

By 1961, when Maris eclipsed Ruth's "unbreakable" record by one homer, the circuit clout was no longer the novelty it had been in Ruth's era. The home run output in the ten-team American League in 1961 had skyrocketed to 1,534—almost quadruple the total achieved in the landmark season of 1927. The Kansas City Athletics had the league's lowest home run total in 1961, and even they managed to hit 90. The next lowest total was the 112 homers notched by the Boston Red Sox. An average AL game in 1961 produced 1.9 home runs. Back in 1927, when the Babe's bat had the sporting world abuzz, there was approximately seven-tenths of a homer per game. Ruth, in 1927, had arguably done the equivalent of netting 150 goals in the space of a 1990s

NHL season or scoring 50 touchdowns in one autumn in the modern NFL. Quite properly, a new adjective entered the English language to describe colossal feats: Ruthian.

Further enhancing Ruth's claim to immortality (regardless of Maris's accomplishment 34 seasons later) is that baseball in 1927 was far and away the most popular sport in America. There might be some debate as to what sport had the second-greatest following that year, but whatever it was, it paled in comparison to the attention that baseball received. Most major daily newspapers regularly featured boxscores and detailed accounts of every major league contest, plus linescores and standings from minor leagues large and small. Serious fans—and there were millions of them—could easily recite from memory the regular eight starters from all 16 big-league clubs.

Although Ruth died half a century ago, he continues to cast an unending shadow over the sport he dominated back in the 1920s. The May 1998 issue of *Baseball Digest* featured letters from two fans who were still fixated with Ruth's accomplishments. One fan from Florida, Lewis S. Bennett, had a question. He wanted to know how many home runs Ruth would have hit had he come to bat as often as Hank Aaron did during the latter's long career. (The answer, by the way, is mind-boggling. Ruth, over the course of his illustrious career, averaged one home run every 11.76 official at-bats. If, and it's a big *if*, he continued to belt homers at this heady clip until he reached Aaron's lifetime total of 12,364 at-bats, Ruth would have walloped the staggering total of 1,051 regular-season home runs!)

The second letter was written by a Texan named John McCormack who was baffled by the seemingly endless controversy over who should be hailed as the greatest ballplayer ever to step on a diamond. McCormack thought the debate was utterly unnecessary. He wrote,

> Until someone has a better ERA than 2.24 over 1,220 innings [sic], bats higher than .342 lifetime, slugs more than .690, and hits more than 714 home runs, choosing the best all-around player ever is a no-brainer.
>
> It has to be George Herman Ruth. If we were both back in the schoolyard choosing sides, and you had the first choice of all the game's players, whom would you pick?

On America's most conspicuous stage, the Babe had been the grandest player of them all. In a year when Charles A. Lindbergh had shortened the distance between continents and ushered in modern aviation; in a year when a president startled his country when he announced he would not seek reelection; in a year when movies learned how to talk; in a year when a thousand other noteworthy events occurred, perhaps the greatest news story in America was generated by its badly flawed, out-of-shape, high-living, garrulous and most recognizable athlete. George Herman Ruth did more than just smack 60 home runs in 1927. He achieved a Ruthian feat.

Appendix A

Summary of
the Home Runs

HR No.	Club's Game	Ruth's Game	Date	Inning	Site	Opponent	Pitcher	Leftie/ Rightie
1	4	4	Apr. 15	1	home	Philadelphia	Ehmke	right
2	11	11	Apr. 23	1	road	Philadelphia	Walberg	left
3	12	12	Apr. 24	6	road	Washington	Thurston	right
4	14	14	Apr. 29	5	road	Boston	Harriss	right
5	16	16	May 1	1	home	Philadelphia	Quinn	right
6	16	16	May 1	8	home	Philadelphia	Walberg	left
7	24	24	May 10	1	road	St. Louis	Gaston	right
8	25	25	May 11	1	road	St. Louis	Nevers	right
9	29	29	May 17	8	road	Detroit	Collins	right
10	33	33	May 22	6	road	Cleveland	Karr	right
11	34	34	May 23	1	road	Washington	Thurston	right
12	37	37	May 28	7	home	Washington	Thurston	right
13	39	39	May 29	8	home	Boston	MacFayden	right
14	41	41	May 30	11	road	Philadelphia	Walberg	left
15	42	42	May 31	1	road	Philadelphia	Quinn	right
16	43	43	May 31	5	road	Philadelphia	Ehmke	right
17	47	47	Jun. 5	6	home	Detroit	Whitehill	left
18	48	48	Jun. 7	4	home	Chicago	Thomas	right
19	52	52	Jun. 11	3	home	Cleveland	Buckeye	left
20	52	52	Jun. 11	5	home	Cleveland	Buckeye	left
21	53	53	Jun. 12	7	home	Cleveland	Uhle	right
22	55	55	Jun. 16	1	home	St. Louis	Zachary	left
23	60	60	Jun. 22	5	road	Boston	Wiltse	left
24	60	60	Jun. 22	7	road	Boston	Wiltse	left
25	70	66	Jun. 30	4	home	Boston	Harriss	right
26	73	69	Jul. 3	1	road	Washington	Lisenbee	right
27	78	74	Jul. 8	2	road	Detroit	Hankins	right
28	79	75	Jul. 9	1	road	Detroit	Holloway	right
29	79	75	Jul. 9	4	road	Detroit	Holloway	right
30	83	79	Jul. 12	9	road	Cleveland	Shaute	left
31	94	90	Jul. 24	3	road	Chicago	Thomas	right
32	95	91	Jul. 26	1	home	St. Louis	Gaston	right

HR No.	Club's Game	Ruth's Game	Date	Inning	Site	Opponent	Pitcher	Leftie/ Rightie
33	95	91	Jul. 26	6	home	St. Louis	Gaston	right
34	98	94	Jul. 28	8	home	St. Louis	Stewart	left
35	106	102	Aug. 5	8	home	Detroit	Smith	right
36	110	106	Aug. 10	3	road	Washington	Zachary	left
37	114	110	Aug. 16	5	road	Chicago	Thomas	right
38	115	111	Aug. 17	11	road	Chicago	Connally	right
39	118	114	Aug. 20	1	road	Cleveland	Miller	left
40	120	116	Aug. 22	6	road	Cleveland	Shaute	left
41	124	120	Aug. 27	8	road	St. Louis	Nevers	right
42	125	121	Aug. 28	1	road	St. Louis	Wingard	left
43	127	123	Aug. 31	8	home	Boston	Welzer	right
44	128	124	Sept. 2	1	road	Philadelphia	Walberg	left
45	132	128	Sept. 6	6	road	Boston	Welzer	right
46	132	128	Sept. 6	7	road	Boston	Welzer	right
47	133	129	Sept. 6	9	road	Boston	Russell	right
48	134	130	Sept. 7	1	road	Boston	MacFayden	right
49	134	130	Sept. 7	8	road	Boston	Harriss	right
50	138	134	Sept. 11	4	home	St. Louis	Gaston	right
51	139	135	Sept. 13	7	home	Cleveland	Hudlin	right
52	140	136	Sept. 13	4	home	Cleveland	Shaute	left
53	143	139	Sept. 16	3	home	Chicago	Blankenship	right
54	147	143	Sept. 18	5	home	Chicago	Lyons	right
55	148	144	Sept. 21	9	home	Detroit	Gibson	right
56	149	145	Sept. 22	9	home	Detroit	Holloway	right
57	152	148	Sept. 27	6	home	Philadelphia	Grove	left
58	153	149	Sept. 29	1	home	Washington	Lisenbee	right
59	153	149	Sept. 29	5	home	Washington	Hopkins	right
60	154	150	Sept. 30	8	home	Washington	Zachary	left

STATISTICAL BREAKDOWN OF THE HOME RUNS

By Ballpark

Yankee Stadium (New York)—28
Fenway Park (Boston)—8
Shibe Park (Philadelphia)—5
Dunn Field (Cleveland)—4
Griffith Stadium (Washington)—4
Navin Field (Detroit)—4
Sportsman's Park (St. Louis)—4
Comiskey Park (Chicago)—3

Allowed by Team

Boston—11
Cleveland—9
Philadelphia—9
St. Louis—9
Detroit—8
Washington—8
Chicago—6

Frequency by Month

April—4
May—12
June—9
July—9
August—9
September—17

Frequency by Day

Sunday—12
Monday—3
Tuesday—15
Wednesday—9
Thursday—6
Friday—7
Saturday—8

Frequency by Inning

1st—16	7th—5
2nd—1	8th—9
3rd—4	9th—4
4th—5	10th—0
5th—7	11th—2
6th—7	

By Type

Inside the Park—1
Outside the Park—59

Runners on Base

No Runners—29
One Runner—22
Two Runners—7
Three Runners—2

Pitchers Who Allowed Ruth's Home Runs

4 Homers

Gaston, Milt (St. Louis)
Walberg, Rube (Philadelphia)

3 Homers

Harriss, Slim (Boston)
Holloway, Ken (Detroit)
Shaute, Joe (Cleveland)
Thomas, Tommy (Chicago)
Thurston, Sloppy (Washington)
Welzer, Tony (Boston)
Zachary, Tom (St. Louis and
    Washington)

2 Homers

Buckeye, Garland (Cleveland)
Ehmke, Howard (Philadelphia)
Lisenbee, Hod (Washington)
MacFayden, Danny (Boston)
Nevers, Ernie (St. Louis)
Quinn, Jack (Philadelphia)
Wiltse, Hal (Boston)

1 Homer

Blankenship, Ted (Chicago)
Collins, Rip (Detroit)
Connally, Sarge (Chicago)
Gibson, Sam (Detroit)
Grove, Lefty (Philadelphia)
Hankins, Don (Detroit)
Hopkins, Paul (Washington)
Hudlin, Willis (Cleveland)
Karr, Benn (Cleveland)
Lyons, Ted (Chicago)
Miller, Jake (Cleveland)
Russell, Jack (Boston)
Smith, George (Detroit)
Stewart, Lefty (St. Louis)
Uhle, George (Cleveland)
Whitehill, Earl (Detroit)
Wingard, Ernie (St. Louis)

Appendix C

1927 BATTING AND PITCHING STATISTICS OF THE YANKEES

BATTING STATISTICS: 1927 NEW YORK YANKEES

NAME	BA	SA	AB	H	2B	3B	HR	R	RBI
Regulars									
Lou Gehrig	.373	.765	584	218	52	18	47	149	175
Tony Lazzeri	.309	.482	570	176	29	8	18	92	102
Mark Koenig	.285	.382	526	150	20	11	3	99	62
Joe Dugan	.269	.362	387	104	24	3	2	44	43
Babe Ruth	.356	.772	540	192	29	8	60	158	164
Earle Combs	.356	.511	648	231	36	23	6	137	64
Bob Meusel	.337	.510	516	174	47	9	8	75	103
Pat Collins	.275	.418	251	69	9	3	7	38	36
Substitutes									
Ray Morehart	.256	.328	195	50	7	2	1	45	20
Johnny Grabowski	.277	.328	195	54	2	4	0	29	25
Cedric Durst	.248	.326	129	32	4	3	0	18	25
Benny Bengough	.247	.353	85	21	3	3	0	6	10
Julie Wera	.238	.381	42	10	3	0	1	7	8

PITCHING STATISTICS: 1927 NEW YORK YANKEES

Name	G	IP	W	L	SV	ERA
Waite Hoyt	36	256.1	22	7	1	2.63
Wilcy Moore	50	213.0	19	7	13	2.28
Herb Pennock	34	209.2	19	8	2	3.00

Name	G	IP	W	L	SV	ERA
Urban Shocker	31	200.0	18	6	0	2.84
Dutch Ruether	27	184.0	13	6	0	3.38
George Pipgras	29	166.1	10	3	0	4.11
Milt Thomas	21	88.2	7	4	0	4.87
Bob Shawkey	19	43.2	2	3	4	2.89

BIBLIOGRAPHY

The Baseball Encyclopedia (9th edition). New York: Macmillan, 1993.

Cataneo, David. *Peanuts and Crackerjack*. Nashville TN: Rutledge Hill, 1991.

Creamer, Robert W. *Babe: The Legend Comes to Life*. New York: Simon and Schuster, 1974.

Daniel, Clifton, editor in chief. *Chronicle of the 20th Century*. Mount Kisco NY: Chronicle Publications, 1987.

Dickson, Paul. *Baseball's Greatest Quotations*. New York: HarperCollins, 1991.

Fischler, Stan and Shirley Fischler. *The Best, Worst and Most Unusual in Sports*. New York: Fawcett Crest, 1977.

Hollingsworth, Harry. *The Best and Worst Baseball Teams of All Time*. New York: S.P.I., 1994.

Honig, Donald. *Baseball America*. New York: Macmillan, 1985.

Kavanagh, Jack. *Walter Johnson: A Life*. South Bend IN: Diamond Communications, 1995.

Keene, Kerry, Raymond Sinibaldi and David Hickey. *The Babe in Red Stockings*. Champaign IL: Sagamore Publishing, 1997.

Maltin, Leonard. *Leonard Maltin's Movie and Video Guide 1992*. New York: Signet, 1991.

Nash, Bruce, and Allan Zullo. *The Baseball Hall of Shame*. New York: Pocket, 1985.

Nemec, David, et al. *20th Century Baseball Chronicle*. Lincolnwood IL: Publications International, 1993.

Okkonen, Marc. *The Federal League of 1914-15: Baseball's Third Major League*. Pittsburgh PA: Mathews Printing, 1989.

Okrent, Daniel, and Steve Wulf. *Baseball Anecdotes*. New York: Harper & Row, 1989.

Reichler, Joseph L., ed. *The World Series: A 75th Anniversary*. New York: Simon and Schuster, 1978.

Ritter, Lawrence S. *The Glory of Their Times*. New York: Vintage, 1985.

Robinson, Ray. *Iron Horse: Lou Gehrig in His Time*. New York: W. W. Norton, 1990.

Ruth, Babe. *The Babe Ruth Story*. New York: Scholastic Book Services, 1948.

Shatzkin, Mike, ed. *The Ballplayers*. New York: Arbor House, 1990.

Sobol, Ken. *Babe Ruth and the American Dream*. New York: Random House, 1974.

Vincent, David W., ed. *Home Runs in the Old Ballparks*. Cleveland: Society for American Baseball Research, 1995.

Wagenheim, Kal. *Babe Ruth: His Life and Legend*. New York: Henry Holt, 1974.

INDEX